Imagined Places

MICHAEL PEARSON

Imagined Places

Journeys into Literary America

With photographs by John Lawrence
and Joel Mednick

University Press of Mississippi   Jackson and London

Manufactured in the United States of America

94 93 92 91   4 3 2 1

The paper in this book meets the guidelines for
permanence and durability of the Committee on
Production Guidelines for Book Longevity of the Council
on Library Resources.

Photographs by Joel Mednick appear on pages 17, 40,
47, 50, 53, 57, 60, 242, 245, 252, and 256.

Photographs by John Lawrence appear on pages 76, 83,
106, 108, 110, 112, 120, 134, 152, 156, 158, 165, 172, 179,
181, 275, 280, 301, and 306.

Library of Congress Cataloging-in-Publication Data

Pearson, Michael, 1949–
    Imagined places : journeys into literary America /
  Michael Pearson; photographs by John Lawrence and
  Joel Mednick.
        p.   cm.
    ISBN 0-87805-526-6
    1. Literary landmarks—United States.   2. Authors,
American—Homes and haunts.   3. Pearson, Michael,
1949–   —Journeys—United States.   I. Title.
PS141.P36   1991
810.9′0052—dc20   91–16920
                                              CIP

British Library Cataloging-in-Publication data available

Contents

For my mother, who long ago sparked my sense of adventure and love of journeying beyond the known;

For my sons, who have always been the best and truest of traveling companions;

And for Jo-Ellen, who—no matter how far I ranged from home—was always my reason to return;

This book is dedicated with love.

Here's to the field and streams
Here's to the hopes and dreams of America.

Aztec Two-Step, "Living in America"

How do people imagine the landscape they find themselves in?

Barry Lopez, *Arctic Dreams*

Travel is a vanishing act. . . . But a travel book is the opposite, the loner bouncing back bigger than life to tell the story of his experiment with space.

Paul Theroux, *The Old Patagonian Express*

Acknowledgments

I would like to acknowledge the National Endowment for the Humanities, the Old Dominion University Research Foundation, and the Old Dominion University College of Arts and Letters Research and Publications Committee for financial assistance during the writing of this book. I am grateful to Robin Winks of Yale University and Charles Morrissey of the Baylor Oral History Project for reading and commenting on early versions of the manuscript and to friends like Peter Huidekoper who read parts of the book, offered pages of brilliant comments and suggestions, but, most importantly to me, encouraged me to keep going in the same direction. My appreciation also goes to Elaine Dawson, the Michael Jordan of word processing, who typed many manuscript versions and never failed to tell me that she loved the story. My special thanks goes to Willie Morris for a welcomed early-morning wake-up call and to JoAnne Prichard for being a wonderful editor.

In particular I'd like to thank Ray and Ginny Hartwick for too many reasons to mention just one. But most of all I owe a debt to the people I met on my journeys who were generous with their time and stories and who made these six places ones that will remain in my imagination forever.

Before the Journey: A Preface

One fine day in early summer a young man lay
thinking in Central Park.

Walker Percy, *The Last Gentleman*

The spirit of adventure is strong in me. It always has been. My inclination, which is surely American, is never to be fully satisfied with any place I've lived, be it New York or Pennsylvania or Virginia. There are either too many people or too few of the right ones, too many condominiums or not enough bookstores.

My impulse has been to travel, to see for myself what lies on the other side of the mountain, not to accept hearsay but to see with my own eyes. The only places that didn't seem to have an ever-enticing hill just beyond them were imagined places, those I'd dreamt up or read about in books. As Northrop Frye has said, "No matter what direction we start off in, the signposts of literature always keep pointing the same way, to a world where nothing is outside the human imagination."

I guess I wanted a world as filled with sound and fury as Faulkner's, as cradled in promises and dark mysteries as Frost's, as populated with oddballs and heroes as Steinbeck's. I wanted the mountains and the sea, the brutal winters that froze desire and the unchanging tropical heat that fed a lazy anticipation. I wanted the perfect memory of childhood that Hannibal represented, but I wanted the violent awakenings of O'Connor's Georgia as well. In books and legends these worlds existed for me, but I wondered whether, if I stepped beyond the magical circle of imagining, these worlds would disappear like a mirage shimmering into memory.

A few years ago I overheard one of my sons talking with a group of his friends about their fathers' professions. I recall him saying, "My father reads books." I felt sorry for him then for not being able to say something more exciting or even more reasonable, but he was close to the truth. That's exactly what I've done for a good part of my life—read books and talked about them with mostly captive audiences in classrooms. But for me books have always been adventures, a slipping off into unknown territories, a way to lose the world for a time and a way to find it again.

Attempting to describe my reasons for writing this book, I feel a bit like the protagonist of Saul Bellow's *Henderson the Rain King*, who started his story by saying, "What made me take this trip to Africa? There is no quick explanation." Henderson went on a longer single journey than I did, but my explanation finally, like his, is meandering and in the book itself.

If I went deeply enough into the past, I could probably say that the impulse to do this book reaches as far back as my love of reading or even my love of words. Like most in my generation, I learned to read in the first grade, but the only vivid memory I have of that seminal year is not of the process of learning to read or of any specific books but of the letters themselves. In St. Philip Neri Elementary School all first graders were given a box of letters, like K-rations to a foot soldier. Each box contained hundreds of letters, smooth little cardboard squares about the size of Scrabble pieces. I have no idea what we were supposed to do with them, learn the alphabet or make words, I suppose, but the only thing I clearly recall is seeing the letters fly around the room. When Mother Concepta was out of the class, letters flew, they fell like snowflakes in February, a storm of Z's and L's floated everywhere. They were thrown like Frisbees and splintered the air like confetti. Words soared, banged into one another, and drifted down into poetry and nonsense on the classroom floor. At the end of the year I had only three letters left—an S, a B, and a Q—but I learned to love the sight of words, the sound they made as they hissed through the stale schoolroom air.

Growing up in New York City, I sometimes felt books were my

sole means of seeing the sunlight. The apartment buildings allowed only glimpses of the sky. In our games, my friends and I learned to play in narrow spaces. We played intensely and used what the environment offered—stoops and fire hydrants and alleyways. But books offered imagined environments, worlds where anything was possible. There were great open spaces, enormous floods of sunshine, not merely broken shafts of light angling between buildings. Of all the adventures I remember—as safe as ring-a-leavio and hunter or as dangerous as roaming the construction sites or jumping from one roof to another—books always offered the most satisfaction.

In fifth grade I was given the Grosset and Dunlap children's edition of the biography of Kit Carson for Christmas. I read the book eight times in half as many months and for all practical purposes became Kit Carson. I answered to my legal name with the same grudging acquiescence with which I took out the garbage. I was lost in dreams of high adventure, knowing that if a five-foot seven-inch mountain man could achieve greatness, so could I, no matter how small I was. The buildings disappeared, transformed into Colorado mountains, the smog faded into purpling New Mexican sunsets.

My taste in literature got better. I moved on to *Tom Sawyer* in the seventh grade and *Lord of the Flies* in the eighth. By high school it was Salinger and in college Brautigan and Vonnegut, then Percy. But as sophisticated as my tastes became—Joyce and Woolf and Nabokov—I never fully escaped from the same impulse that Holden Caulfield had—to meet an author if I really liked his or her work.

When I became a journalist, I developed other desires—to see some of the places where great writers had left a mythic imprint through their personalities or their writing and to meet the residents of those places. Books first took me, in my curiosity, *from* the world with their smell of acetate and wood pulp and the faint, alluring sound of different voices. They offered new people and unknown places. Those same books, along with my curiosity, led me *back* to the worlds they described.

A few years ago I took an assignment from the *Atlanta Journal and Constitution* to go to Oxford, Mississippi, to write an article about Faulkner's influence on his hometown. It became a story for me in which all points converged: my desire to travel, my love of literature, and my interest in other people's lives. I began to think about other American writers whose poems and stories had led me dreaming through my boyhood and into college. I began to think about those writers who, through the power of their words or the strength of their legends, held certain places in the grip of myth.

When I thought of the chiseled beauty of Vermont, its scrupulously handsome villages, its wintry character, its sharply ironic people, I thought of Robert Frost. Vermont and Frost were one in my mind. But the place, like the poet, was not uncomplicated, and probably as May Sarton suggested, the New England landscape captured the American heart partly because for all its beauty, life had never been easy there. The whiteness of Vermont, similar to what Melville in *Moby Dick* called "a dumb blankness, full of meaning," is both a mantle of loveliness and a shroud of death. In his poetry Frost described the beauty, but he also wrote of "a blanker whiteness of benighted snow/ With no expression, nothing to express." I wondered if Frost's Vermont of shining surfaces with darker mysteries beneath was something I could find.

I first journeyed through the South, encountering its poverty and humor and violence, its racism and sense of community, its propensity to talk, its ignorance and eloquence and fervent beliefs, in the fiction of William Faulkner and Flannery O'Connor. Her voice was a razor-sharp jackknife, his a broadsword, but both showed me the South, which at that time seemed to me as far away from New York City and my experience as Saturn. Faulkner depicted the individual entangled in southern culture. No one in Faulkner's world escapes the inherited web of violence and racism or the complicated ties of blood and community. In Flannery O'Connor's fiction an austere religious sensibility comes exploding through a comic vision. Her South is a living paradox, where deeply felt mystery and deep-rooted manners crash into one another on dusty country roads.

Someone once said to me that Faulkner always wrote about those around him, but Hemingway always wrote about himself. Most likely, Hemingway was one of his own best creations. At a certain point in his career it seemed as if he spent as much time on his legend as he did on his writing. His was the literature of escape, of characters cut adrift or saying farewell. Although many places have claimed him—Michigan, Illinois, Idaho, Paris, and Spain—in America it was Key West that was most often linked to his legend. The man and the place seemed perfect partners in their unkempt, slightly disreputable artistic reputations.

Both Steinbeck and Twain were writers I had read avidly as a boy and had grown to admire more as an adult. The Salinas Valley was a world that existed for me in the sheer power of Steinbeck's reimagining it, and Hannibal, Missouri, was a place as surely rooted in everyone's memory and desire as Ithaca or Troy. I needed to see Twain's boyhood home, the town he transformed into St. Petersburg, on the mile-wide, majestic Mississippi, and to meet Steinbeck's bindle stiffs who roamed the golden foothills of the rocky Gabilan Mountains. I wanted to know if migrant workers still bent in the fields of the Salinas Valley and if the scions of Tom and Huck strolled along the streets of the peaceful hamlet.

I was drawn by what Robert Coles described as "the call of stories" to see these imagined places myself. I was determined to go where the stories started, but I wanted to listen not only to the famous authors but to the stories of the people who lived there now, people who might open their lives to me like the pages of a book. Would their lives reflect the writers' legends or the literature they left behind? Would Key West turn out to be the perfect escape? Would Salinas hide the shattered dreams of an American underclass? Would Hannibal, like Twain, have a split personality?

Each of these writers had written in universal terms, but as Flannery O'Connor once said, "The best American fiction has always been regional." Great writers always read "a small history in a universal light." Each of these six writers had explored his or her postage stamp of ground, but it was a representative corner and reflected the world at large. They all wrote honestly about their own culture, in New England, the South, or California. Each breathed life into the idea of place. Steinbeck's California was the West of golden dreams and false promises. O'Connor's South was not the Dixie of storybooks but an impoverished community in the shadows of pridefulness and hypocrisy, a region at "a peculiar crossroads where time and place and eternity somehow meet." Robert Frost's Vermont was a rustic encyclopedia, a compendium of country things, a series of rural epiphanies. He offered no comforting picture of the natural world or man's place in it; instead, his carefully ironic verse suggested that to know ourselves we must first know the natural world and then discover our place in it.

Before starting out on my journeys, six separate trips over a period of fifteen months, I thought of Annie Dillard's sojourn at Tinker Creek. She said, "It has always been a happy thought to me that the creek runs on all night, new every minute, whether I wish it or know it or care, as a closed book on a shelf continues to whisper to itself its own inexhaustible tale." The call of literature whispered its inexhaustible tale to me. Steinbeck's stories of sad-eyed dreamers called. O'Connor's fiery-eyed believers called. The picture of Faulkner staring fixedly across the Oxford square or Hemingway brawling in a Key West saloon called.

Over the year and a half I traveled a number of times to each place. Two photographers, John Lawrence and Joel Mednick, came along. John, a Mississippi native, came with me to Oxford and Milledgeville. His mellifluous southern accent often helped me gain access to places my New York City tones might never have allowed. He came with me to Key West and Hannibal, too. There his accent didn't help, but his photographer's eye often aided me in noticing things I might have otherwise overlooked. Joel traveled with me to Vermont and California. As we stood among the pickers in the field, Joel's knowledge of Spanish often proved invaluable. My younger sons came with me to Vermont and Missouri. They offered companionship and insights. I needed both.

The trips themselves were a blend of plan and improvisation. Whenever I could, I tried to set up some meetings in advance. For instance, I knew I wanted to meet Steinbeck's old friend Bruce Ariss in Monterey, talk with Gandhi's grandson in Oxford, Mississippi, or spend some time with Flannery O'Connor's mother in Georgia. But many of my most interesting and moving encounters— with Norman Lear and Andy Thompson in Vermont, with Bill Appleton in Mississippi, or with Stephen Roy Aiken in Salinas— happened serendipitously. I was just in the right place at the right time, or at least I waited patiently in the wrong places long enough until something or someone turned up. In this respect, I was just a pilgrim on the back roads.

The six writers that stimulated my search—Frost, Faulkner, O'Connor, Hemingway, Steinbeck, and Twain—have created a deep and lasting sense of place in American literature. In the last century they have, as much as any of our writers, given us a sense of what it means to be American and how place informs our understanding of who we are. With the voices of these writers whispering behind me and their ghostly images beckoning me forward, I went looking for a sense of place, particularly in the lives and the stories of ordinary people. For years I had read the books, finding myself over and over again in those stories. In those American places and in the people who lived there now, I hoped once again to find myself, and perhaps, as Paul Theroux had said, bounce back bigger than life.

Imagined Places

I

A Beginning Place

. . . words are for beginnings.

Ursula LeGuin

SOMEONE ONCE SAID that a journalist is like a beachcomber on the shore of another's experience. The coastline I follow begins with actual oceanfront in Virginia Beach in the summer of 1989. From late May on, the strip, especially along Atlantic Avenue, is lined with cars and people. The day I leave people are everywhere, carrying beach chairs, coolers and canvas bags, from landside to the ocean. The smell of suntan lotion is more pungent than the sea breeze.

Pacific Avenue curves around at 83rd Street and becomes Shore Drive, following the ocean as it leans into the Chesapeake Bay. The road cuts a path through one of the few natural wooded areas left in Virginia Beach, a city that has more than tripled its population in the last twenty years to over 350,000. Seashore State Park has miles of trails and dozens of inlets for crabbing. Other than the bay or the ocean, the state park offers one of the only places in the city to escape the encroachments of carbon monoxide and civilization. Many wonder how long it will be before the wildness of the state park is displaced by another, more modern, wildness. More cars, more Wendy's restaurants.

This is where English America started, not far from the point of land named Cape Henry by Captain John Smith and his fellow explorers shortly after they came to the New World. Riding into the forty-mile-wide mouth of the Chesapeake Bay one spring morning in 1607, gliding past the undisturbed dunes, the Virginia Company's three ships—the 100-ton flagship, *Susan Constant*, and the two smaller escorts, *Godspeed* and *Discovery*—sailed along the sun-sparked waterway that separated what were to become known as Virginia Beach and the Eastern Shore. The ships anchored off the coast probably near what is now called Lynnhaven Bay. Captain Newport of the *Susan Constant* took a group ashore where they were assaulted by a band of Indians, and two Englishmen were wounded. For John Smith, though, it was a "vale of plenty," a paradise of meadows and streams and wildlife. The four-month trip across the Atlantic had brought them to Jamestown, "a thick grove of trees," uninhabited and ready for settlement. Paradise was theirs.

According to most accounts, seafood flourished in size and abundance—sturgeon up to seven feet long, crabs that four men could feast on, and an apparently unlimited supply of mussels. Of course, recent years have proven that the supply of crabs is not unlimited, that even the Chesapeake can be polluted, and that the fish population can be decimated. In a little less than 400 years the 150 prospective colonists have become over 1.5 million people. Neither the crabs nor the Indians had a chance.

In writing about the English in the New World, William Least Heat Moon described colonization as an old world gone tired and corrupt trying to exploit a newer land. England wanted to emulate Spain's financial success in pillaging America but learned nothing from Spanish mistakes in dealing with the Indians. "The privateers did not come to build a new society," Least Heat Moon writes, "for Raleigh was no utopian like Thomas More or Roger Williams. Rather he was merely an intelligent man who envisioned an expansion of Elizabethan mercantilism." The American dream may have always been gold plated.

Greed and a lack of concern for the land and its people may have been the snake in the garden from the start. The developer's mentality was in place in the seventeenth century in England when creative spirits were turned loose on the idea of America, picturing fancy as fact. In a performance of *Eastward Hoe* at Blackfriars Theater in London, the playgoer could hear about Virginia: "Gold is more plentiful than copper with us. . . . Why, man, all their dripping pans and their chamber pots are pure gold; and all the chains with which they chain up their streets are massive gold; all the prisoners they take are fettered in gold; and for rubies and diamonds they go forth on holidays and gather them by the seashore to hang on their children's coats, and stick in their children's caps. . . . You shall live freely there, without sergeants, or courtiers, or lawyers."

If the playwright were alive, he would have to eat those words, there being enough lawyers and sergeants in the Hampton Roads to restrict anyone's freedom. Courtiers, like the dinosaurs, have disappeared or been born again as Washington lobbyists.

Smith's "vale of plenty" has swelled into a seven-city megalopolis. Highways have replaced foot paths, and condominium complexes have rooted in the ground where clusters of pines once stood. The dangers are not the ones Smith foresaw. No one fears natives. There aren't any. People move in and out like nomad tribesmen. The typical family stays put for about two years. Then it moves on. There are no wild beasts, except perhaps on the highways. The rolling hills and meadows that Smith saw in the early seventeenth century are gone. Rows of townhouses and a seemingly endless supply of gas stations and car dealers have sprouted instead. In America's beginning place, the present has bulldozed the past into a new, often nightmarish shape, with stretches of indistinguishable buildings on land stripped of all trees, one subdivision after another connected by a slithering mass of highways carrying a never-ending line of commuters. This is America's present, a future John Smith could never have predicted for his Eden. But this may be the perfect point of departure for time travel, for a look at the rest of America.

Shortly after Seashore State Park comes to an end, the real Virginia Beach begins again, Pizza Hut, Dunkin' Donuts, and Be-Lo Groceries. And miles of townhouses and resort hotels. Within a few miles the Chesapeake Bay Bridge-Tunnel looms ahead, just beyond the brightly colored sails of the catamarans dotting the sand, like a designer's splash of colors against a scene with too much blue and gray.

The bridge itself stretches out, a seventeen-mile-long magic carpet across the expanse of water from Norfolk to Cape Charles on the Eastern Shore, sailboats and cabin cruisers, coal barges and oil tankers going in various directions. Completed in 1964, the Bridge-Tunnel runs north from Chesapeake Beach, the trestles standing like centipedes between the two tunnels that dip below the ocean floor to allow ships to travel in and out of the bay. Coming across to the Eastern Shore is like crossing a border into a new world, no houses or people, just a sign for Fisherman's Island. Head boats and skiffs dot the north channel. The old salts keep saying that fishing in Virginia Beach is gone, that the fish that were there twenty years ago aren't anymore. They've been lost to pollution or the nets of the trawlers that harvest the coast. So those who know head for the less populated Eastern Shore, which, it seems, will stay sparsely populated. The nine-dollar toll each way will keep the population of Hampton Roads from making it a bedroom community. And the distance from Washington, Baltimore, and Wilmington holds those hordes back.

Route 13 runs through the flatlands of the Eastern Shore, through St. Charles and Cheriton and Eastville. The towns along the side roads resemble each other and seem far away from cities and from the present. In Cheriton, for instance, the welcome sign says "1886—Worship at the Church of Your Choice" and the first place is a tiny white house with a sign that reads "The Eastern Shore Lutheran Mission." There are a number of other churches and houses with white clapboards in various stages of disrepair.

Route 13 is another story. It slices like a scar through the flatlands. Every thirty miles or so the American strip reappears. Family Auto Sales ("All Sales Final"), Zenith TV's, Texaco, Paul's Restaurant, Stuckey's, Holiday Inn, Larry's Mobile Center. The gauntlet ends and the flatlands return, bringing farms and occasionally a brick house and a trimmed lawn, a feed-and-seed store, or a small yellow house with the requisite yellow school bus in the side yard. The country stretches out as flat as the desert, so low and flat that you can see the weather changing half an hour ahead, the dark clouds rolling in. The towns appear and disappear like apparitions: Pocomoke City, Temperanceville, Exmore, all moving toward Salisbury, Dover, and Wilmington.

During the summer the heat seems to make the land even flatter, adds to the gravity. But it doesn't affect the baseball games going on at the local high school fields. The grass is parched and scorched brown, but the players look cool and dreamy, imagining their imminent heroics. The heat shimmers up from the asphalt, no wind at all; the tall grass beyond the outfield is a still life, and the players look like peasants from Millet's *The Gleaners*.

Route 13 may not be a superhighway, but it is an artery going through the heart of America—abandoned gas stations, corn fields, peach orchards, trailer parks. Whitman's multitudes and contradictions. In rapid succession I pass a McDonald's, a Burger King, a Roy Rogers, and a rooster standing mournful sentinel over a dead hen by the side of the road.

The road continues into Delaware and onto the St. Georges Bridge, which arches over a body of water and places the New Castle skyline squarely in view, a collection of church spires and factory smokestacks. Sulphur and hosannas rise together. From the New Jersey Turnpike to New York on Route 95 it's all a blur of blacktop and eighteen-wheelers. Driving through New York City is something beyond Dante's darkest imaginings. Even the sun's rays seem to turn gray as soon as they enter the New York City atmosphere. The buildings are gray, the people are gray, the garbage on the side of the highway is gray. It's the underworld that Odysseus had to enter before he could continue on his journey. It is Ishmael's damp, drizzly November of the soul. And, as I pass through, it's only June.

Ishmael turned to the sea to drive off the spleen and regulate the circulation. I turn to the road, to the dark, dreamy, meditative American road. In his recent book about his travels around America, Ian Frazier wrote, "For fantasies, the Great Plains are in many respects the perfect place. They're so big that you never know all there is to know about them—your fantasies could never wear them out." The road I travel is lined with fantasies as big as the Great Plains, strewn with metaphors and images from Twain, Steinbeck, Hemingway, O'Connor, Faulkner, and Frost. The road leads back to them.

2

Country Things:
Frost's Vermont

It would be a mistake to expect the stone walls
and woodpiles, the farms and the mountains, the
hired men and farm people will be interpreted or
explained to us. We must go, as Frost's speaker
in "The Pasture" goes, to observe and reflect on
rural New England.

John Kemp,
Robert Frost and New England

Nearly everybody has to live two lives. Poets.
Sculptors. Nearly everyone has to live two lives at
the very least.

Robert Frost speaking to Roger Kahn
in *The Boys of Summer*

And if you're lost enough to find yourself
By now, pull in your ladder road behind you
and put a sign up CLOSED to all but me.

Frost, "Directive"

IT'S A CORD OF MAPLE cut and split and piled—measured, four by four by eight—that is the first thing I see as I get off the main road and enter Vermont. It might just as well be a sign: Frost Country. It's all highway up to Brattleboro, Vermont. Route 95 becomes Route 91. But around Northhampton, Massachusetts, the countryside starts to be New England. The mountains rise up more, the colors become greener, the road seems carved through rock. It's an overcast day and the fog hangs in smoky drifts from the treetops above the line of hills as I get off the highway and start west on Route 9, the road that winds over Hogback Mountain toward Bennington.

It's not the mountains or the maple trees or the sheep farms that give the clearest sign of modern Vermont. It's the inns that offer the clue: Nutmeg Inn, Homestead Inn, Dovetail Inn, Ormsby Hill Inn, Willoomsac Inn, Longwood Inn, Equinox Inn. In some towns the only competition the inns have for sheer numbers are the real estate offices.

Vermont is also graveyards on sloping hillsides, firewood stacked against weathered barns, and stone walls in the shadows of mountains. Although Vermont is known for its neat, well-kept houses and towns, what makes it seem different from such manicured places as Bronxville or Scarsdale is the sense of things in flux, life in motion—a truck filled with fencing parked in front of a white Cape Cod, a snowmobile angled against a barn, an axe cut into a chopping block, stacks of hay, ladders leaning against window sills.

Shaped something like a funnel, Vermont is bordered on the west by a sprawling New York State. From Rouses Point in the northwestern corner of New York to Whitehall in the south, Lake

Champlain serves as a natural boundary separating the two states. More than 400 mountain peaks, part of the Appalachian chain, rise within the 9,614 square miles of the Green Mountain State. It's a spine of hills, in some places as much as thirty-six miles wide, running from north to south. From 1777 to 1789 New Hampshire and New York wanted to divide Vermont in half. Without the wisdom of Solomon, they proposed to split the state along the crest of the Green Mountains. But Vermonters do not shift their ground readily, and the mountains remained the backbone, not the dividing line.

A little under one mile high, Mount Mansfield is the tallest peak in Vermont, but before prehistoric glaciers reshaped the landscape, mountains rose to over 15,000 feet. There's plenty of evidence of that glacial movement in Vermont—granite outcroppings, scratched rock surfaces, and the oldest coral reef in the world on Isle La Motte in Lake Champlain.

The lake is a watery funnel that, like Vermont itself, slowly narrows towards its southern end. To the east of Vermont, New Hampshire is its mirror image, an inverse twin. It's shaped like a cone, the narrow end on top and the wide one below. The southern section of Vermont balances precariously on the rural northwestern portion of Massachusetts, a short distance from the Boston area. The northern edge of Vermont touches the province of Quebec, which leads to the frigid waters of Hudson Bay and the Labrador Sea and eventually to the Queen Elizabeth Islands and frozen North Pole. With ice above and megalopolis below, Vermont is a land in-between.

Vermont is small, but it has more square miles than six other states—Connecticut, Delaware, Hawaii, Massachusetts, New Hampshire, and Rhode Island. Along its eastern border Vermont runs 157 miles, following the course of the Connecticut River. On the west, Lake Champlain stretches 120 miles, keeping New York and the Adirondacks at a safe distance. At its widest point Vermont stretches about eighty miles between Lake Champlain and the Connecticut River. In population it is the third-smallest state, with about half a million people. Only Alaska and Wyoming have fewer.

Frost once wrote that "America is hard to see." Vermont is no easier, caught as it is between myth and history. The myths come from many sources, an advertisement in *The New Yorker* or a friend's recounting an October drive through Smuggler's Notch. Vermont is pictured as a pristine retreat for the last of a breed, rugged individualists. According to Charles Morrissey, it is "an island in space and time." It's small-town America, white picket fences and neatly painted clapboards. It's stone walls and taciturn farmers, town meetings and a final stand for mall haters.

There's some truth to all of this. Vermont is beautiful, ablaze with colors in the fall and blanketed by white in the winter. Many of its towns are a postcard photographer's dream. Armed with Act 250 as part of the State Land Use and Development Plan and a basic antipathy for developers, Vermonters have made a number of mall promoters turn tail, blueprints between their legs. But although once there were more cows than people in Vermont, the balance has slowly shifted. In the early nineteenth century sheep was the main industry, but in the 1860s dairy farming replaced sheep herding as the primary activity of Vermont farmers. One hundred years later tourism became central to the state's economy. The figures dotting the hillside changed over the years, from sheep to cows to tourists. And as one Hinesburg farmer sardonically said to me, "At least the last two can be milked." But Vermont is still one of the few states that shows a great respect for a rural ethic. Like Frost himself, many in the state value the natural world.

For years Vermont's biggest export was its own natives. It was a tough place to live, rocky, cold, and far from the rest of the industrial world, it seemed. It is a landscape of extremes, both in beauty and hardships. It can be a lonely environment, which breeds a solitary, tough-minded individual or one who is ripe for defeat. According to Charles Morrissey in his history of Vermont, between 1850 and 1900 two out of every five Vermonters left the area. By 1880 over 50 percent of all Vermonters lived outside the state. The mountains, which now serve as a natural playground for skiers and hikers, were then walls to bound over to get to real opportunity. Stephen Douglas suggested that Vermont was a great state to be born in, as long as one left early. It wasn't until the 1950s that people began to outnumber the cows.

In 1945 the state had 26,490 operating farms. Now it has fewer than 5,000. Every major industry in Vermont is now owned by out-of-state firms. The largest landowner in Vermont is the St. Regis Paper Company, with its corporate offices in New York City. Ben and Jerry's Ice Cream Company may get more publicity but they don't compete in the same corporate league.

In certain respects Vermont is still part of the nineteenth century. Except in Burlington and a few other towns, there is little traffic. Factory smoke doesn't darken the sky. Violent crimes, when they occur, still have the power to shock the populace. Maple syrup buckets are more visible than Burger Kings. And even if Ben and Jerry's doesn't make as much as IBM, they give one percent of their profits to World Peace.

But there's another side to Vermont. The silken silence in the mountains is intermittently broken by the metallic rumble of snowmobiles. Land prices are rising beyond the point where natives are able to buy. People from Montreal and New York can control the market. Bernie Sanders, of Burlington, was the only socialist mayor in the country in the late 1970s, and the town had its fifteen minutes of fame when Gary Trudeau in his Doonesbury strip declared it "The People's Republic of Burlington."

It is not a bucolic paradise without violence. Within recent memory, a young woman sitting on the steps of a church enjoying her lunch break in downtown Burlington was killed by a man who strolled along the street with a lead pipe. In Essex Junction two pre-teen girls were raped and one was killed. Vermont, too, has been touched by the modern world.

There is also poverty. Vermont ranks forty-fourth in per capita income but nineteenth in taxes levied. Vermont is a brutal place in the winter and some barely subsist. There are trailer parks and unpainted shacks on dirt roads off the main thoroughfares. There is hopelessness. Fewer Vermont high school students go to college than students from any other state. There is incest and ignorance. As Charles Morrissey suggests, step off the Appalachian Trail in some parts of Vermont and one steps into Appalachia. As with any paradise, the hiker must be careful not to tread on the snake.

But step off the road in other places and it is close to Eden, as seen by Thoreau if not the authors of the Bible. Soon after I reach

Writer helps to mend walls

Vermont I stop on a back road to help two men move a boulder that has slipped from a stone wall bordering their property. Like the woodpile, the image seems left for my attention. Besides, my joints are stiff from driving, and this seems a perfect way to combine a neighborly instinct with simple reportorial nosiness. The two men are both much older than I am, and although they express their gratitude differently, both are happy to have some help. With shoulders and crowbars we roll and slide the rock back into position.

In a way these men resemble the two farmers in Frost's "Mending Wall." One holds back. His language is plain and laconic. "Oomph" is the most colorful syllable he utters. The other chatters away, a droll wit and a devious grin. I half expect him to say, "Something there is that doesn't love a wall/ That sends the frozen-ground-swell under it," but instead he talks about the other man's stony stare.

Like the figures in Frost's poem they seem to represent the two sides of the mythic New England character, a sensibility that has been described as down-to-earth and shrewd, as affable and dour, as cheerfully sarcastic and coldly humorless. The people, like the region, are defined in extremes. And not even "Mending Wall" suggests which perspective is right. One wants to tear down walls, but the other feels that such fences make good neighbors.

I leave the men to finish closing the gaps in the wall, and head on thinking of the conflicting views in Frost's poetry, the sly mysteries, the unanswered questions, the state itself, which seems both cold and friendly, beautiful and treacherous, and the people, who seem both neighborly and isolated. Frost's poems such as "Mending Wall," "Out, Out—," "The Road Not Taken," "After Apple Picking," and so many others, do not explain the New England experience as much as they describe its complexity and offer a simple and eloquent "momentary stay against confusion."

Vermont myths probably started with a somewhat confusing historical record. Samuel de Champlain sailed into the lake that now bears his name in July 1609. Most argue that he was the first European to see that stretch of water. However there are other stories. For instance, in 1853 two workers uncovered a lead tube with a message written on coarse brown paper near a sand pit on the banks of the Missiquoi River, which empties into Lake Champlain near Swanton, Vermont. The message, dated November 29, 1564, said: "This is the salme daye I must die this is the 90th day sine we lef Ship all have perished on the Banks of this river I do to [or, *so*] farewells may future Posteritye knowe our end." It was signed John Graye. But historians have questioned more than Graye's aversion to good grammar and punctuation. The story itself has been discredited by, among others, the Harvard historian Samuel Eliot Morison. But even if the story doesn't tell much about Samuel de Champlain, it at least suggests that Vermonters may have had a playful sense of humor lurking beneath the beards and the Calvinist cool.

There even seems to be something of a debate about how Vermont got its name. Reverend Samuel Peters, an Anglican clergyman who traveled through Vermont in 1763, claims the distinction of naming the state. Supposedly, Peters climbed Killington Peak, which affords a view of Lake Champlain to the west and the Connecticut River to the east, and christened a rock with a bottle of good whisky. According to his account, he dedicated the new land with "a new name worthy of the Athenians and ancient Spartans—which new name is Verd Mont, in token that her mountains and hills shall be ever green and shall never die." There was quite a fiery debate during his lifetime about the truth of his account. His detractors said he had a keen eye as a land speculator rather than a poetic nature. Also, they suggested he had a certain skill in telling prodigious lies. But Peters said the state was named Verd Mont for the Green Mountains and not Vermont, as his opponents claimed, because *Vermont* translates from the French as "Mountain of Maggots."

Whatever the truth of how Vermont was named, there is not much debate about who its most famous sons are. The Allen brothers, Ira and Ethan, are the Daniel Boone, Davy Crockett, Paul Bunyan, and Mike Fink of the Green Mountain State. Ira and Ethan each wrote "histories" of the state, but both seemed more concerned with their own exploits than anything else. Ira's *Natural and Political History of the State of Vermont* was published in 1798 and many historians still go to it to discover information about the beginnings of the state. Ethan Allen wrote his own accounts, even more concerned with himself. Ethan was a big man, much bigger than his younger brother Ira who was nicknamed "Stub" because of his shortness. In one of his stories Ethan describes how he lifted two opponents off the ground, one in each hand, and beat them together until they begged for mercy. An optometrist's and dentist's nightmare, he supposedly could shoot the horns off a buck deer at one hundred yards or chew nails into bits. Once, as he told the story, he strangled a mountain lion that had the audacity to leap onto his broad shoulders. But skill and strength were only part of his talents. Along with his brother, he was the original shrewd Yankee businessman. In one of his reminiscences, he described a farm in Charlotte he and Ira wanted to buy. He got his friend the sheriff to announce that the auction was postponed until "one o'clock tomorrow." The crowd left, planning to come back the next afternoon, but Ethan and Ira returned at one in the morning. Ethan bid a dollar. Ira bid two. And the sheriff said, "Sold to the short man in the coonskin cap."

Ethan and Ira were part of the official history of the state as well as being subjects of tall tales. Vermont is one of the few states to start as an independent republic. From 1777 to 1791 it was a separate nation with Thomas Chittenden as its president. The British established the first settlement in Vermont in 1724, but during most of the first half of the eighteenth century they vied with the French for control of the territory. In 1763 the Treaty of Paris made Vermont part of the British Empire. However, none of the king's colonies seemed interested in taking jurisdiction over the land in between, that is until the royal governor of New Hampshire, Benning Wentworth, began granting land parcels to his friends. Then New York State got interested.

Litigation followed. New York won title to the land. This didn't mean much to Ethan Allen and his companions, called the "Green Mountain Boys" or more harshly dubbed the "Bennington Mob" by New Yorkers. Allen's men kept New York surveyors out, ran sheriffs off the land, burned cabins, and sent New Yorkers scurrying home with Ethan reportedly shouting, "Complain to that damned scoundrel your governor. God damn your governor, laws, king, council, and assembly."

Warrants were issued for Allen's arrest, but the outlaw wasn't cowed. In 1772 he offered his own reward for the capture of important New York officials. It was a bitter battle, mostly of words, at which the Allens seemed particularly good. But the battle ended with the greater struggle—the American Revolution. The New Hampshire Grants, as Vermont was known, became independent. On March 4, 1791, it was admitted as the fourteenth state of the Union.

Vermont had a contrary streak, it seems, right from its beginnings with the Allen boys, a streak that can still be seen in the people's defeat of the Pyramid Mall in Williston recently. The picture of Vermonters—hard-working and unemotional—comes partly from myth and partly from history. Their humor is wry, sometimes as cold and dry as a February wind off Camel's Hump. Dorothy Parker once said that the Vermonter Calvin Coolidge was weaned on a pickle. Some feel the same could be said about many of the other residents of the state.

Without question its most famous inhabitant was neither warrior nor politician but a poet who didn't begin living there until he was forty-six years old, a man as caught between legend and reality as Vermont itself—Robert Frost.

Boris Pasternak once said that no bad man could be a good poet. It's goodness we expect of poets, I guess. They can be wild-eyed drunkards or raging lovers, but we assume it's their free spirits that trigger such explosions. Their anger is fired by truth. The sparks of personality are inspiring. So we expect wildness in our poets, and if we can't have that we take the next best thing: wisdom. Perhaps a white-haired sage, with a meditative and philosophical tone and a wickedly playful smile.

Robert Frost was and is our image of the American poet. He lasted long, wrote poetry that echoes clearly across the three decades since his death, and permanently imprinted his image upon American culture. His poetry conjures up his deep-set, pale blue eyes and throaty New England twang. He was the American poet-father, gentle, loving, and unflappable.

Even Frost might have wanted to believe in his image. In a conversation with Van Wyck Brooks he said, "You want to believe that writers are good men. It's an illusion that dies hard." Maybe the illusion dies hard because on some level we all fancy ourselves poets. If it weren't for our jobs as municipal clerks or bank tellers, we'd be writing poetry and living in cabins in Vermont. We'd front the essential facts of life and learn what they had to teach . . . if only things were different. We imagine the poetic side of our nature to be the best of us, the part that despises and speaks out against all that is wrong with the world and recognizes and cherishes all that is beautiful. Like Frost, we'd have our epitaphs read, "We had a lover's quarrel with the world."

But we may suspect this isn't the whole story about poets or ourselves. The famed editor Maxwell Perkins said all writers are sons of bitches. And this is close to the final estimate that Lawrance Thompson offers in his three-volume biography of Frost, the view that James Dickey appears to share when he says we will never again be able to believe in the Frost myth of the good-neighborly and forebearing writer. We are left instead, Dickey feels, with a small-minded, vindictive, ill-tempered, egotistic, cruel, and unforgiving man. But the original Robert Frost story, as Dickey points out, is still a "secular myth of surprising power and tenacity."

The Robert Frost story is an American story, and its moral might be that we expect too much of our heroes, literary or otherwise. We demand that they be perfect saints or perfect sinners. Nothing in between. Probably, though, Robert Penn Warren had it right when he said writers should only have relatively pure hearts, for if their hearts were truly pure they wouldn't be in the book-writing business in the first place.

The Frost myth, a collaborative creation of the poet and his readers, goes deep and it goes right to the beginning of his story. He's been called the farmer poet, the Yankee bard, and the poet of New England, but he was actually born in San Francisco and lived there for his first eleven years.

The three great influences on the young Frost's life were his mother, his father, and the city of San Francisco itself. This may sound fairly typical, family and environment shaping character, but it's the blend of influences that is interesting. The poet's mother, Isabelle Moodie Frost, was born in Scotland and raised by her devout Presbyterian grandparents. Her tendencies ran toward the mystical and the poetic. William Prescott Frost, Jr., the poet's father, had another set of inclinations. A Massachusetts native and a Harvard graduate, his enthusiasms were aroused, it seems, by the Confederacy, women, drinking, gambling, and adventure. After Harvard he settled down to teach school but just long enough to save some money, marry Isabelle, and head off for a career as a journalist and politician in the West.

William Saroyan once called San Francisco the genius of American cities, "all-fired and hard-boiled, delirious with energy, incoherent because of the many things it has to say, broken-hearted with sorrowful memories." In many ways this describes the young Robert's eleven-year sojourn in the city.

When William Frost moved to San Francisco to begin his career as a writer, the city had barely shaken off its dusty image as a frontier town with muddy streets and murders in broad daylight. Most men still carried guns, and the city still carried a reputation as a dangerous place, especially for newspapermen. People had witnessed editors horsewhipped in the streets and reporters shot in the back. In 1879, six years after William Frost moved to San Francisco, Charles de Young, co-publisher of the *Chronicle*, was shot and killed by the mayor's son.

According to many accounts of the period, drinking was an art and fighting was a recreational activity. Frost's father fit in very well. His was a temper made for the place and times. Even the weather often seemed to complement his nature. The night before the birth of William Frost's first child had been stormy, with thunder, lightning, and rains "besieging" the area, according to one newspaper account. On March 26, 1874, the weather began to stabilize but the elder Frost's temper did not. A few hours before Robert's birth a doctor came to the house to assist in the delivery. But before he could get to Mrs. Frost's bedroom, her husband pointed a pistol at him and warned that if anything went wrong he would suffer the consequences. Mother and doctor survived and Robert Lee Frost entered the tempestuous world of San Francisco.

Shortly after this episode William Frost returned with full force to his youthful ways, drinking, womanizing, and gambling. He was dead from tuberculosis before he turned thirty-five. During his twelve years as a family man he had managed to make a middling career as a journalist, including nine years as city editor on the *San*

Francisco Post, but his political aspirations went sour and illness made his moods even darker than they would have been normally. This frightened Isabelle and left its shadow on Robert. More than once she ran from the house clutching her young son, afraid for both their lives. In 1876 she fled back to New England where her daughter Jeanie was born.

Mrs. Frost returned to her husband but he had long since transformed himself into a "Heathcliff" and her absence altered his behavior for only a short time. Frost's memory of his father's black temper finds its way into his apocalyptic description of San Francisco in "Once By The Pacific." The exaggerated terror at the heart of the poem is the child's fear of the darkness, but it suggests the uncertainty and fright that were surely present in his early years. Robert was educated at home, his indulgent mother most certainly overcompensating for her brutal husband.

With eight dollars to her name after her husband's death, Isabelle Frost borrowed money from her in-laws and returned to New England. There, in Lawrence, Massachusetts, Robert went to school, in the town his father had sought so desperately to leave behind less than twenty years before. His first published poem, "La Noche Triste," appeared in the *High School Bulletin*. His career had started, but it would be twenty-three years before his first book of poetry, *A Boy's Will*, was published. But Frost was surely not idle during that time. Those were years of flight in two ways. His flights were both escapes from restrictions and daring leaps into the unknown. First, there was his brief enrollment at Dartmouth College after high school. Lonely for his high school sweetheart Elinor White, who attended St. Lawrence University, and bored with classroom routine, Frost quit Dartmouth in December, but not before he had a ritual leave-taking party with one of his classmates. They locked themselves in their dorm room, ate Turkish fig paste, and occasionally shouted insults out the half-opened window at the sleeping world. The next day he left Hanover. Years later he remembered what he liked about his first try at college life: "Much of what I enjoyed at Dartmouth," he said, "was acting like an Indian in a college founded for Indians."

For the next few years he worked at a series of odd jobs: cobbler, hired hand, light-trimmer, gate tender, bobbin-boy, and part-time teacher. He continued his pursuit of Elinor White and his pursuit of poetry. In 1894, at twenty years old, he had his first professional success, receiving fifteen dollars for "My Butterfly" from *The (New York) Independent*. Elated by his success Frost wanted to make a life writing poetry. He also wanted to marry Elinor, but she was determined to finish college. His importunings being unsuccessful he decided to win her favor with his poetry. He took "My Butterfly" along with four other poems and had a printer make an edition of two copies of a book titled *Twilight*; the gift did not persuade her to give up her college plans.

This precipitated Frost's second flight, this time toward a place that seemed to be named for his state of mind—the Dismal Swamp in Virginia. In November 1894 he took a train from Massachusetts to New York City and boarded a steamer for Norfolk, Virginia. From there he walked into the wilderness, the unrequited lover looking to punish himself or the woman who rejected him. In the darkness he came upon a group of fishermen, went along with them to Nags Head, and stayed three days with a family in Elizabeth City, North Carolina. After a few days riding the rails toward home, a brief stay in a Washington jail and a short-lived job in Baltimore, the young poet found himself back in Massachusetts.

Within a year he married Elinor White and began teaching again. The next year his first child, a son named Elliott, was born. In 1897 Frost entered Harvard as a special student, staying there two years until, as he put it, he "caught on." Then he left. Actually he was suffering from several physical ailments and a doctor prescribed outdoor activity over scholarly pursuits. He turned to chicken farming, possibly hoping that the birds would take care of themselves and leave him to the business of poetry.

The years from 1900 to 1912 were a time of both tragedy and growth for Frost. Elliott died from cholera and Frost's mother from cancer. He was to see another child die during that decade, but Elinor was to give birth to four others. Frost spent those years farming and teaching to support his family. And although he had little success finding publishers, he continued to write poetry. In 1912 he made his third and possibly most important escape. He put the world of full-time teaching and full-time farming forever behind and left with his family for England. He had been writing since he was eighteen, and now, nearing forty, he decided to sell his New Hampshire farm, which he had kept for the ten years stipulated in his grandfather's will, and cross another threshold—the Atlantic Ocean—to settle in the land of Palgrave's *Golden Treasury*.

During the decade or so he had lived on the New Hampshire farm with his family he had spent more time learning the craft of poetry than he did the art of farming or teaching. Manuscripts piled up. He burst forth as a relative newcomer but he had been practicing his song for years. He never intended to stay in England, only to be discovered there. And he was. He said in one of his letters: "I went away to save myself and fix myself."

He was a man with a plan but fate helped some. A month after he arrived in England he found a publisher for his first book, *A Boy's Will*, which was issued in 1913. A year later one of his most important books, *North of Boston*, was also published. Most of the poems in both volumes had been written long before he landed in England, but Frost's declaration of independence came when he sailed *away* from America, at least for a time. As William Pritchard has said, it was Frost's way of "believing the future into existence." It was a performance, like his departure from Dartmouth or his trek into the Dismal Swamp, part of his writing into fact the poet's story he wished to create. Robert Lee Frost was determined to be the Yankee poet, despite his middle name. He wanted, as James Cox has said, to rise to poetry but bring language down to earth.

When the six Frosts returned to America in 1915, Robert was a poet with the beginnings of a literary reputation that was to continue growing for the half century he had still to live. By 1924 he had won the first of his four Pulitzer Prizes. His return to America was the initial step toward a tidal wave of honors, awards, and public adulation. When he stepped off the SS *St. Paul* in New York Harbor the seeds were being planted for the Frost myth. On the newsstands in Manhattan were copies of the *New Republic* with Amy Lowell's words of praise about *North of Boston*, and Henry Holt and Company had already arranged to bring out the American edition of his works. In the years to come the legend would blossom magnificently.

He had waited a long time for it, but once fame arrived it seemed to come overnight. *North of Boston* was acclaimed by the American critics. *Mountain Interval*, his third book, was published by Henry Holt in 1916. Frost had found a publisher he would stay with for the rest of his life. And he had found a home—New England—with which he would always be identified. It was in 1916 that he began his campus lectures and readings at Harvard and other schools in the area. The next year he took a professorship at Amherst, the first of many academic positions he was to hold during his career. By 1917 he was already on the way to literary stardom; universities were ready to pay for his presence on campus and groups were eager to listen to him "say" his poems. Louis Untermeyer's phrase "the rustic from the Northeast corner" stuck and Frost became the natural genius from New England.

The 1920s were a good time for Frost. His family moved from Franconia, New Hampshire, to South Shaftsbury, Vermont, and his literary ascension continued. He spoke at the Bread Loaf School of English in Ripton, Vermont, in 1921, beginning a pleasant association that was to last the rest of his life. *New Hampshire* won a Pulitzer, and he held enviable positions at Amherst and the University of Michigan. *West-Running Brook* was also published during these years. *Collected Poems* won another Pulitzer, and he was elected to the American Academy of Arts and Letters. He had become an American institution.

Although only five feet nine inches tall, by most accounts Frost was an imposing figure, the center of any room he entered. In a conversation with me, Alf Mapp, renowned biographer of Thomas Jefferson, remembered meeting Frost at the peak of his fame. Mapp, an undergraduate at William and Mary at the time, came into a room where Frost was reciting one of his poems to a small group. The voice was conversational, but Mapp recalls, "a head like a New England boulder, frost on top and over the eyes. Deep-set, sunken eyes but with a conspiratorial twinkle when he looked at you." Frost held his students, his audiences, and the American public within the hypnotic power of those pale blue eyes and that crackling New England twang.

The 1930s were productive poetically but tragic personally for Frost. His sister Jeanie died after spending nine years in a mental institution in Maine. His favorite daughter, Marjorie, contracted puerperal fever after the birth of her first child and died shortly after the Frosts arrived, unable to do anything but watch the pain of her final moments. Elinor Frost died four years later in 1938, and his son Carol committed suicide a few years after. In the years to come Frost was also to see his daughter Irma institutionalized because of mental instability. He was truly one "acquainted with the night."

Frost's last two decades were filled with honors: another Pulitzer, a consultancy to the Library of Congress, goodwill missions for the U.S. State Department, six more books, and innumerable performances as the Vermont sage. He had done pretty much what he had said he intended to do when he was in England, and that was to return to America, buy a farm, and as he said, "grow Yankier and Yankier." He was "never undesigning," as William Pritchard has said, never more than a symbolic farmer. He was a born poet, consciously forging, often with a bit of humor, the myth of the country versifier. Eventually he became his own myth perhaps. But his best poetry refuses to be stereotyped. His poems, he said, were voices behind a door that cuts off the words. He intended his poems to be parables "so that the wrong people can't read them, understand them, and be saved."

According to Philip Gerber, the public saw Frost as the "epitome of the benevolent farmer-sage, a type of ideal regional figure whose communion with nature purified him and raised him to the status of seer, but whose total humility rendered him approachable to all." With his thick workmanlike hands and his silver tongue, he was both intellectual and man of the people.

It is more than coincidence that John F. Kennedy chose him to read at his inauguration, a reading that was the culminating performance of his career. Neither the blustery wind nor the sun's glare could lessen his success on that day. The moment seemed a dramatic tableau, a poet's final appearance, memory conquering chaos in his reciting of "The Gift Outright." At eighty-eight years old, the mythic American poet proved himself capable and versatile. For the public there was no reason to doubt the legend.

From the time he won his fourth Pulitzer Prize in 1943 until his death twenty years later, Frost was a public figure whose writing seemed to take place in his life as an American icon. He was, in Randall Jarrell's phrase, "the Only Genuine Robert Frost in Captivity."

The true story of Robert Frost is somewhere between Lawrance Thompson's picture of the petulant, selfish child-man and the public's image of the literary saint. The picture found in his poetry is more complex than any biographical oversimplification. Frost's favorite figure of speech was synecdoche because he most loved figures in which a part stood for the whole or the whole suggested a specific part. As a poet he was a "synecdochist." New England was for him the whole world, much as Oxford, Mississippi, was for William Faulkner.

Frost appeared to be the archetypal reticent New Englander, but as Reginald Cook remembers the poet, he was more reserved than reticent. His natural dignity didn't allow him to say too much about personal sorrows. Cook said, "The scars, like those of Hawthorne and Melville, were on the soul. Only on occasion did the exposed fractures show lines of stress." In actuality he was not reticent at all. He was a brilliant conversationalist, with marathon sessions sometimes going through the night, a Dr. Johnson on top of Bread Loaf Mountain. As one of his contemporaries put it, epigrams fell like split maple from his sharp mind.

His best poems offer a picture of New England and the people who live there, a world impoverished and beautiful, generous and miserly. As Archibald MacLeish said, they are New England poems because "they use New England for their purposes, and because the look and feel and smell of things in New England is so profoundly and yet so intimately usable: because the landscape lets the human meaning through: because the human asking is reflected here as nowhere else I know."

I decide to start at the conclusion, at the cemetery where Frost is buried with his wife and children. The most direct road, Route 9, goes through Bennington, past the 360-foot-high tower rising atop Mount Bennington in honor of the famous Revolutionary War battle. It's impossible to miss it, a stone erection unlike any other in the area or in the state. Near the tower is the Old Bennington Cemetery, where Robert Frost and his family are buried. There's a sign that points the way and a few arrows to lead tourists, but it's a fairly quiet place—no neon signs or ticket takers. The Old Church looms above and a few houses suggest a settled air of permanence. It's like an outdoor museum without contrivances and without the tour guides.

Frost's grave is situated under a towering maple and beside two clusters of young birches, in the bowl of the mountains. Driving to the cemetery I watch a field mouse scurry across Old Silk Road like a wind-up toy on slick ground. As I step out of the car, a scarlet tanager, a burst of black and red, flies across my line of vision and toward the entrance to the churchyard. I stop about ten yards from the grave because it seems nature has one more performance in mind for me. A red-tailed fox eyes me disdainfully, then darts into nearby woods. The graveyard itself is filled with Minervas and Hirams and Nathans, markers dating from the Revolutionary period.

Frost's gravestone has the chiseled poetry "I had a lover's quarrel with the world," but on my way out of the grounds I notice his is not the only poetry. Nearby is the stone of another respected American writer, William Ellery Channing, whose inscription reads: "In this quiet village among the hills/ William Ellery Channing/ Apostle of faith and freedom/Died at Sunset/October 2, 1845."

Before I turn off the path I notice a man and woman placing a red rose on Frost's grave. The poet's lines "The living come with grassy tread/To read the gravestones on the hill; /The graveyard draws the living still/But never more the dead" seem written for the moment. The man, a professor of physics at Berkeley, and the woman, a graduate student in nursing at Johns Hopkins, decided to celebrate their engagement vow by placing the rose on their favorite poet's grave. The woman remembers the day she heard about Frost's death and cried all morning. "He makes the smallest things in nature seem important," she says.

From Bennington it's Route 7A to South Shaftsbury and Frost's first Vermont house. A shadow from a two-hundred-year-old maple in the yard slants across the "1769" on the front door. It's what the locals call a half-stone cottage, the flat stones coming up to meet the white clapboards on the sides and the steeply pitched gable roof in the front and back. In the back of the house are a few Norway spruces that were probably there when Frost owned the place. There are also the remnants of an apple orchard out back. A stone wall borders the southern edge of the property, once the main entrance to the land. The present owner, Gordon Steck, is a reserved man in his sixties. Balding and portly, he looks a bit like a gentleman farmer and seems more comfortable with his sheep, goats, and pigs than he does with strangers. He bought the house in 1988, but he remembers coming up from Connecticut as a teenager and passing the Frost place, the poet selling apples across the road. Now there's a white ranch-style house over there, and on busy weekends the traffic pours by in a blur of exhaust and a whir of tires.

In ways the stone cottage is much as it was in Frost's time. Frost bought the house in 1920. Dorothy Canfield Fisher, the Vermont novelist, showed the Frosts what was called the Peleg Cole place. The old farmhouse had no furnace, no running water, no bathroom. Frost made some improvements, as have the more recent owners—an addition on back of the house, a new garage near the old barn, a white picket fence out back. But the house still rests, as Lawrance Thompson describes it, on the brow of a hill not far from South Shaftsbury, halfway between Norman Rockwell's Arlington and Bennington College. The ninety-acre farm is now ten acres, the barn that was across the road is gone, the apple orchard out back is diminished, but even for Frost the farm never became what he had hoped. He bought it so that he could set his son up as a farmer, particularly in the apple business. In a letter to a friend, Frost wrote, "I mean to plant a new Garden of Eden with a thousand apple trees of some unforbidden variety." That never happened, but the farm retains much of the character Frost saw in it seventy years ago, a stand of birch, the aged maple, to the west a brook that could have been the model for his lines:

> It is this backward motion toward the source,
> against the stream, that most we see ourselves in,
> The tribute of the current to the source.
> It is from nature we are from.
> It is most us.

To the north of the stone cottage on Route 7A is Howard's "Art" Museum, and the owner, seventy-five-year-old Franklin Howard, a farmer by birth and a poet-painter by inclination, recalls playing in the brook with Prescott Frost, the poet's grand-son. "There's no question that Frost cast a spell over this area," Howard says. Although he seems unaware of it, the spell touched Howard too. The quotation marks around "art" in his sign suggest that Howard may understand his limitations but, like Frost, farm-ing was never more than a preoccupation for Howard. First there was painting, then poetry. He sits in his "museum" six days a week, rubbing the white stubble on his chin and painting his images of Orpheus and Eurydice and of the Vermont countryside as if both were a reasonable subject for a Vermont farmer-artist. His work is better than the velvet Elvis school but is not quite ready for Manhattan's Museum of American Art. His poetry is stacked in boxes by his easel—hundreds of poems about the countryside, about Greek myths, about the ocean. As I'm leaving he says, "You can feel the spell of Frost most clearly at the Gully Farm."

About a mile and a half as the road curves or three quarters of a mile through the fields and woods is Frost's second house in this part of Vermont, the Gully Farm. Although the house sits out of sight from the road, high on one of the rolling hills in the area, it is nestled among ridges in a hollow or gully. Its name is minimally descriptive, not nearly adequate to capture the beauty of the place. As Lawrance Thompson describes it, the eighteenth-century house was tucked away "as though the original builder had thought of ways to protect himself from northeast and southwest winter gales...snuggling down in this hillside pocket without losing the best view of all." According to Thompson, Frost liked the coziness of the "little and ancient house."
  The view is still magnificent. Frost took down most of the outbuildings and barns that obstructed the views down the hillside. Now the grass, along the 100-acre sloping roller coaster of a front yard, is manicured like a golf course. It's a hidden world with a perfect angle of vision. A beautiful setting for anyone, it may have been the ideal location for the writer, allowing him to see without being seen, to be in the world and separate from it at the same time. Gully Farm has what geographer Jay Appleton calls "prospect" and "refuge." It has both a long sweeping vista that allows infor-

mation gathering and a hidden perspective. Few environments have both.

In a letter to Louis Untermeyer Frost wrote, "I bought a farm for myself for Christmas. One hundred and fifty three acres in all, fifty in woods. The house a poor little cottage of five rooms, two ordinary fireplaces and one large kitchen fireplace all in one central chimney as it was in the beginning.... My farm probably doesn't compare with yours for views."

Unless Untermeyer had a palace in the Alps, Frost was being modest. He bought the farm in late 1928 for $5,000. Today someone would have to pay ten times as much for a one-acre building lot. Frost moved into the house with his wife in October 1929 and was, according to Thompson, "delighted with the lofty isolation of it." In 1944 the poet deeded the farm to his daughter-in-law and grandson. There have been a number of owners since then, but the most famous after Robert Frost is the present owner, Norman Lear.

Lear, the producer of "All in the Family," "Maude," and "Mary Hartman," bought the house in 1978 and lives in it part of the year. He was once a door-to-door salesman, hawking among other things a novelty ashtray, and that might account for his ready smile and immediate "Come on in" when he sees me at his side door in the rain. He remembers what it feels like to be standing on the outside waiting to get in.

In a way Lear has always been on the outside. Born in New Haven, Connecticut, the sixty-six-year-old writer-producer moved in and around New England as a boy. His father, Herman K. "King" Lear, was a traveling salesman, always on the search for a quick dollar. He came close to finding it once, but ended up instead in Deer Island federal prison in Massachusetts, convicted of trading fraud. When "King" Lear got out of prison, he went right back into business, selling two-burner hot plates and whistling teakettles. And although he told his son that he could "put shit on a stick and sell it for lollipops," he never became successful.

In his youth Norman followed in his father's footsteps. After a year in college and four years as a radioman and gunner in the Air Force during World War II, Lear returned from New England and worked for his father until "King" Lear went bankrupt. That's when Norman tried selling a combination ashtray-coffee saucer-cigarette holder. After one good season, sales plummeted and the novelty wore off. Lear went to California and started selling lamps and ships' clocks, and then gags and one-liners to comedians in Los Angeles. He soon found that there was more money per hour selling jokes than selling furniture, but he was his father's son and wanted the big score.

It came when he telephoned Danny Thomas's agent and made believe he was a reporter from the *New York Times* who needed some facts in a hurry. They were facts only Thomas could verify. The agent gave him Thomas's private number. Lear called, tried to sell him a few jokes, and when Thomas asked how he got his number, Lear told him the truth. Instead of getting angry Thomas admired the young man's ingenuity. His career had started.

The rest is television history, shows that outraged, shocked, and amused millions of viewers. In 1978, the year "All in the Family" won the Emmy for best comedy series, he retired from television, bought his Vermont farm, and made plans to produce a few movies. Part of each year he makes those plans as he walks the woods behind his Vermont house. In the caretaker's cabin a few hundred feet from the main house he has his office, and there he returns to the writing desk that began his career. A cross-stitch hangs over one door: "By all accounts this should be the place."

Lear's description of how he came to purchase the farm suggests that for him it is *the* place. He was visiting a friend in Pasadena, a modern art collector, and they sat in his living room discussing painting and sculpture when the man's daughter walked in, introduced herself, and asked her father if Ken Nolan had sold his house yet. Lear says he doesn't know why but his heart turned over right there. "It didn't stop racing until three days later," he says. "That's when I finally got to see the property. But somehow I knew I wanted to live here before I even saw it. I think I know what Frost loved about this place. It's the most female piece of land I've ever seen, the way the land moves, all hips and bellies and thighs." Lear tries unsuccessfully to light one match, then another, raises his eyebrows as if to acknowledge defeat, and continues, "The planet is being raped, but in Vermont it feels that things have changed less than anywhere else in this country. Vermonters haven't changed."

The farmhouse, which from a distance looks as if it too has not changed much since 1929, has been renovated Hollywood style. The huge country kitchen is all shining white tile, sparkling pans, and modern appliances. The barn out back was renovated into a studio, and an addition larger than the original house connects the barn and the cottage. Skylights, lofts, and rooms big enough for square dancing make up the new "farmhouse."

I wait in the breakfast room while Lear speaks with an architect and a steady stream of handymen. One group of workers walks in discussing possible reasons for the poor TV reception in the house. They are there to repair the satellite dish that lies hidden about five hundred feet back in the woods. For thirty minutes workers move in and out as I ponder the red, white, and blue character of the house. There are flags or pictures of them everywhere. A red, white, and blue quilt hangs on the wall, a poster of the American flag from the Whitney Museum on another, a painting of a Revolutionary War soldier on a third.

The real Lear seems to be dramatized in all this, part salesman, part poet. A New Englander raised to fame and fortune in Hollywood, Lear is sentimental about what he describes as the magic of Vermont. But then again he's just sentimental. He once said, "I know I wear my emotions on my sleeve—sometimes I think I must sound like a walking soap opera—but frankly, I can't find anything wrong with that, personally or professionally. . . . I like wet people." He may be a more logical heir to the Gully Farm than he at first glance appears. His white hair and gentle eyes have something of Frost in them, and his puckish grin has the poet's mischief in it. He seems to have the same love of the land that Frost had. And even if Frost would not have sanctioned the satellite dish, he probably would have understood Lear's wish to "provide, provide." For Lear, as for many Americans, Frost's poetry represents a rural ideal, even though there are few idylls in his verse. His poems do not depict the country as a comfortable escape from a frenzied, complicated urban situation. Instead, like Thoreau, Frost suggests that a rural world is the place to live deliberately, to front the essential facts of life, to drive life into a corner and reduce it to its lowest terms. The satellite and the additions are Lear's concessions to Hollywood, but he hopes that for him, as it did for Frost, the Gully Farm offers a perspective on Vermont.

My last view of Lear is in his living room, which overlooks the sloping front yard. He looks, as Frost did sixty years before, over the mountains and valleys before him. Frost would certainly have appreciated the modified lines from *King Lear* that hang framed on the wall near the window:

> Come let's away
> We two alone will sing like birds i' the cage
> ...so we'll live
> In the ebb and flow of the moon.

Vermont is not only a land in between, it is a land divided. Near East Rupert in an old marble quarry fed by underground springs, I meet Bill Lewis. While he watches his twelve-year-old daughter dive off the blocks of rough-cut marble that line this man-made crater, he complains about rising land prices and low wages. Bill, a car salesman in Manchester, tried to buy land two years ago but was unable to do it. "I've thought about buying in New York State," he says. "It's so much cheaper. When you buy in Vermont you pay 30 percent more because you're buying the Vermont mystique."

The quarry is Vermont in microcosm. On this lazy summer afternoon people loll upon the marble ledges like seals on the California coast. Long-haired teenagers, flashbacks to the sixties, stretch out and listen to music. Some of them leap from thirty-foot precipices or swing from ropes knotted to birch trees, a new version of Frost's swingers. Catapulting themselves onto a point in space, they appear to stand still, and like cartoon characters on a crest of air, they glance toward heaven and fall back to earth, which after all, as Frost said, is "the right place for love." Young people make up the majority, but there are farmers after a day's work, waiters and waitresses from local inns, and tourists, plenty of tourists like myself who have sniffed out the local hideouts. This may be the modern Vermont—Pabst Blue Ribbon cans and the awful strains of Metallica booming from radios. An older Vermonter walks around the rim of the quarry, a plastic garbage bag in hand, collecting bottles and cans and other debris. Old and new strike a precarious balance.

Robert Williams, the curator of the nearby Shaftsbury Historical Society, tries to strike the same equilibrium but finds the myth and realities of Vermont at times hard to balance. Born in 1944, Williams spent his first thirty years in West Shaftsbury on a dairy farm. He went to college at the University of Vermont, leaving in 1974 to get a master's degree at San Francisco State. He stayed there seven years, until the pull of home became too great. Both Frost and Vermont have had profound influences on his life, Williams claims, but he is certain that he doesn't romanticize the people or the place any more than Frost did. He agrees with Ezra Pound: "Frost has been honestly fond of the New England people. I dare say with spells of irritation. He has rendered their lives honestly and seriously. He has never turned aside to make fun of it. He has taken their tragedy as tragedy, their stubbornness as stubbornness."

Williams is fond of disagreeing with Archibald MacLeish's statement about how usable Vermont is for artists. "This state isn't so much usable as it is used," says Williams. Williams, who looks quite a bit like Oliver Hardy without the whisk-broom moustache, is also fond of telling an old joke about Vermont. "There's this New York City fella traveling through Vermont," he begins. "And he stops at a Vermont farmhouse to ask directions. 'Can you tell me where Putney is?' 'Nope,' says the farmer. 'Can you tell me where the road to Rutland is?' 'Nope,' says the farmer. 'Can you tell me where the next main road is?' 'Nope,' says the farmer. The city man, who has gotten increasingly frustrated, says angrily, 'You don't know much!' 'Well, I ain't lost,' says the farmer."

For Williams the joke tells a lot about Vermont and its people. "People here are always building walls," Williams says. "Frost was right when he had that farmer say 'Good fences make good neighbors.' That's the Vermont mentality. People live within walls here. And maybe we have to. The economy and the environment are in a downward spiral. In 1790 the population in Shaftsbury was at its peak. We have fewer people now. The area was settled in the 1760s, and by the 1790s they had depleted the thin layer of topsoil.

Many of the people left are part of that used character. Frost wrote about this loss and sadness, but he made poetry out of us. Some of the women's clubs see only what they want to see in his writing. They look at only the comfortable poems, but that's not the real Frost. It's like the joke—there's something more to it."

As he talks about Frost, Williams's rutted face becomes thoughtful. He seems to be speaking more about himself than anyone else. The pathos he speaks of may be his own. When he leaves at four this afternoon from the Historical Society, he will return to his house in Bennington and to his part-time job as a night watchman, what he calls security work.

On my way toward Middlebury I stop in Manchester Center long enough to visit the stores—Ralph Lauren's, Liz Claiborne's, Anne Klein's. It's a Disneyland for wealthy adults. The license plates invariably read Connecticut or New York. I decide to take in the flow of people and traffic from the park bench in the center of town, a front row seat I share with Andy Thompson. Andy looks eighty-five but he's only fifty-seven. He works at Angelo's Restaurant as a dishwasher. He watches the cars go by until it's time to go to work at five.

Thompson is out of place in Manchester, or seems to be, among the Polo shirts and Rolexes. Three of his front teeth are missing and the rest are stained brown from tobacco. White hairs, which look as stiff as porcupine quills, grow along the ridge of his nose. An oil-stained red baseball cap rests precariously, tilted to the right, on his head. The word "POISON" covers the front, but when I ask him about it, he says it could stand for anything. His left arm is filled with tatoos. One says "Hell Driver." The forearm is lined with initials—DL, PC, WC, KC. Initials of friends, he says. "I put them on so long ago, I've forgotten who they all were."

Intentionally or not, Andy has forgotten a lot. He grew up in Orwell and Shoreham, Vermont, where his father worked as a hired man on farms. He says he can't remember exactly when his father died. His mother is still alive, though, and lives in the Castleton Meadows Senior Center. As far as he can recall, Andy visited her four or five years ago. Castleton is about an hour up the road. Because he hasn't spoken to her in a number of years, he's not actually sure if she's alive. A brother lives in Wallingford or Danby, "one of those towns," he says. Andy has a sister in Manchester, but they don't talk. Sometimes she drives by the park bench, but she never stops. "I don't even know where she lives. She's a stranger like the two people who just drove by in that car," he says, pointing to the road.

Andy is not caught up by the mystique of Vermont. He seems to personify May Sarton's remark about the difficulties of living in New England. For him Vermont is just like any other place. He's never left the state because he's never had the chance. Andy's not sure what he makes per hour right now, but he knows he pays $150 a month in rent for a one-bedroom apartment. "I don't know how many times I've shot for broke in my life," he says. "It's hard to make ends meet. Years ago I had a dream about being a book writer, but I got used to washing dishes."

As I drive toward Middlebury the lines from *King Lear* that hung near the window in Norman Lear's living room return to me:

> We two alone will sing like birds i' the cage
> . . . so we'll live
> In the ebb and flow of the moon.

Somehow it feels especially good to be on the road, away from that bench in Manchester. But before I get far out of town I am destined to meet three women whose lives and memories are very different from Andy Thompson's.

Barbara Comfort emigrated to Landgrove, Vermont, in 1943 when she was twenty-seven years old. Among other things she's a mystery writer who is touted by the Northshire Bookstore in Manchester. In what is described as the best bookstore in Vermont, her mysteries are prominently displayed near the main cash registers. I find copies of four of her novels neatly stacked on the center table in Northshire. When I express an interest in finding out more about her, I am directed toward a woman whose desk is in the back of the store. Our conversation is pleasant enough until she notices a notepad in my back pocket. "Are you a *journalist?*" It comes out like *Nazi war criminal*, so I talk about the book I am writing. Things relax a bit. After all, I'm not exactly a journalist, but what

Leaning silo in Manchester, Vermont

Andy Thompson would call a book writer. There's no newspaper editor lurking in the shadows. Softening, she says, "Barbara Comfort lives in Landgrove."

"Where's that?"

"I won't tell you."

Journalists are like detectives or at least, as historians do, they like to play detective, but this seems a strange mystery, absurdly easy to solve. I understand the isolationism that is behind her refusing to tell me where the town is, but I think she should notice the irony of her position. She is working in Northshire Bookstore in Manchester, Vermont, the sort of store that sells Stephen Dobyns's mysteries and Osip Mandelstam's poetry, the kind of place you might expect in Berkeley or Greenwich Village but not in the Green Mountains. She is trying to preserve the innocence of the place by keeping me out, but she is working in a store that exists mainly for tourists and the New York-Connecticut crowd. Not many farmers are reading Mandelstam. She also fails to realize that I have a copy of Rand McNally in my car.

What I fail to realize is that Landgrove isn't on the map, any map I can find. But I know that wouldn't have stopped Lew Archer, so I ask a few questions at some gas stations, and lo and behold there is Landgrove over the mountain, a left toward Peru, and down a dirt road. It's near the Bromley ski area, and according to some of the natives a few people left in disgust a couple of years ago when Bromley built the "world's longest alpine slide." Some others left when the center of Manchester turned into such a traffic jam that the natives began to call it "Malfunction Junction."

Barbara Comfort likes it, though. Her home has a view of Bromley Mountain and she's close enough to visit "Mallchester" (what she calls Manchester) if she wants. Like many of the wealthier Vermonters, Comfort lives half the year in Vermont and half the year in New York City. At seventy-three years old, Comfort finds herself spending more and more time in Vermont. What used to be four months a year is now closer to eight. In New York City she lives in a historical district of brick town houses where her apartment overlooks what used to be Aaron Burr's yard. She is co-owner of the town house, which is on the edge of Soho. In Vermont she lives on the chin of a mountain in a small house with cathedral ceilings and rolling glass walls. The house is built in a circle of sorts, the circle bulging out as rooms have been added on.

Comfort started out as a painter of portraits and landscapes and she still is. She writes all winter and paints all summer. She studied in the École des Beaux-Arts in France and has had a number of solo shows, but she made her money as a designer-inventor. Early in her career as an artist she opened her own plastics factory in New York. She made enough money to buy thirty acres on a mountainside in Landgrove and build a house. In recent years she deeded five-acre lots to her godchildren so that she's surrounded by friends.

There's a lot of New York City still in Barbara Comfort. When she meets me at the door of her house, she looks more like a suburban mother than an artist-factory owner-mystery writer. Her white hair is carefully combed. She's attractive and looks far younger than her seventy-three years. Seeming more a part of Park Avenue than Vermont, she wears a white blouse, blue pants suit, and a blue scarf with white dots. Her white earrings sway like leaves in the breeze as she bends to pick up one of her two small dogs.

Her self-portrait sits on an easel in her living room. Nearly finished, it is a realistic portrait, not sentimentalized and not modest. The eyes in the painting look undaunted, the mouth looks ready to speak. When Comfort does speak it pops with a New York idiom. She "borrowed some dough" to buy this place, or it "ain't worth hot spit," or her friends "are all moving out of the city or corking off." Like Frost's West-running Brook, she seems to trust herself to go by contraries. She invented a holder for the Cuisinart blade and a special container for ice cubes. Both were money makers. She also invented the "edible toothpick," which never made a profit.

In the back of her house is a shed. The sign over it reads "Landgrove Press." It's the publishing company she founded with friends. It's also her publisher. To hell with New York City publishers, she says. Her books will never win an Edgar, but they're fun to read—and a bit shocking—lesbianism, seduction, and murder in small-town Vermont.

Near the shed in the back yard is a maple tree with a blue ladder propped against it. "I made that ladder," Comfort says. "I like a ladder against a tree. Kids need something to climb when they visit me. I climb it myself occasionally." A little behind the tree is a small clearing and in the grove is an eight-foot-high plastic Statue of Liberty, which she bought during the bicentennial celebration. As I leave, she smiles and hands me an edible toothpick. "Try one on the way down the mountain," she says.

Maxine Atherton lives in Dorset, Vermont, and at eighty-five years old feels she can rightly claim to have caught more salmon than any other woman in the world. When she recounts the past, her eyes widen and she seems to forget the present. She has a schoolgirlish lilt in her voice that seems somehow to match the pink bow tied in the back of her hair. When she decides not to answer a question, she looks down at her blue sneakers and then abruptly raises her head, looks right at me with her big, moist eyes, and tells the story she wants to tell, whether it has anything to do with the question or not. She's fished all over the world, in Ireland and France and Norway. She started fishing with her first husband, John Atherton, who was, according to Maxine, the greatest fisherman who ever lived. He wrote a book about fishing, but he was known as a commercial artist, a good friend of Norman Rockwell, and a regular contributor to the *Saturday Evening Post*.

She grew up in California and married Atherton in 1927, when she was twenty-three. Like Frost's family, her ancestors started in New England and ended up in the West. And like Frost, she eventually travelled back to New England. In 1929 she moved with her husband to New York City, where he went into advertising. Their only daughter was born in 1932 and shortly after that they moved to Ridgefield, Connecticut. In 1944 they moved to Arlington to be near the Rockwells and the renowned fishing in the Battenkill, a river famous for its trout.

Soon after their move to Vermont, John had a skiing accident at Bromley, suffering a concussion, and Maxine is certain that his personality and his work changed right after the accident. She won't say much about it, but he became mean at times, in public and in private. But she will talk about the change in his work. "He conceived things differently after the accident," she says. "He saw things in another way. His paintings became abstract." She points behind her at a painting on the wall, a group of clowns after the circus. The painting has an eerie magic to it, a Dali-like quality, dark and surreal.

While she was married to Atherton, she met many famous people, Robert Frost among them. He came to dinner once at her house with the musician Carl Ruggles. All she can remember about Frost is that "he looked like his work." But musicians are far more interesting than poets, she feels. The only interesting literary story she has, she says, is the one about her fight with Robert Penn Warren. Fire comes into her eyes when she recalls the moment. She seems ready to fight again.

"I was at a dinner party in New York at the Haas house. A lot of literary people were there. William Faulkner sat across from me. He didn't say much. But Robert Penn Warren did. I think he was taken with me. Well, everybody was talking about what they'd written, what they were working on, what they'd produced. He asked me what I had done and I told him I'd just produced a baby. He said, 'Well, that isn't hard to do.' I hit the ceiling. I looked him right in the eye and said, 'Well, you can't do it.'"

Soon after John Atherton died, Maxine took off to fish the chalk streams in France and Spain. She went to the Klondike because her father had once gone there. And she went to Labrador just to see about the fishing. In 1960 she met a man who was handsome and charming until she married him. "He wasn't an artist and he was a lousy fisherman," she recalls. She divorced him and concentrated on salmon and trout and the book that she's now finishing. "It's a book dedicated to ladies who want to fish and never had the chance," she says. "It's not only a fishing book, though. It's a book of essays about my adventures, about John Atherton, and fishing. There are twenty-six important rivers that I've fished and there are twenty-six essays. The main theme is the need for conservation. I've seen the salmon disappear in the last ten years. My real hero is nature. It's a story about nature and what we've done to our resources."

Right before I leave, the mail comes and she opens a letter from a publisher who is interested in seeing more of her book. She lets out a yell of joy and jumps into the air. As I drive across the little bridge over her stream I catch a glimpse in my rearview mirror of her heading back into her house, her hair shining in the sunlight and the ribbon askew on the back of her head.

Before I leave Dorset, I stop in H N Williams Department Store. Actually, there seems to be something of a difference of opinion about the nature of the store. A sign over the front door says "General Store" but a sign over the barn attached to the left side says "Department Store." It's not much of either and some of both.

H N Williams Store is a time machine into the past. When it was built in 1840, William Williams ran it as harness shop. Sweat pads, lead ropes, and halters were the order of the day. One hundred and fifty years later sweat pads and halters still hang in the narrow entranceway, just below the exposed wiring and next to the "Sure Shot Ribbon Cut" chewing tobacco sign. It's the sweet, earthy smell of grain that fills the corridor.

The store has eight rooms and enough variety to make Woolworth's blush. The old thermometer on the wall reads ninety-two degrees and a handwritten sign under it says, "We have cold soda now." If it weren't for the heat, the present would seem far away, because the store is cluttered with the past. Old advertising posters for Bag Balm, a fast-healing, all-purpose ointment. Salada Tea. Dr. Naylor's Veterinary Products. Pyrex Ware. Nebo cigarettes—5 cents a pack. In most stores this sense of the past would be carefully calculated, old posters consciously placed to create a chic feeling of heritage, but it's clear that these posters and signs have been there for years, covering holes in the walls or simply becoming too familiar a part of the place to be torn down. The atmosphere of this store has not been manufactured. It has grown of its own accord, shaped from the inside out like a human personality.

The difference between the tourists and the regular customers is easy to see. The regulars walk in unamazed and act as if they had all the time in the world. They sit around as if it were a pub and they were on their way home after a hard day, even if it's only 7:45

in the morning. The tourists walk in and their eyes grow big as moons and they begin to talk louder. One woman comes in and says, "This will boggle your mind, dear. Come see this place, Harry. Now this is a country store!" She turns to the woman at the table and asks, "Did you buy the store this way or put it together like this?" What the tourist doesn't seem to realize is that a store like this one can't be controlled. It takes on the shape of its customers and owners over the years. Like a child, it was at first somewhat governable. But after a century or so it became an adult, set in its ways. It would take a fire or a bulldozer to change it significantly.

At 7:30 in the morning when Ruth Bromlee, the thirty-eight-year-old owner, opens the store, the only sounds are birds chirping and the awful whine of a chain saw. Every few minutes, like a chorus, the sound becomes a momentary silence, then a sharp crack as a tree falls. Ruth, who owns the place with her forty-six-year-old husband Dennis, is there every morning, wearing jeans and a T-shirt and carrying a leather change bag over her shoulder. As far as Ruth can remember, there's never been a cash register in the store, only a change bag. Theirs was made fifteen years ago by a neighbor down the road.

But many of the local customers charge, and for that purpose Ruth and Dennis use a "McCaskey," a metal box with a series of flaps to keep track of accounts. An alphabetical order combined with a number system allows them to follow accounts and add them up at the end of the month. The case for the McCaskey is fireproof, but a hinge has been sprung for six or seven years, and they just leave it open at night. The Bromlees work on trust.

A customer walks in and asks if they take MasterCard. They don't but they will take a personal check. For a moment this seems too much for the tourist to comprehend, but eventually she smiles and opens her checkbook. Dennis Bromlee strolls in to help out. He's been cleaning his garage. He's tall and heavy with a boyish face, red hair and freckles and a shy smile. He looks like an Idaho farm boy and he once was. "This business is built on good intentions," he tells me. "You have to trust people. You can't be in all eight rooms at once."

H N Williams Store in Dorset, Vermont

The eight rooms seem to be an example of chaos barely held in check. There are hardware, paint, crowbars, rolls of chain, screws and rusty nails, and some bolts over two feet long. Candy, baseball hats, shoes, work clothes, postcards, horsewhips, sliced beets, and Wyman's wild blueberry pie filling. People roam around and browse while a rat casually nibbles on a bag of grain. "There's generally a method in where things are," Dennis says, "but I'm not sure what it is." For Ruth, the method is clear: put things wherever you can find a place. That means, in the main room, around the wood stove that seems to be the heart of the store, there are piles of gloves and marshmallows, Doan's pills and lanterns, suspenders and canned mushrooms, Blistex and potted meat.

Each room has a name: the clothing room, the main room, the grain room, the old grain room, the hardware room, the cellar room, the upstairs room, and the northend room. But the names change periodically, and the name of the room depends upon who is speaking. Ruth and Dennis may use many of the same descriptive phrases, but Ada Rumney, Ruth's mother, may use her own names when she helps out each day.

Dennis and Ruth bought the store from Ruth's parents, Ada and Austin Rumney, in 1983. The store has been in Ruth's family for five generations, and it's important to her to keep it that way. Ruth and Dennis met at Brigham Young University, where Ruth went to school after living her first eighteen years in Dorset, Vermont. She married Dennis, became a Mormon, and they moved to Richfield, Idaho, to start a dairy farm in 1972. But after a visit to Vermont, Dennis fell in love with the countryside, and in 1977 they started working at the store. They have four sons and a daughter, but none of them works in the store. Their seventeen-year-old son works as a dishwasher at Mistral's Restaurant, and their fifteen-year-old daughter works as a clerk at Liz Claiborne's. When I ask who will take over the business, Ruth says, "We'll see."

Today business is thriving, a steady flow of customers buying Charleston Chews, cans of V-8, bales of moss, horse masks, 100-pound bags of fertilizer, lengths of copper tubing, and bottles of mane and tail conditioner. People come in, lean against the wood stove, and spend some time talking about the weather or the town police waiting down the road on the lookout for speeders. One man walks in and dramatically throws his hands in the air, saying, "God bless you, Dennis. I need some sanding paper. You haven't been here the last few times I've been in." When Dennis explains that he's been cutting wood, the man laughs and says, "That's no excuse. But it's good to see you here. To see that you're working sometimes."

In order to make ends meet during the past year, Ruth worked as a teacher in a nearby school. This year Dennis hopes they can get by with her doing only some substituting. Dennis graduated from Brigham Young with a major in political science and a minor in English. At one time he wanted to go to law school, but decided he had had enough of school. He seems happy where he is, five acres and a house across the road from the store and next door to his in-laws. He has a good-sized garden and he helps his father-in-law with the maple syrup business. And he has the store. "For me the store means people," he says. "It's good to have a lot of friends." Ruth doesn't disagree, but she says, "I could be happy almost anywhere."

It's taken me two days to travel the two hours from Manchester to Middlebury, but I get there in time to speak with Ron Powers. Dressed in a white sport coat and beige pants, Powers walks into the nineteenth-century atmosphere of the Middlebury Inn looking a bit like Mark Twain. Powers, with a Pulitzer Prize and an Emmy for his television commentary and criticism, is now teaching at Middlebury College and researching a book on small-town life in America in the 1980s. His most recent book, *White Town Drowsing*, examined life in Hannibal, Missouri, 150 years after Twain's birth. With poetic irony Powers describes his growing up on the banks of the Mississippi and the entrepreneurial midwestern spirit in the town that made Twain's name a marketing idea in the 1980s. Hannibal, a town Powers describes as a place on the way to nowhere, was slowly becoming a ghost town. With some public relations advice, the town fathers decided to resurrect the most famous ghost they had—Mark Twain.

Twain's name peered at motorists and pedestrians from produce

Ron Powers on the front porch of the Middlebury Inn

trucks, bakeries, and movie theaters. Theme parks were planned and the sesquicentennial organizers found marketing strategists parachuting in from all over the United States. In his book Powers makes it dramatically clear what Hannibal meant to him as a boy and what it had become in the struggle to survive.

"There's no theme park mentality in New England," Powers says, "and probably that's why I'm here. America has jettisoned its sense of history, but in Vermont there seems to be a tense, living memory of its past. Vermonters know where they came from, how the land should be used, how to do things with their hands."

Vermont and the small town of Middlebury where he lives remind him of the past. Before he first came to Bread Loaf for the writer's conference in 1979, Powers was a good staunch, corn-fed midwesterner, even if he lived in New York City. He expected Bread Loaf to be filled with pasty-faced intellectuals discussing post-modernism. It wasn't. He's been there every summer since and in 1988 he became a full-time resident of Vermont. "My experience connects with Frost in a fairly tangible way," he says. "You feel his presence at Bread Loaf and all over this community, but he hasn't been appropriated as a marketing symbol as Twain has in Hannibal."

Powers realizes that it's easy to over-romanticize Vermont and the Bread Loaf community. The summer conference becomes Brigadoon for some. Writers are recognized and appreciated. The environment, Powers says, is close to heaven. Bread Loaf, like Vermont itself, becomes an escape from the dislocation and terrors of the city. For those like Ron Powers, leaving the city and looking perhaps to recapture childhood's dreamy serenity, small-town Vermont may satisfy an important need. Sitting in the Middlebury Inn, fittingly under a painting of the white-haired Robert Frost, Ron Powers talks about corporate relocation, a modern plague that he says is partly responsible for America's becoming a nation of strangers. For him, Vermont is a return to a remembered time of tree-lined streets and neighborliness. It is a reimagining of the past.

Powers senses a loneliness pervading Frost's work, a loneliness that is in the cold mountain landscape itself. It's an environment that teaches limitations but also offers tremendous possibilities. It's the sort of land that demands alertness and might allow an individual to be "whole again beyond confusion" as Frost said. Many come to Vermont to refashion their lives from the lines of a dream of small-town or rural America. Some come to escape the violence and indifference of the city. Like Frost they are fugitives, not farmers. Others come, Thoreau echoing in their minds, to live deliberately in the world, to be awakened by the extremes in the landscape. Vermont is a place to come to, the balance of numbers clearly swinging from the native Vermonters to the immigrants from New York, New Jersey, Connecticut, and other states. Many of them are city-born and -raised, like Robert Pack, poet and director of the Bread Loaf Writer's Conference.

Before meeting with Pack in his office at Middlebury College, I drive up to the Bread Loaf Campus. Route 125 is a winding mountain road that follows the course of the Middlebury River. Every now and then the river appears on the left, a narrow stream with big boulders and raging white water. Frost is everywhere. Driving up the mountain, I go over the Robert Frost Memorial Bridge, past the Robert Frost Interpretive Trail, and stop briefly at the Robert Frost Wayside of the Green Mountain National Forest. I expect to meet picnickers and poets, but instead I meet a man with a two-year-old monkey. Her name is Cassie and she's wearing a pink shirt and diapers. The monkey is friendly or at least wants part of my sandwich. Cassie climbs over my shoulder, down my arm, and grabs a piece of the bread. I ask the man about monkeys as pets. He doesn't like the question much and says, "Monkeys and children don't make good pets. Cassie is my daughter." I have visions of Tarzan for a moment, but the man is wearing khaki pants, an Oxford shirt, and boating shoes. Not even in Vermont would Tarzan dress like this. This is his fourth monkey, he tells me. He raises it until it is three years old and then it is sent to the Boston Medical Center to be trained for one year. The monkey is then given to a quadriplegic, helping to feed its master and do other necessary chores. Before I can ask any other questions, the man is off, the monkey on his shoulder, into the woods.

Frost's cottage in Ripton, Vermont

A short drive farther up the mountain is Frost's cabin, within walking distance of Ripton and the Bread Loaf Campus. In 1938 Frost began living part of each year in the three-room cabin that was part of the Homer Noble Farm. The farm had a house and the cabin on 150 acres bordering the national forest. *Walden* was one of Frost's favorite books and this was his cabin in the woods.

Unlike Thoreau's Walden Pond, Frost's little place hasn't changed much over the years. The cabin looks exactly as it did in 1938, right down to the phoebes sitting on a branch of a white birch near the little house. Like Keats, I wonder if the voice I hear this passing day was heard on a similar day by another, by Robert Frost perhaps. Only the slightest breeze stirs the air near his cabin but the woods are alive with sounds, seeds and leaves falling through the green canopy, a steady sound like raindrops. The cabin is a few hundred feet up the path from the farmhouse. There are no ticket takers or tour guides to destroy the effect of traveling back in time. But there is one obstacle to dreamy serenity: the black flies. They swarm around me as I walk up the path, drawing blood and curses. They don't stop me from going to the cabin, but they make me change my leisurely pace. The doors to the cabin are locked, but the screened-in porch is open. Safe for a moment from the insects, I peer through the triangle of glass left unblocked by window curtains. I can't see much, a table, a few chairs, but I do see a copy of *Robert Frost: The Early Years* by Lawrance Thompson. Frost's ghost, if it roams the premises, probably won't approve of the reading matter.

I race down the path and into the car. Bread Loaf campus is about a mile up the road. The mountain road rises to a plateau. The elevation is about 1,000 feet and the Green Mountains rise to the east and west. Ron Powers was right. This does seem like Brigadoon. The Victorian Bread Loaf Inn, which overlooks a field of wildflowers that leads to the western branch of the Middlebury River, is the center of things. All of the buildings that were part of the original inn owned by Joseph Battell are painted yellow and green. The rest are painted white. Buildings dot the 300-odd acres of the campus, and students and writers talk in clusters or stroll along the grounds.

In 1915 Joseph Battell donated 30,000 acres of land near Ripton to Middlebury College. Five years later the land became the college's Bread Loaf campus, used for a graduate program in literature and what was to become the first writers' conference in America. Frost's first performance at Bread Loaf was in 1921 with a reading of his poems. Within a few years he was a traditional part of the summer program. Soon he was the center of it. He liked people to see him as the godfather of the place, the spiritual father. The institution of Bread Loaf and the institution of Robert Frost dovetailed. It was the perfect place for the "professor of conversation," as Frost liked to call himself.

Frost's original idea for the conference, established writers living on equal terms with younger writers, is still very much alive. Thompson described Frost's plan:

> In such a course, the teacher would no more think of assigning work to the student than they would think of asking him to write something for them. In discussions, such a teacher would expect to take as well as give, insofar as an exchange of ideas was possible—if not ideas of form, at least observations of life. Such a teacher should address himself mainly to the subject-matter of the younger writer. Instead of correcting grammar, in red ink, he would try to match experiences of life and experiences of art with his students. Individual conferences could best be conducted during long walks into the country or, on rainy days, long talks before the fireplace. ... The manuscripts offered to the author-teacher would not be 'exercises,' because the young writer's whole nature should be in every piece he set his hand to; his whole nature should include his belief in the real value that the piece would have when finished.

Since Frost's time there have been many famous writers taking part in the program, including Richard Wilbur, John Irving, and Joan Didion. But nobody has replaced Frost as the center of the Bread Loaf universe. His name, his poetry, and his legend still provide the gravitational pull. David Bain, who is writing a history of Bread Loaf, tells me, "This place is populated mostly by ghosts, but Frost's ghost is unquestionably the most significant."

David Bain and I have our conversation on the lawn between

the milkhouse and the woodshed. The Inn is to the west and Bread Loaf Mountain, rising nearly four thousand feet, looms in the east. We're sitting on Adirondack chairs that are exactly like the ones Frost and his students sat on in the 1930s and 1940s. "They may be the same ones," Bain says and smiles. Sitting in this pasture is somehow like being in outer space. We are alone in the field. No distractions but an occasional bird flying in the distance or some background chirping. We are out in the open as if we were on a stage, but I feel as if we are secluded, the space cutting us off from the rest of the world. This spot is a fitting reminder of Galway Kinnell's lines about Frost, calling him "Poet of the country of white houses, /Of clearings going out to the dark wall of woods."

Bain first came to Bread Loaf in 1980. And he came with more than a little trepidation. He expected the atmosphere to be something like a gathering of writers at a New York City party, a lot of jockeying for attention, "a patina of pleasant chatter with a lot of malice underneath." Before he came to Bread Loaf he had worked as an editor for six years in New York City. One day he got fired from his job and went home to type up his resume. He put a sheet of paper into the typewriter but about halfway down the page he tore it out, put in another, and began typing a book proposal. It was a book about a Vietnam veteran who returned from the war with post-traumatic stress disorder and murdered a Vietnamese refugee who came over during the air lift in 1975. The book, *Aftershocks: A Tale of Two Victims*, in his words, "encompassed much about the Vietnam era, the problems with American imperialism, and our inability to learn from our own mistakes." He went to Bread Loaf on a fellowship about the time the book was being published.

At first he resisted the experience at Bread Loaf. The night after he arrived he called his wife in New York City and said he was going to come home. But a few days later he called with another story, one about friendships, poetry readings, and a gathering of writers. That's when the seeds for his book about Bread Loaf were planted. In 1982 he began the book and he's been working on it for the past eight years, a labor of love. In the meantime, to pay the bills, he's written a number of articles and books, but the story of

Stone wall on Bread Loaf campus

Bread Loaf seems to be his story, the one he would write full-time if he could.

In 1987 he and his wife moved from Brooklyn, New York, to Shoreham, Vermont, and onto a 150-acre farm with two barns, horses, and sheep. Although Bain never uses the word "home," Vermont is clearly it and Bread Loaf is the hearth. His conversation keeps coming back to the phrase "kindred spirits" as if he's talking about his family, those he loves or understands. His loyalties are clear. He sits back in his chair, puts his palm against his reddish-gray beard as if he's contemplating an interesting piece of sculpture, and speaks about one of the cottages on the grounds.

"I could see the ghosts around this place before I could even recognize who they were," he says. "Treman Cottage, through tradition, became the faculty lounge in the 1930s. It was the social vortex of the faculty and the visitors who came up here. That's where you would go and see Robert Frost talking with Archibald MacLeish, Katherine Anne Porter talking with Carson McCullers or Eudora Welty, James T. Farrell getting into a political debate with Bernard DeVoto, W. H. Auden presiding in a corner over a gin and tonic with the eighteen-year-old Truman Capote listening to his every word. There was a parade of accomplished writers coming in and also the younger ones listening to what they had to say and being treated almost as equals or very often as equals. There was, and still is, that sense of a community, a welcome to a community and a welcome to a calling. The philosophy is one of helping out new talent, of nurturing it."

There is something of a priesthood in all this, shamans teaching each other the magic. We walk toward the front porch of the inn, acolytes and priests circling about. On the porch David looks across the road, beyond the stone wall, at the trails leading toward what he calls "Widow's Clearing." He talks about the sweat lodges that used to be there but have now deteriorated, places travelers used to go to clear the bile and refresh themselves. Maybe not all that different from Bread Loaf itself.

Robert Pack, the director of the writers' conference since 1973, is described by David Bain as "tremendously practical," an odd way perhaps of describing a man who has written eleven books of poetry. But romantic myths about poets aside, it takes some practical sense of organization to teach, direct a writers' conference, and publish over a dozen books as well. Pack is a man who has, in Frost's terms, united his avocation and his vocation. In discussing his writing, he is apt to quote from Frost's "Two Tramps in Mud Time": "Only where love and need are one,/And the work is play for mortal stakes, /Is the deed ever really done/For Heaven and the future's sakes."

Frost once said that his poems were written in parables so that the wrong people wouldn't read them, understand them, and be saved. Robert Pack too writes in parables, and a preacher's gleam comes into his eyes when he speaks about Frost, with whom he feels a kinship. Like Frost, he is a city boy come to Vermont. "For Frost the description of a place at first appears to be simple, literal description," Pack says, "but the more you read his poems, the more you realize that those descriptions have overtones. In his poem 'Directive,' where Frost mentions hiding the truth so that the wrong ones can't be saved by it, the whole landscape is mythologized, more overtly than in any of his other poems. It's a journey back in mythic and geological time. In that poem the setting is clearly rendered as a symbolic place. But although Frost's landscapes always have this symbolic aspect, one of the hallmarks of his poetry is the accuracy and literalness of his descriptions. Frost knows his nature and he knows his New England landscape. And he knows what flowers and what trees grow here. He gets his natural facts right all the time. And there are a lot of names and details, nouns and proper nouns, things that you have to know and be able to identify. He had a little poem which says 'it takes all sorts of indoor and outdoor schooling to get accustomed to my kind of fooling.' I think he's saying to his reader that you have to know the landscape, the difference between an oak and a maple tree, and you also have to have read a couple of books. Frost reads nature as a book. But in order to read nature as a book, you have to read a few books as well."

Pack speaks about the need to be versed in country things. Then he talks about Frost's realistic view of New England and the world. He quotes the concluding lines of "The Need of Being Versed in Country Things":

Robert Pack on Middlebury campus

For them there was really nothing sad.
But though they rejoiced in the nest they kept,
One had to be versed in country things
Not to believe the phoebes wept.

Pack's voice is mesmerizing. It's a poet's voice. It rolls like soft, distant thunder, only with a New York accent. His eyes are hooded, somewhat like Frost's. At about five feet eight inches tall, he is roughly the same size Frost was, but at sixty Pack barely looks middle-aged. He reminds me of Frost at forty-five. Pack is slim and muscular. The sleeves on his short-sleeve brown shirt have been rolled up, and his arms are those of a farmer. Like Frost, though, he is no farmer, although he lives on a 100-acre farm, chops his own wood, grows his own vegetables, and raises fruit trees. "I'm a teacher and a poet, an academic," he says. "The guy down the road chops wood and grows vegetables out of need. I do it out of love. When I work in my garden, I'm really cultivating metaphors." Like Frost he follows his own rules but explains himself only in mischievous asides. "Writing before breakfast," he says, "is like making love to a girl whose name has slipped your mind."

Vermont has the soil where metaphors grow best for him. He begins to talk about two different kinds of writers and their relationship to place. He says some writers write very much out of their imaginations, creating landscapes. They are great fabricators, making up people and places. Then they live in them and have their literary world fill out from these inventions. It's more likely, though, he thinks, that most writers have a basic place, a particular landscape. "It's certainly true of Frost and it is also true of me," he says. Like Frost, Pack finds nature's presence preserved in Vermont and like Frost he sees the natural world as a tutor.

Pack admits that he couldn't live any place but Vermont, but he has a theory about antithetical landscapes. He believes everybody has his ideal landscape but an antithetical landscape, as well, a place that the person is drawn toward. It's a place, he feels, that fascinates and startles with the difference from our own home ground. There's a positive and a negative pole. For him Arizona is his positive antithetical landscape, with its wide spaces and dark shadows. It's the other side of Vermont for him. His negative landscape is New York City. All of his poems about the city are what he calls paranoid poems, filled with fear and violence.

Pack moved to Vermont in 1964. He grew up in the Bronx, and his first taste of New England came for him when he went to college at Dartmouth. He knew during his college years that he would eventually return to New England, but it was not until he was thirty-five, had received his master's degree, and taught at Columbia that he got the job offer at Middlebury and the chance to return.

A gravelly sound comes into his voice as he speaks about his past. He'd rather talk about Frost's poetry than his own life. He doesn't think poets should have biographies, only their poems. He smiles guardedly and says that when it comes time for someone to write about his life, he'll be willing to compromise and give his approval, as long as the writer makes it all up. Paul Mariani, the biographer of William Carlos Williams and John Berryman and Pack's friend, wants to write his life story, and Pack says he'll let him as long as there's nothing true in it. "My life's a fiction," he says. But then he admits that he's afraid he won't "stack up with Williams and Berryman as a sinner."

Pack speaks about the relationship between New Englanders' taciturnity and the poet's need to withhold, to speak in parables. To help make his point he tells the old story about Mark Twain's visit to Vermont on one of his lecture tours. The tour had been a great success. Audiences had roared with laughter. During his Vermont talk, however, all Twain heard was silence broken by an occasional cough. At the end of the speech he stepped down from the stage, a little confused and quite depressed, and positioned himself to listen to comments from the crowd. He saw one man turn to a companion and heard him ask, "Well, what did you think?" The man looked at him and replied, "It was the funniest talk I've ever heard. It was all I could do to keep from laughing."

Like the Vermonter in Twain's story Pack will not expose too much of himself to the world. He keeps his time for teaching, writing and cultivating his various gardens. He will not have leisurely conversations right before the two-week-long Bread Loaf Writers' Conference. He's getting ready for all the talk. During the two weeks of the conference, he lives totally immersed in that event. For three days after the conference he allows no words in his presence. He escapes to his study and listens to classical music. "No words. I've had enough of words," he says. The close of one of his poems, "The Mountain," suggests this part of his personality:

> And a shadow from within
> Draws me back closer to myself—
> Dwindling in my own mountainside shade,
> Forgetting, trying almost not to remember,
> Almost welcoming the isolation,
> And the dark, the dark, the dark.

He tells me he would be willing to talk about his life at another time, but already I see him glance at his office door and draw himself closer to his own shadow, towards isolation. Like one of Frost's silent farmers, his eyes turn from me toward the distances to the east. It wouldn't surprise me to hear him say, "Good fences make good neighbors." But he remains silent.

As I'm leaving his office Pack mentions his new book, *Before It Vanishes*. He walks me outside and directs me toward town. His eyes sweep the stone buildings of Middlebury Campus and the mountains surrounding it. "In this new book I want to treat the cosmos as if it were Vermont," he says. For some, like Robert Pack, perhaps it is.

The drive back to Virginia takes twelve hours, and the road rushes by like a swiftly moving stream. The country roads turn to highways, and the stream widens until it's a river. Vermont, that island in time Charles Morrissey described, seems years away as the miles float by. The Green Mountains and the voices of the people I've met swirl behind me, but it's Galway Kinnell's words that I recall:

> We see your old footprints going away across
> The great Republic, Frost, up memorized slopes,
> Down hills floating by heart on the bulldozed land.

3

The Sound of the Past: Faulkner's Mississippi

Once I had escorted Robert Frost in a taxicab to Rhodes House for a talk. "Where are you from, boy?" he had asked. "Mississippi," I replied. "Hell, that's the worst state in the Union," he said. But, I argued, it had produced a lot of good writers. He said, "Can't anybody down there read them."

Willie Morris, *North Toward Home*

Tell about the South. What's it like there. What do they do there. Why do they live there.

William Faulkner, *Absalom, Absalom!*

AS I PACK A SUITCASE to take with me to Mississippi, I think of Lena Grove in *Light in August*, climbing out of her bedroom window into the "pinewiney silence" of an Alabama night, carrying a palm leaf and a small bundle tied neatly in a bandanna handkerchief. With thirty-five cents and a pair of worn shoes, Lena journeys for four weeks from Alabama to Jefferson, Mississippi, in search of the father of her unborn child. Thinking of her, I decide to leave that extra pair of shoes and that cashmere jacket in the closet. I fill the empty spaces with Faulkner's books.

Originally I had planned to drive from Virginia to Mississippi, but the most obvious route is south on Interstate 85 by way of Route 58 west. There are two problems with that route. First, 58 west is a two-lane nightmare that twists through the Virginia flatlands and is quite seriously called "Suicide Strip." There are enough head-on collisions between tractor trailers and Ford Escorts each month to make the nickname convincing. Once safely past Route 58, I would be on Interstate 85 with its never-ending Stuckey's and Exxons and mini-marts. Only the giant peach along the roadside in Gaffney, South Carolina, makes the driver readjust his eyes to the miles of highway. My choices seem to be: get slammed by a truck on 58 or be bored to death on 85.

Faulkner once wrote "Between grief and nothing, I'll take grief." My choices are less romantic, so I decide that between routes 85 and 58, I'll take a plane and fly into the Atlanta airport. Atlanta is the new South in all its glory: the rising copper peak of the IBM building, glass walls holding the towering skyline like an icon, Mercedes and BMW's, and repulsively splendid shopping centers. The airport is probably the pièce de résistance. It is a futuristic city of walking sidewalks and ever-running trains, of microchip voices and space-age art. It is the twenty-first century, crowded and anonymous. No accents, just the voices of robots: "The doors will be closing now!" A soft Georgia twang replaced by a metallic alien dialect.

A friend picks me up in Atlanta, and I head by way of Newnan, Georgia, toward Mississippi. In Newnan, I eat in Sprayberry's Barbecue, what must be the best in the South, perhaps on the planet. The beef and the pork have a sweet smoked taste, like hickory and honey laced together.

It is December and the first winter storm of the season has struck. Snow falls like balls of cotton, huge flakes two inches across disappearing into the wet road. Two older black men wearing blue hooded sweatshirts cook slabs of pink meat in pits outside the restaurant. Inside, young white men, around high school age, wait on tables. Even though it is three in the afternoon, most of the tables are filled and the sweet, ashy smell of barbecue mixes with the hum of conversation. I half expect Flannery O'Connor's fat Red Sammy Butts to peek out from the back room. Just in case, I keep an eye out for the Misfit as well.

From Sprayberry's we drive to the center of Newnan. My friend has to pick up a carved wooden fish at a printmaker's house in the heart of town. The house, about 150 years old and once part of the now-defunct Temple Women's College, is one in a row of columned mansions lining the street. The printmaker, tall and overweight, seems to be all roundness and no angles. If he were dressed less like a butcher and more like a nobleman, he might remind me of the duke in Browning's famous poem as he leads me through the decaying house, pointing out a sixteenth-century Dutch landscape and an eighteenth-century English portrait. It's dark and musty enough to give me the feeling that I'm working my way through a catacomb. He points, gestures, explains as we move past couch springs and cat shit, Greek statues in the hall, a two-foot-wide cameo on one wall, and a cupola (once on the roof) that sits incongruously in the garden like a man in a tuxedo in the bleachers at a baseball game. The printmaker's father lies in bed watching television in one of the rooms off the foyer. We walk past as if he were another piece in the museum and we jaded tourists too tired to do anything but glance and raise our heads acknowledging the sick-room smell. It has taken only thirty minutes—the time to drive from the airport and tour the house—to travel from the space-age new South back, back in time to the house in Newnan, onto what could be a stage set for a Tennessee Williams play.

Carved fish in the trunk of the car and John Lee Hooker singing a scratchy, mournful version of "Tupelo" on the radio, we head out of Georgia on Interstate 20, one of the main roads that stretch out from Atlanta like the tentacles of an octopus. The six-lane highway goes into Birmingham and then the road narrows and the past truly seems to come out of hiding. As Atlanta and Birmingham recede, Route 78 winds toward Mississippi and towns like Jasper, Carbon Hill, Winfield, and Sulligent. The names read like lyrics in a country-western song: Tocopola, Iuka, Itawamba.

The bare, wintry kudzu vines hang from pine and oak trees like an alien blight. Small country churches appear with the regularity most of us have come to expect of McDonald's in the suburbs. The messages are not city messages. A sign along the road says, "Life is a puzzle. Come in here to find the missing peace."

As we get deeper into Alabama the red clay begins to take on the shade of dried blood, baked in the sun. The grass seems yellower, the poverty more brutal. This is the country of unpainted shacks standing tipsily on crumbling cinder blocks, of tin roofs, and hand-painted signs. One sign, a piece of metal with flecks of red paint splashed across it says "Genes" and has an arrow pointing toward a cabin about 200 yards off the road. I can't imagine either DNA experiments or Levis sales in such a spot, but who knows? Another sign, a weathered piece of plywood canted against the hillside says, "Watch King Jesus is Coming." Another: "Mrs. Lamarr, Reader and Advisor."

An afternoon moon hangs like a surprised expression in the northeastern sky as we get close to the Mississippi state line. In Pickens County, Alabama, we stop to stretch our legs at the Tabernacle Methodist Church and Campground. It's empty, nothing but a chill stillness now, but somehow it's easy enough to imagine preaching and laughter and the aroma of fried chicken and the screams of children playing. The sounds, the people, seem to be waiting at the tree line, a dim echo of the past. There's also something terribly austere about the place, like a concentration camp. Stripped of color and extravagance, the twelve cabins that surround the center of the campground are no more elegant than barns. The bedrooms are stalls with mattresses lying on the saw-dust floors. In the kitchen are old, unpainted picnic tables. The ceilings are barely seven feet high.

Beside the outdoor arbor, the center of worship, is a basketball goal, the hoop facing the cemetery on the hill and the brick church across from it. The basketball court makes this ground seem too happy for a character like Faulkner's McEachern to have stopped here, but it's possible to see Byron Bunch spending a week with his family during a long, hot summer.

A local man tells me about the cemetery. There's a story for every tombstone, he says, and I believe him, but he tells me only one. A man in the early 1800s came home one day to find that his wife had been killed by Indians. He found her sitting on the front porch. At first he thought her expression was a bemused gaze but upon coming closer he realized it was wide-eyed terror frozen into her very flesh. She sat slumped in a rocking chair on the front porch, her head tilted to one side, scalped. He picked her up, chair and all, carried her down to the cemetery, and buried her in the rocking chair.

It's only a short drive through flat cotton country into Columbus, Mississippi. The bleak day seems custom-made for the town with its grays and browns, the dirty brick and peeling paint. Partly renovated antebellum mansions stand next to shacks, rusted Chevys next to shining vans. A Siamese cat with fur like a worn blanket slips under a crawl space but not before turning to look at me a little arrogantly like a fallen aristocrat who remembers the past.

I drive through Catfish Alley with its Taekwon Do Club and abandoned garages on my way to St. Paul's Episcopal Church Offices, a small yellow-and-gray Victorian house with gingerbread trim and a fresh coat of paint. The sign out front reads: "First Home of Tennessee Williams: One of America's Leading Play-wrights, Tennessee Williams Was Born Here On March 26, 1911. He

Received The Pulitzer Prize for *Streetcar Named Desire* and *Cat On A Hot Tin Roof*. Both Stories Set In the South."

There are probably two ways for southerners to respond to such a town, to the South in general perhaps, to a culture that holds mansion alongside shack, that has Catfish Alley adjacent to the Episcopal Church. A southerner can reject or embrace the mysterious culture that places "Janice's World of Beauty" and a sign for Tennessee Williams's home together in the same perspective. Most southern artists, like Williams, made use of such tension and from their own ambivalence created art, recording with love and disgust the world they saw.

The artist of record right now in Columbus, Mississippi, is Birney Imes, a photographer who uses color the way Faulkner used metaphors. He is fast becoming one of the most highly regarded photographers in the South. Part of the fascination with his work may be the element of taboo that courses through most of his images. His photographs give people a way of entering those worlds that seem closed to them. His photographs of juke joints and the people who own them or frequent them are like Nelson Algren's record of Chicago's lost souls, except that Imes's images are less didactic. His photographs take people into the bars, the places many would like to peer inside, the people they would like to meet, but usually don't. Many wonder what it's like in the Whispering Pines, Monkey's Place, or the 45 Club. Imes lets them know.

I half expect the man who gains entrance to such places to have a jagged scar from his eye to his unshaven cheek, to have a tattoo on each arm, to wear black leather. His office in Columbus seems as if it might house such a man. Above the Princess Theater, a defunct vaudeville palace and movie house in the center of town, across the street from McLure's Furniture Store, and next door to Laws Drugs ("The House That Knows No Dull Days"), Imes's studio could be a haven for Sam Spade. Up a narrow flight of stairs and into a corridor lit nervously by a fluorescent bulb I hesitate on the creaking floorboards like Peter Lorre about to break and enter.

But if I expect Humphrey Bogart to greet me, I have to readjust to a sandy-haired Michael Sarrazin. Birney Imes could not play a villain, not with his wide and wondering blue eyes or his boyish good looks. After a view of his work space, the four rooms he rents and the few others he squats in, we head downstairs to take in Steve's Pizza Place. It's 10:30 in the morning but the place is about half-filled, twelve customers sitting in the booths and at the counter. As we walk in, every head turns, appraises me, and then one by one focuses on my companion, "Hi, Birney." I don't seem to interest them much anymore. I'm with Birney.

Steve's Pizza seems to sell every type of food but pizza. It looks as if it were a luncheonette that might have thought adding pizza to the menu in the 1960s would add a cosmopolitan flavor to the atmosphere. Steve's is clearly a gathering place, and I'm convinced that if I returned ten years later to speak with Birney the same people would be sitting at the counter, turning to see the new people who enter.

Birney is a minor celebrity here. A few people come over to ask about how his book is coming along. One man sits down with us and tells Birney about some photographs he's taken. Birney smiles. Michael Sarrazin transformed into James Stewart. The door opens as a couple comes in, bringing along with them a few seconds of the Christmas music that is now blaring from the speakers hanging from the marquee of the Princess Theater. This could be a scene from *It's a Wonderful Life*.

And Birney Imes may have something in common with George Bailey, both recognizing the riches in their backyards. Imes grew up in Columbus, where his family owned and still operates the local newspaper. He is a product, he says, of the segregated South, a two-culture system in which whites only saw blacks peripherally. When he was a sophomore at Lee High School in 1968 the schools were integrated. This opened a new world to him. He became friendly with a young black man, one of his teammates on the high school football team. There is a connection between this friendship and his gravitating toward photography. "People photograph things they want to know more about," he says. "Integration lifted a veil for me and showed me a rich culture I was barely aware of. I wanted to know more about that culture."

After high school, Birney went on to major in history at the University of Tennessee. He graduated in 1973, lived for a while in Cambridge, Massachusetts, and took a motorcycle trip across the country. But he ended up back in Mississippi and started "making photographs." He worked for his family's newspaper for a couple of years. He says he still gets a lot of calls on Sunday morning from people who haven't received their newspaper that day. But being a newspaper photographer opened a lot of imaginative doors for him. It gave him a reason to explore and a license to investigate, everything from a day at a carny show to a night at the bus station. He also began to drive over to the Delta and, as he says, "stumble about, letting things show themselves to me."

He got married and left the newspaper, lived in New Orleans, and then bummed around Europe. But he ended up back in Columbus, Mississippi, to raise his three children and to make his photographs. "Photography for me is the act of pointing. I'm part of Mississippi, part of this place," he says, making a gesture with his hand that seems to take in Steve's, Columbus, all of the South. "I'm wedded to this area. Photographing any other place wouldn't feel right."

Although he claims to have no political motive, no message, his photographs offer a startling story of rural black culture. Like the historian he may have once aspired to become, he records a passing world. But in using his photographic talent to point at this world, he also points out its value. His photographs suggest no dreamy-eyed, romantic view of place. His images have an edge, clear, striking colors and sharp focus—a country baptism or the unabashed eyes of a drunk in a Mississippi bar. Always, it seems, his photographs try to lift the veil that separates cultures in the South.

In Imes's recent first book, *Juke Joint*, the beautifully crafted photographs open up an unfamiliar world, one which seems far beyond the middle-class, generic realities such as K-Mart and McDonald's that usually obstruct our vision. Since 1983 Imes has roamed the back roads of Mississippi looking for jukes, drawn to them for the same reason people are attracted to his carefully composed images: they are mysterious, beautiful, and menacing. Unlike the readily definable TGIFridays that dot much of the suburban landscape, jukes are at once exotic and commonplace, both funny and threatening.

Of course, juke joints have been around a lot longer than TGIFridays. Southern roadhouses, called honky tonks or jukes, had their beginnings in antebellum taverns. According to historians, these taverns sold questionable liquors to both blacks and whites, probably in separate rooms. The white farmers bought "butt-head" whiskey and the slaves traded for "red-eye" rum. After the Civil War the antebellum groggeries became segregated. Some rural blacks started selling liquor to friends and strangers from their homes. For entertainment they brought in local blues musicians. Couples danced and there was usually a corner for gambling.

The word "juke" is probably a mispronunciation of the word *joog*, meaning "disorderly," used by the Gullah blacks of South Carolina and Georgia. Some linguists believe the word originally derived from the African term *dzugu*, which means "wicked."

Although racial integration in public places in the South has become commonplace, custom seems to keep jukes segregated. Honky-tonks, or honkies, are for whites. Juke joints are for blacks. But Birney Imes has been entering juke joints for the better part of a decade. Like a character in a Walker Percy novel, Imes is a watcher, a listener, and a waiter, a habit of being that is necessary for a man who stalks a precise arrangement of images, striving to capture what Cartier-Bresson called "the decisive moment." Patience, of course, is not enough. Imes also has a receptive and discriminating eye, anticipating—often in a fraction of a second—his prey.

Imes, who admires artists who refuse to explain their work, lets his pictures speak for themselves. And there is a wealth of stories in his dazzling photographs. As the novelist Richard Ford says in his introduction to Imes's book, "Sweet longing drifts through these pictures like heat." For instance, Imes's 1983 photograph "Leland Juke" depicts a man, pool cue in hand, bending slightly into a triangle of light made by an opening in a red curtain which hangs over the entranceway to the bar. Imes captured the decisive moment, the man bending to peer out at the photographer, at us, his eyes still veiled by the sheer curtain, pool table shimmering like red ice under a Budweiser light in the background.

Imes's photographs lay seductive claim to people's attention. The ubiquitous Budweiser cans, the Colt 45 ads, the blurred faces, the ghostly bodies, the primitive murals on the walls. There are stories here. Even the rules above the bars, along the walls, over the doors, suggest a plot—"No Lottering," "No Pot Smoking or Sale in Here," "O Lord Please Help Me to Keep My Damn Nose Out of Other Peples Busness," "No Credit," "No Fighting," and "Be Nice or Leave" (Imes's original title for the book). As the word "juke" suggests, something "wicked" may be happening here.

This afternoon Birney takes me on a tour of some of the juke joints pictured in his book. Our last stop is Mitch's place, in the country outside of Columbus. Mitch's is only a few miles from Waverly Country Club, one of the most famous golf courses in the country, but it might as well be on another planet. The Christmas lights tacked to the roof spell "CLUB." Something resembling a moat has been dug around the building, but only the most far-reaching imagination could see a Camelot here. Inside, two men are lounging by the juke box, glancing at the songs. One points at G3 and G4: "I Want Her" and "I Want Her, Part I" by Keith Smart. I can't figure out the chronology, any more than I can understand the sign that reads: "No Laying, No Partical, No Gambling, No Fighting." Two of the admonitions are perfectly clear, one is ambiguous, but "Partical" sweetly eludes me. The other man pushes the button for Shirley Jones's "Do You Get Enough Love" and turns to his companion: "I remember those days in Crawford," he says. "Those were times. If you had some hot tamales, you had you a woman." The other man, not appearing to listen, says to the darkened room, "Women always look better at closing time."

We've been invited by Leroy of the L & N juke to be judges at the "Big Butt Contest" that evening. About ten o'clock we head out there, and the place is jumping, cars squeezed into the parking lot, a blend of rap and soul music shaking the windows, and a pig roast flaming outside the bar. I'm reminded of the definition of juking Joanne Woodward gives to Marlon Brando in *The Fugitive Kind*—you drink a little and drive a little, then stop at a place and drink some more, and eventually you wind up in a bone orchard and make love on a grave. By one o'clock in the morning, I'm convinced the cemeteries will have their visitors tonight.

Birney Imes works his way around the room, watching, taking photographs. The people are friendly, although some of them wonder if we're there to shut the place down or to buy dope. I don't feel threatened, except in the vaguest way. Birney tells me a story about an experience he had in Percy Walker's Cafe. Two

Birney Imes in Steve's Pizza Place

weeks before he photographed the place there had been a killing. A man had been romancing the d.j.'s girlfriend and a scuffle started. Another man, trying to break it up, fired a gun and killed an innocent bystander by the door. When Birney photographed the place two weeks later, he talked to a man whose mid-section was covered by a bandage. The man had been standing in the middle of the floor when the bullet grazed his stomach on its way to its deadly destination.

But faulty wiring seems more of a threat than bullets in most juke joints. As Birney tells me, "These places are an electrician's nightmare. When I plug in my equipment, I sometimes wonder if I'll survive the experience." He's not only survived the experience tonight but he's gotten some interesting photographs as well.

As I sit at the bar thumbing through a copy of *Juke Joint* with Leroy and watch Birney, searching for another photograph, angle past a group of dancers and a few men shooting dice on the pool table, I think about his remark about the picture he took of the Leland Juke. Although he tried a number of times, he was never able to find the place after he photographed it. It's as if, as Richard Ford says, these photographs were unearthly things, pure gestures of the photographer's imagination. Leroy leans toward me to make himself heard over the music and, as if he can read my mind, says, "Those photographs are beautiful. One of these days the juke joints will all be gone, but that book will still be here."

The next morning, back at Steve's, the photographer I am with takes some shots of Birney in one of the red-and-green booths; the yellow table top and lime green walls make a dizzying combination against his blue chamois shirt. This is exactly the sort of place Birney would photograph, I realize, the bright colors, the cereal boxes on the shelves, the coffee cups stacked like a pyramid next to the stove, the men lounging at the counter. As he stares into the eye of the camera, Birney looks a bit uncomfortable and asks, "What do you want me to do?"

"Just look at me," the photographer replies. Birney does, shifts again uneasily in his seat, rubs his hand across the khaki pants, and, always the photographer, asks, "Is that a 50 mm you're using?"

† † †

As I leave the outskirts of Columbus, the strip of motels turns within a few miles into what is called "The Prairie," a flat plane of rich black soil. There are miles of cotton rows, bits and pieces of white lingering on the stalks. There are cotton trailers and cotton gins along the roadside. A kestrel hawk sits on a telephone line patiently eyeing the ground for a mouse. Dove hunters stand at the edge of a field dotted with bales of hay rolled into cylinders.

I head across the Tombigbee Waterway and into Tupelo, eat a hamburger, and keep a careful watch for Elvis. I'm on the Pontotoc Road into Oxford, the road Lena Grove probably strode along into Faulkner's Yoknapatawpha. I pass the Paradise Club and the Magic Bar. Juke joints are as prevalent in Mississippi as country inns are in Vermont. I go under the Natchez Trace, daydreaming about highwaymen and the beautiful Rosamond in Eudora Welty's *The Robber Bridegroom*, and see two more sparrow hawks on opposite sides of the road, one in front of the Immanuel Baptist Church and the other perched on the domed tornado shelter built alongside a frame house.

As I cross the invisible line into Lafayette County, I feel I've really entered Mississippi, where "The past is never dead—it's not even past." This is the birthplace of the blues, of Howlin' Wolf and B. B. King, and the beginnings of great southern writing with Faulkner, Wright, Welty, and Percy. Elvis Presley and Charlie Pride started here. Jefferson Davis lived and died here.

As every schoolchild learns at some time or another, "Mississippi" is a Choctaw word meaning "father of waters." The big river cuts a curling line along the Arkansas and Louisiana border. Mostly forest and swamp, the magnolia state stretches north from the Gulf of Mexico for nearly 400 miles, from the sandy soil of the Gulf Coast to the dense swamps of the Delta. Before the 1850s there were no towns except for a few river settlements. It was wilderness, the old Southwest. After the Civil War there were two major worlds in Mississippi, two societies, the Delta and the hills. In the Delta a few white plantation owners controlled the labor of black farm workers and became quite wealthy. In the hills, farm families worked their own land, usually making just enough to support themselves. Cotton was king in the Delta, but hill soil was quickly worn out by cotton, and farmers had to switch to other crops to subsist.

The Indians were in Mississippi before the Europeans came or the Africans were forced to come, before written history. The story in Mississippi is the same as the story for the rest of America; the coming of white people brought about drastic changes in the old civilization and finally destroyed it. In the sixteenth century when Hernando de Soto came through the Mississippi territory, he encountered three major Indian tribes: Natchez, Chickasaw, and Choctaw. By early in the nineteenth century all the tribes were stripped of their land as whites failed to honor treaties and promises. The ground was cleared and Indians were bulldozed west of the Mississippi River through bribery and threats. In 1830 when Congress, spurred by Andrew Jackson, passed the Indian Reform Bill, the Choctaws' spirit was broken.

The end came for the Choctaws in 1830 at Dancing Rabbit Creek. United States agents set up booths with food and drinks, and gamblers and con men filled the site. Missionaries weren't allowed because the commissioners were afraid they would advise the Choctaws not to sign the treaty. With the help of their main negotiator, Greenwood Le Flore, the Choctaws appeared at first to make a better deal than most of the other southern tribes at the time. But of course that's not saying much. Besides, when the negotiators realized that removal was inevitable, they made the best deals they could for themselves. For instance, Le Flore got, among other things, 2,500 acres of Delta land. And the Choctaws got cheated.

In 1831 the first removal began and the trail of tears started. Winter, cholera, and broken hearts left a trail of dead between the Mississippi and Oklahoma. Many of the thousands of Choctaws and Chickasaws who remained were persuaded to leave by white raiders who tore down fences, burned homes, and attacked families. For all practical purposes the Indians who survived and stayed in the state were as segregated as the blacks were.

The last act in the story of the Indians' encounter with the white man was a replaying of the first act. The first European exploration of the Mississippi territory was led by Hernando de Soto, and his three-year stay in Mississippi was described by one historian this way: "Everywhere they went, they raped, robbed, and killed the Indians, including even those who befriended them. Indian hospitality to whites was repaid with wholesale slaughter of men, women, and children. The Spaniards burned unsuspecting villages in which they had slept, taking the chiefs as hostages and the village children as slaves."

Such violence often turned back on these adventurers. In March 1541, after de Soto demanded that 200 Chickasaws carry his supplies, they rebelled and attacked his sleeping camps with pots of hot coals. His men ran naked from the burning huts and would have been slaughtered had it not been for de Soto's gathering a few men on horseback and charging the Indians. Many of the men and most of the supplies were lost. After wandering in Arkansas, de Soto returned to Mississippi, died and was buried in the river.

Unlike Ike McCaslin in Faulkner's "The Bear," de Soto never discovered his own guilt. For de Soto, Indians were possessions, like the land, to be used and discarded. Whereas Ike sacrificed everything to expiate the crime against the land and the violation of the people, de Soto, like so many of the characters Faulkner imagined in his Mississippi fiction, never repudiated the enslavement or murder at the center of his world. De Soto's hold on the land was trivial, but he never realized that. Faulkner understood this, and through the characters of Sam Fathers, part Chickasaw Indian, and the boy Ike McCaslin, he makes this point: "... until at last it would seem to the boy that he himself had not come into existence yet, that none of his race nor the other subject race which his people had brought with them into the land had come here yet; that although it had been his grandfather's and then his father's and uncle's and was now his cousin's and someday would be his own land which he and Sam hunted over, their hold upon it actually was as trivial and without reality as the now faded and archaic script in the chancery book in Jefferson which allocated it to them and that it was he, the boy, who was the guest here and Sam Father's voice the mouthpiece of the host."

For most people, though, the history of Mississippi has less to do with Indians than it does with blacks. In many ways, the history of Mississippi is the history of race relations in America. Although during the peak of slavery in Mississippi only 5 percent of the white population owned thirty or more slaves and most whites owned none, cotton was king and the plantation system existed on slave labor. The image of the South as a place filled with gentlemen sipping mint juleps, ladies gliding about in crinkling crinoline sighing "la de da," and slaves sweating in the fields simply isn't accurate. But by 1860, Mississippi produced almost one-fourth of the nation's entire cotton crop. The powerful had no intention of doing away with a system that kept them wealthy.

Of the 78,000 Mississippians who marched off to war to defend their way of life, more than 27,000 were killed or wounded. At home there were hardships and burned cities. Reconstruction brought violence, race riots, the KKK, and a series of horrors— Republican officials whipped, blacks hanged, black sympathizers shot. As with slavery, many Mississippians rationalized the Reconstruction-era subjugation of blacks. Lynchings, mob violence came first. Then such violence was institutionalized in segregation and Jim Crow laws. In 1896, with the Supreme Court's "separate but equal" ruling, segregation fully replaced slavery, and an elaborate social etiquette developed in the parks, at dances, in stores, playgrounds, schools, and churches, so much so that in 1937 sociologist Bertram Doyle was able to write: "Tradition thus assigns the Negro his place in the South, law defines it, sentiment supports it, custom and habit continues it, and prejudice maintains it in those instances where it seems to be breaking down."

Most whites in Mississippi had it little better than blacks during the early part of the twentieth century. Sharecropping and worn-out soil made most Mississippians a poor lot. Public schools were scarce. The only thing more scarce, probably, was industry.

Some things haven't changed much. Fiftieth in per capita income, under $11,000 in 1988, Mississippi still has frightening poverty. There is still heartbreaking ignorance in the state that is fiftieth in per pupil expenditure each year. With more than one-third of the population black, the highest percentage in the nation, Mississippi still bears a heavy burden of discovering how the races should best live together.

In many respects Mississippi has made remarkable progress in the last quarter of a century. In the 1960s Mississippi and Ole Miss in particular were symbols of racism. The images of Ross Barnett and James Meredith played across the television screens. Many remember Governor Ross Barnett's declaration: "I refuse to allow this nigra to enter our state university, but I say so politely." Rednecks and racism seemed part of the landscape. On June 12, 1963, Medgar Evers was killed, and although there were two trials, his murderer went unpunished. In 1962 there was a race riot at Ole Miss over Meredith's entrance onto the campus. Three more civil rights workers were killed on June 21, 1964, in Neshoba County. During that same summer racist groups burned thirty-seven black churches, bombed thirty homes, and beat more than eighty civil rights workers.

Some Mississippians spoke out, but many who did paid a dear price. When one insurance salesman in the southern part of the state invited some civil rights workers into his home to talk, his dog was poisoned and his family threatened. Eventually he lost his business and had to leave town.

A quarter century has brought an acceptance of public integration and a silencing of racist rhetoric. Other things have changed as well. The years have brought farm mechanization and some industry. The family farm still exists but it appears to be disappearing, as it is in most states. Mississippi has felt some of the economic warmth of being close to the center of the Sunbelt.

As I drive along thinking of Mississippi's history and its present, I recall a passage from Walker Percy's *The Last Gentleman* that describes the new South: "The happiness of the South was very formidable. It was an almost invincible happiness. It defied you to call it anything else. Everyone was in fact happy. The women were beautiful and charming. The men were healthy and successful and funny; they knew how to tell stories. They had everything the North had and more. They had a history, they had a place redolent with memories, they had good conversation, they believed in God and defended the Constitution, and they were getting rich in the bargain. They had the best of victory and defeat."

I greatly admire Walker Percy's work. His books, more than Faulkner's, first introduced me to the South. *The Last Gentleman* is my particular favorite, and I reread it every few years, but the first place I stop in Lafayette County doesn't fit his ironic description.

Deer on a swing set outside Trula Threlkeld's house

About ten miles outside of Oxford I stop at a ramshackle house about fifty feet from the road. I'm drawn to a pair of eyes which stare at me from the front yard. The eyes, wide and mournful, belong to the disembodied head of an eight-point buck. The body, skinned and eviscerated, hangs in the center of a swing set. The head leans to the right, twisted around, mouth frozen in a snarl and eyes appearing to focus on its own carcass.

I knock on the cabin door and ask if it's all right to take a photograph. Trula Threlkeld, a tiny seventy-one-year-old woman, opens the door and invites me in, even though she doesn't know who I am and can't see me. Trula has no eyes in her sockets and has been blind for forty-five years. Her nephew Philip shot the deer, and Trula praises his abilities as a hunter. He's off right now, she says, somewhere in Colorado hunting. She gestures in the direction of the torn sofa where her niece Kay McKay, a retarded teenage girl she cares for, sits curled up, eyeing me. Trula tells her to get some photographs of Philip's other kills, but Kay just stares. "She's mad at me," Trula says, and repeats her request. Kay brings the pictures and I look at them. "She loves Philip," Trula says about her and Kay looks away.

There are trophies dotting the walls. A deer on one, a bass on another, a coyote on a third. The cardboard ceiling is falling down in places. Trula says she's going to move soon. She can't stand the smell of cat urine in the place anymore, she says.

She tells me she knew Faulkner, saw him a few times before she went blind. When the doctor first told her about her eye disease they said it wasn't inherited, but she says, "Come to think of it now, my granddaddy was blind."

She points me in the direction of Oxford from her front porch, her niece eyes me from the sofa, and as Trula closes the door, the warm air from the wood stove mixed with the acrid smell of cats lingers in my nostrils.

The first thing I see as I enter Oxford is the courthouse and the statue of the Confederate soldier. Faulkner's words haunt the space like a distant train whistle: "But above all, the courthouse: the center, the focus, the hub; sitting looming in the center of the country's circumference like a single cloud in its ring of horizon, laying its vast shadow to the uttermost rim of horizon; musing, brooding, symbolic and ponderable, tall as cloud, solid as rock, dominating all."

I wonder how many times Faulkner sat on one of these benches in front of the courthouse and looked up, pondering this magnificent columned building. I think of him raising his dark, hooded eyes some time in 1928 as he was writing *The Sound and the Fury* and imagining Luster and Benjy in the Compsons' surrey, approaching the square, "where the Confederate soldier gazed with empty eyes beneath his marble hand into wind and weather," imagining Jason's taking over the reins, imagining Ben's voice roaring in "horror; shock; agony eyeless, tongueless; just sound."

Because of Ole Miss and perhaps because of the spirit of Faulkner, Oxford is different from most towns its size in Mississippi and probably in the South. For many of the writers and artists who are there, it is the only town in Mississippi in which they could live. In writing about Oxford's uniqueness, Willie Morris once said, "The courthouse in the middle of the square and the Lyceum at the crest of the wooded grove are little more than a mile apart, which is appropriate, for it is impossible to imagine Ole Miss in a big city, and Oxford without the campus would be another struggling northeast Mississippi town. One can drive around the campus and absorb the palpable sophistication of a small southern state university, and then proceed two or three miles into a countryside that is authentic boondocks upon which the 20th century has only obliquely intruded." The name of William Faulkner, too, accounts for the town's special character. Although during his lifetime, to many in Oxford he was at best an eccentric and at worst a drunkard, he is now, according to some, an industry that competes with timber and soybeans.

Oxford is a town of about 20,000, half of them students at the University of Mississippi. Willie Morris says he finds too little loneliness here among the "goldfish" (his word for the achingly beautiful blond coeds who seem to be everywhere on campus). Maybe this is the happy, successful South that Walker Percy referred to in *The Last Gentleman*. When school is in session, fraternity brothers and sorority sisters cover the landscape, driving their baby blue BMW's and red Buick LeSabres. One New York writer described Greek rush week: "What screams, what cries, what an amplitude of passion. The proceedings are more exotic than the Romswarmnivian rites of the primitive Sherentes of Brazil's rain forest."

The Ole Miss college students give this oasis in the middle of the boondocks a cosmopolitan atmosphere and in some spots a bohemian one. The square in the center of town at first glance looks like any of the hundreds of other squares in southern towns from Greenville, Georgia, to Opelika, Alabama, only a bit better tended. But it goes much deeper than a few coats of paint.

Some of the stores around the square are typical fare: Plaza Shoes, The Village Tailor, Oxford Family Vision Clinic, Neilson's Department Store. But it would be difficult to find a Victor's Ristorante or an elegant Downtown Grille in Greenville. And it would be impossible to find a Square Books in Opelika or in just about any other southern town or city and most northern ones as well. Square Books is a bookstore that the novelist Barry Hannah calls the best in the entire South. It's probably the only bookstore outside of Greenwich Village or Berkeley, California, where a browser can have a cup of homemade soup, read Terry Pringle's latest novel, overhear a conversation between Tom McGuane and Ellen Douglas, and watch Mahatma Gandhi's grandson walk past the front door. Just off the square is the Hoka, a coffeehouse named after a Chickasaw princess, run by Ron Shapiro, described as a "white Jewish Rastaman," and Jim Dees, a Mississippian who writes essays under the name of "Dr. Bubba." The Hoka offers coffee and other things. The back room serves as an auditorium that shows American and foreign films (I lounge on one of the couches and watch Michelle Pfeiffer sing a version of "Making Whoopee" that makes me dig my fingers into two of the many tears in the couch. By the time she's finished I wipe my sweating brow with globs of stuffing.) Across from the Hoka is the Gin, a bar converted from an old cotton gin.

It's in the Gin that I meet Larry Brown, fireman and novelist. When Brown walks through the swinging saloon doors, I recognize him immediately, even though he doesn't look much like his book jacket photos. A shade under six feet tall and thin as a Mississippi reed, Brown would look like a kid even at thirty-eight years old if it weren't for his widow's peak and a network of lines etched into his face. There's nothing shy about him but nothing arrogant either. His smile is clear and unguarded, like his speech, a country drawl that says "stoof" for "stuff" and "thang" for "thing."

He wasn't on duty today at the firehouse, so he's unshaven. He sits down across from me in a booth in the back. He looks comfortable, as if he's been here many times before, a beer in one hand and a cigarette in the other, wearing a worn blue plaid shirt and jeans and a bemused smile half hidden by a scraggly moustache. A fireman for sixteen years in Oxford, he's recently become a celebrity, appearing on CNN and "The Today Show." He's been treated something like the poet Robert Burns was, as a sort of divine ploughman, an unschooled genius. In a sense, that's exactly what he is.

Born in 1951, he grew up mainly in Mississippi, graduating from Lafayette County High School in 1969. He was never much of a student, and when his father died when Larry was sixteen, he gave up on school and, for a while, on life. He failed English in his senior year of high school and didn't graduate with his class. The escape route seemed to be the service, and he joined the marines in 1970. One of the lucky ones, he never went to Vietnam. Instead he was stationed at Camp Lejeune in North Carolina and then Philadelphia. In Philadelphia he met a number of wounded veterans. His second book, the novel *Dirty Work*, came from this experience.

After military service he returned to Mississippi, got married, and became a fireman. In 1980, just before he turned thirty, he began to write fiction. "I'm not exactly sure why I started writing," he says. "I'd always loved reading, but it may have had more to do with approaching thirty.'

Approaching thirty or not, Brown was an innocent. The chances of a fireman from Oxford, Mississippi, making his way in the sophisticated world of publishing were about as good as, well, a postmaster from Ole Miss winning the Nobel Prize. But Brown was either too naive or too optimistic to consider the long odds. Instead he "decided to just try and see if I could do it." So he wrote a novel. As he remembers it, even the title was horrible, but he was convinced the book would be published. It was rejected enough times to persuade him otherwise. He wrote four other novels and over 100 short stories in the next few years, some of them rejected as many as fifteen times, before one of his stories, "Facing the Music," caught the careful eye of Shannon Ravenel, the editor of the Best American Short Stories series. She contacted him about publishing a book. In 1988 *Facing the Music*, a collection of ten stories, was published. A year later *Dirty Work*, his first published novel, was critically acclaimed. And although he hasn't won a Nobel Prize yet, he's had enough of a taste of fame, and the crank calls that accompany it, to get an unlisted telephone number, mainly to avoid speaking with the people who want to write books with him or have him write books about them. The strangest call he's received recently is from a woman in California who said she was a Jewish-Choctaw granddaughter of slavemasters from Mississippi. Her name was Snowdove and she wanted him to write a book about her. The next day he changed his telephone number.

At first his wife thought writing might be another of his whims, like rebuilding car engines. He smiles at that, the wrinkles around his eyes deepening, looking like grooves cut in dry ground. He says, "But I didn't give up. I was in for the long haul. Besides I got to use the only course I paid any attention to in high school: typing."

He begins to talk about books and the writers he admires. Faulkner's name is sounded early. After all, this is his postage stamp of earth. He began to read Faulkner, he says, at sixteen but appreciated him only much later. Despite the similarities between himself and Faulkner, both self-educated and both from Oxford, Brown's hero is Cormac McCarthy. He lifts his eyes toward the beamed ceiling as if he's singing a hymn when he mentions McCarthy's *Suttree* and *Child of God*. He's written only one fan letter in his life, and that one unanswered, to McCarthy.

He's also learned a lot from reading Raymond Carver, and Brown's stories show it. They are spare, cutting language and emotion to the bone. "Facing the Music," the title story of his first book, begins: "I cut my eyes sideways because I know what's coming." At first the reader can only guess but finds out it's a story about the changed relationship between a husband and wife after the woman's mastectomy. The story is unrelenting in its honesty, and like some of Carver's and Hemingway's stories, it has great power in its silences, in what's left unsaid. At one point the wife says, "Well, you don't want me since my operation," and the husband thinks, "She's always saying that. She wants me to admit it. And I don't want to lie anymore, I don't want to spare her feelings anymore, I want her to know I've got feelings too and it's hurt me almost as bad as it has her. But that's not what I say. I can't say that. 'I do want you,' I say. I have to say it. She makes me say it."

There are other stories in the volume that are as tautly written, as purely powerful as "Facing the Music." How did this man who failed senior English and spent sixteen years fighting fires in Lafayette County, Mississippi, find such stories inside him? From what source did he imagine the pain and loneliness that he writes about? He doesn't seem to know the answer to that question, and he's not the type who analyzes things in such a way. But for the past sixteen years as a fireman in Oxford, as a man living in a town populated by Faulkner's ghosts, by Joe Christmas and Quentin Compson and Caddie and Dilsey and Thomas Sutpen, Larry Brown has been listening to the living voices around him, to the jokes in the fire station, to the sad musings in local bars, to the conversations at parties. He's paid attention to what he's heard.

Ten cigarettes and four beers later, Brown is ready to head home. One day he'll use all those years as a firefighter in a novel, but for now he's waiting for his next book, titled *Big Bad Love*, a novella and eight short stories, to be published. He's also working with PBS on a dramatic version of *Dirty Work*.

"Heat Wave" playing on the juke box in the Gin, Brown stands, tells me to meet him at the firehouse the next morning, and goes off into the shockingly cold Mississippi night. Nothing, it seems to me, is exactly what I expect it to be—this fireman or the climate.

When I get to the firehouse, the engine is out, the firefighters investigating some smoke at the Dunkin' Donuts about a mile down the road at the mall. The entrance to the mall is directly across from the main gate of the Ole Miss campus, as if the architects and planners decided to make it as easy as possible for Willie Morris's goldfish to wiggle across Route 6 and right into Jewels by Annette or J. C. Penney's. I slide past a sad-eyed, skinny Santa and make my way into the Waldenbooks in the mall to see how the search for Faulkner would succeed here. The Waldenbooks in Des Moines would probably serve as well as this one. There are no biographies of Faulkner on the shelves and none of his best novels. But those who want to read *Knight's Gambit* or *A Fable* are in luck. Like American newscasters striving to talk in an unaccented, generic speech, malls strive desperately to be faceless. Once inside, you feel like Will Barrett walking in an amnesiac stupor on a southern battlefield. You're not sure where you are. It could be Arizona or Mississippi, and it doesn't make much difference whether you pick up *Knight's Gambit* or James Michener's *Chesapeake* to while away the time as you eat your french fries.

When I return to the firehouse the truck is back. There was some trouble with the smoke alarm, but it wasn't a wasted trip. A bag of donuts sits on the table. Two firemen look up from a soap opera they're watching and smile. Brown and I go outside and talk until an off-duty fireman stops in front of the house in his pickup truck. A three-wheeler, gardening clippers, a fifty-caliber muzzle loader, and a four-point buck are in the back. The firemen gather around, and one or two push their fingers into the deer's back, near the huge hole the bullet made, producing a sucking noise as the blood gurgles up. The gun is so powerful that the deer's back has been broken, and the men spend some time talking about this phenomenon. One man picks up the rack and lets the head fall, with a metal thump, on the bed of the truck.

Like Faulkner sitting among his cronies on the square, Brown seems perfectly natural in this setting, with these men. But after a few minutes he drifts away toward me and we say our goodbyes. Once again, briefly, he talks about firefighting and mentions Dennis Smith's *Report from Engine Company 82*, a book he admires. Brown, though, has three novels waiting to be revised or burned. Of the five he's written, one has been published and one burned. He doesn't have time right now to write about firefighters. He smiles, rubs his freshly shaven cheeks, and turning back into the firehouse, says, "I'm saving it all up."

Back at the square I cut through Faulkner Alley, between Shine Morgan's Furniture and Promise and Praise Books (now empty and moved to the mall). Other than a painting of Faulkner in the local McDonald's and the small sign put up on Taylor Road outside Rowan Oak, this is the only advertisement of Faulkner's presence.

According to Willie Morris, it's in Faulkner Alley that late-night drunks piss away their wine and beer.

I make my way to the faculty apartments on the campus to speak with Arun Gandhi, the grandson of Mahatma Gandhi. North Mississippi is not the place anyone would expect to find Gandhi's grandson, but he's been here for two years with his wife, in an apartment no larger than an untouchable's hovel in Bombay.

The fifty-five-year-old Gandhi, a journalist for over thirty years, is working on a book comparing the caste system in the South to the places he has lived, South Africa and India. He's published four other books, including *A Patch of White*, about racism in South Africa, and *Kasturba*, a biography of his grandmother. Long before he became a professional writer, journalism was in his blood. In a voice as soft as but deeper than his famous grandfather's, he says, "I was born in a printing press. My father put out a newspaper in South Africa, and he insisted everything be done by hand. I was setting type at ten."

His gentle manner once again recalls his grandfather, but his pink shirt and black corduroy pants are too modern for the image to linger. He has dark Indian skin, a faint moustache, and streaks of gray in his jet-black hair. Like his wife, Sunundu, with her boyishly cropped hair and British accent, he seems to have leapt away from his grandfather's time, in brown loafers and white socks.

His story, though, is deeply connected to the past and immersed in family. Like so many southern homes, Gandhi's apartment is filled with pictures of his family—his wife, his thirty-two-year-old daughter, and twenty-nine-year-old son. There are other photographs on the walls and tables—Mahatma Gandhi, Martin Luther King, Arun's grandchildren, and his parents when they were first married. All of this is in a jumble of images, past and present, plaques from the YWCA, a key from the mayor of Chicago, a calendar from a local restaurant, the Dr. Martin Luther King Freedom Award, and a remote control from a new Magnavox television.

His voice keeps reaching back to the past. He was born in Durban, a port city in South Africa. One of his earliest memories is of the racism that is such an accepted part of that society. It was

1942, and he was an eight-year-old boy visiting some Indian friends who were living in a white residential community. The young Gandhi went off exploring near the center of town. Following a British tradition, towns in South Africa are quiet after one in the afternoon. The center of town was deserted, and Gandhi strolled to a candy store in an all-white area. After buying his candy, he trailed after a black man who was walking along whistling. The eight-year-old Gandhi started whistling the same tune until two white boys came up, threw him down on the ground, and beat him, saying, "This is a white neighborhood and you're not allowed to whistle here." The black man, dressed in a half-trouser made of white cotton and a white shirt with a red border around it, clothes that marked the domestic servant in South Africa, stood by and watched the beating. It was the type of situation the white government supported, Gandhi feels, and in 1952 with the Bantu Education Act, this attitude was institutionalized. The act kept the tribes divided. The one thing that made the government tremble was the possibility of blacks and non-whites in South Africa uniting.

Gandhi was shaken by the beating, a lesson in racial hatred he has never forgotten and one that has been repeated in different ways throughout his life. His experience in America hasn't been much different. Early in 1988 he gave a talk on racism at Jacksonville State in Anniston, Alabama. There were threats from the KKK and tensions ran high. Arun and his wife were having dinner after the speech with two professors when, as Mrs. Gandhi describes it, "A country-looking man came directly toward our table. The color drained from our hosts' faces. One jumped up to intercept the man before he could reach Arun, but he didn't get there in time. The man got to Arun's side of the table, reached out his hand, and said, 'That was a great speech.' We all started to breathe again, but I could tell they were happy to get us on the plane the next day."

In New Orleans a few weeks later, where he was to speak at the University of New Orleans, he was greeted at the airport by six plainclothes security officers. Flashing back to South Africa, he thought he was being arrested, but it was just heightened security. He was marched to a car, three men in front and three in back. During lunch at the university he was encircled by police.

His encounters with the black establishment in Mississippi have not been much more encouraging. Black leaders like Aaron Henry have essentially told him to go back to his own country and teach *them* about racism. Gandhi's book may not be far from completion, but his dream of a Center for the Study of Non-Violence, something similar to but even more activist than Ole Miss's own Center for the Study of Southern Culture, seems far from ever being realized. Gandhi feels that, like Faulkner in his lifetime, he has been ignored by the University of Mississippi, in particular, and the state, in general. His offers to teach special seminars at the university have been ignored. His requests for financial assistance have fallen on deaf ears. His proposals on the state level have been politely received but not acted upon.

His dream for a Center for the Study of Non-Violence began a long time ago. The Phoenix Settlement, started in 1903 by Mahatma Gandhi and continued in 1917 by Arun's father, is where he grew up and learned his grandfather's philosophy. When Arun was twelve he spent a year living in India with his grandfather, a man who accepted non-violence as a creed and poverty as a way of life. But for the teenage Arun his grandfather was not a saint but a warm, affectionate man. "He was very human," Arun remembers. "It's not the tenets of his philosophy that stay in my memory from that year I lived with him, the year before he was killed, it is his arms around me as he hugged me tenderly."

In 1956 Arun left South Africa and returned to live and work in India. There, for nearly a quarter of a century, he worked as reporter for the *Times of India* in Bombay, leaving in 1980 to become the editor of *Imprint*, a monthly literary magazine. After three years, the magazine's financial situation became increasingly precarious and he resigned as editor. The next two years were the most miserable of his life. He did freelance work and had no job prospects. Finally, he took the little savings that remained, and in his 300-square-foot house, roughly as big as an average-size living room in an American home, he began to write and lay out his own newspaper. He was modestly successful until the printer tried to cheat him. As Gandhi tells it, the printer carefully manipulated affairs until the newspaper was dependent on his press. When the paper began to be successful after eighteen months, the printer demanded to be made a partner or he wouldn't print the next issue.

Arun tore up the next issue in front of the surprised man and told him to leave. The next day he shut down the paper.

Soon after, he came to the United States to begin his study of race and caste. A few things have become clear to him. In the United States blacks are considered inferior. In South Africa they are considered dangerous. In South Africa discrimination begins with color. In the United States it is based on race. He mentions Faulkner's Joe Christmas in *Light in August*. "One small part of Negro blood, even one-sixteenth, makes you a Negro," he says. "But what about that fifteen-sixteenths, shouldn't that make you white?"

As he speaks his hands make light brown butterflies in the air, moving out and back as he begins to talk about his life in India. There, the caste system is, in some respects, similar to that in the American South. Like the Indian scourge of untouchability that divides people into four groups (Brahmins, nobles, businessmen, and laborers), the caste system in the South separates blacks, poor whites, and landed gentry. In the American South, of course, there is potential for movement from one caste to another, especially among whites. In India, initially there was the chance of moving from one caste to another, as well. But sometime during the first century a king created a law which prohibited movement. Castes were determined by birth. Family names became caste-based. "But how different," he asks, "is this from caste being determined by race?"

In 1947 in India, after independence and a new constitution, equal rights were provided for everyone, but the caste system did not disappear. Outside of a few large cities, India is made up of 750,000 small villages, closed communities where a person's name is fixed forever, whether the individual has it legally changed or not. "A Snopes is always a Snopes," he says. Civil rights laws came to India in full force about the same time they came to the United States, but Gandhi feels the point is clear: laws alone will not insure rights. Poverty and ignorance fuel the caste machine in both India and the South. When he lived in India, Gandhi was a member of a group that helped the untouchables use government programs. In one town he helped the people organize milk production, form a cooperative dairy, and fend for themselves. He doesn't believe in charity and thinks, "It is far better to teach a man to fish than it is to provide him with free salmon. The man who has the skill is independent." The economy of the town in 1961 was zero. Seven years later it was $80,000.

Poverty in Mississippi often reminds him of India's, but he had not been able to interest local or state organizations in the "adopt a village" program that worked so well in his homeland. Racial considerations, he believes, are behind the resistance. Racism, he's convinced, is at the core of the American character. "But the South has one advantage," he says. "People here are aware there is a problem. Much of America is like an alcoholic who refuses to admit the disease exists." Brown butterflies reach into the slanting winter light that cuts into the room as I get up to leave.

On my way to Rowan Oak I can't help but wonder what Faulkner would have made of such a visitor to his small town. Some things have changed so much and others not at all. The expensive, modern brick homes along Taylor Road are new additions since Faulkner's death, but Rowan Oak looks much the same as it did thirty years ago. It is still a rustic mansion set atop thirty-two acres that slope away from it. The brick path that leads up to the four wooden columns that support the Grecian roof of the house is still lined with stately 100-year-old cedars. When Faulkner bought the house for $6,000 in 1930, complete with a sagging roof, squirrels in the attic, and rumors of a ghost, the house was hidden away on the curve of Taylor Road. It still is hidden. The green historical marker, put up this year at the cost of $900, is inconspicuous. The sign says: "Rowan Oak—Built ca. 1848. From 1930 to 1962 the home of novelist William Faulkner, who named it for the rowan tree, symbol of security and peace. Now maintained as a literary land-mark by the University of Mississippi."

This is the true center of Oxford, perhaps of the South. This is where Faulkner's story seems to be, beating like a heart. Born September 25, 1897, in Ripley, Mississippi, Faulkner moved to Oxford when he was five. He spent most of the rest of his life there. It became the imaginative source for most of his best work for the next sixty years.

Although William Faulkner was no bookworm and was never

fully engaged by schoolwork, writing seems to have run in his family. In 1851 the twenty-six-year-old William Clark Falkner, William's great-grandfather, privately published "The Siege of Monterey," a poem about his exploits as a lieutenant in the Mexican War and his love for his fiance. In the same year he paid for the publication of a novel, *The Spanish Heroine*. In 1867, he wrote a play, *The Lost Diamond*, which had eight scenes, one titled "The Battle of Manassas. Thrilling Scenes on the Bloody Field." It was in 1881, however, with *The White Rose of Memphis* that Faulkner's great-grandfather found literary success. The novel went through thirty-five editions and sold about 160,000 copies in thirty years. It was a potboiler, described by one critic as "a murder mystery plus two romances."

After his death William Clark Falkner became a legendary figure. People remembered his flowing white hair and his goatee, his aristocratic features and piercing, hooded eyes, which his great-grandson inherited. William Faulkner once said, "People in Ripley talk of him as if he were still alive, up in the hills some place, and might come in at any time." A Mississippi once and future king, he certainly lived a life that legends are founded upon. When he was sixteen he left home, studied law and lived by his wits until he went off to the Mexican War at age twenty. He returned from the war in 1847 minus the first joints of three fingers and a good deal of blood from a foot wound. Two years later, now a husband and father, he killed a man in a knife fight. The jury ruled it self-defense. In February 1851 he shot a man to death. Again, he was acquitted. By 1859 he had fathered three more children, bought a number of slaves, farmed, practiced law, invested in land, and run for the state legislature. During the Civil War he led the First Mississippi Partisan Rangers and used guerrilla-style tactics in northeast Mississippi and southern Tennessee. After the war he practiced law and built a railroad from Ripley to Tennessee. By 1889, according to Joseph Blotner, "He had published a book and raised money in New York, shaken Grover Cleveland's hand in Washington and done the grand tour in Europe." In 1889 he also won a seat in the state legislature. But before he was able to serve he was shot in the mouth and killed by a political rival. Not long afterward a monument was erected in his honor, an eight-foot-high statue standing on a six-foot-square pediment, carved out of Carrara marble. It was made from the old colonel's photograph. He had ordered the statue himself. He knew a legend, it seems, when he saw one.

The young colonel, John Wesley Thompson Falkner, William's grandfather, was not the romantic legend that William Clark was, but he was an equally imposing and successful figure. A prominent lawyer, he continued to develop his father's railroad business. He became an assistant U.S. attorney and eventually the president of the First National Bank of Oxford, where he settled with his wife. When the young colonel sold the railroad, William Faulkner's father, Murry, was virtually forced to follow him to Oxford, where he would set him up in business. Murry was devastated. The railroad was his love. He talked about moving west and ranching, but a stubborn wife and three young children made the decision for him. He bought a livery stable in Oxford.

Murry became a cold, distant man, unhappy with his situation, who drank himself into periods of escape and oblivion. His only substitute for his dream of going west were his times at hunting camp or in the woods surrounding Oxford. Maud, his wife, hated drink and loved books more than the woods. In most ways she seemed to be Murry's opposite, particularly in her strong attachment to William, but she too could appear to be unaffectionate. According to one of her granddaughters, Maud masked her insecurity with a cold manner and often seemed brusque and arrogant.

William inherited his mother's love of books and his father's passion for the woods. And as alienated as he felt from his father, as an adult William drank prodigiously, using alcohol much as Murry had. As a young man Faulkner loved sports, played quarterback on his high school football team and enjoyed baseball, but he was never a typical Oxford boy. At an early age he fell in love with his neighbor Estelle Oldham and soon after, he began writing poetry. Writers and poets were less common in Oxford than integrationists. Some people thought Billy Falkner odd.

Like Murry and Maud, Estelle and William were also opposites. She was outgoing, laughing, and self-assured. He was often introverted, silent, and full of self-doubt. He was disconsolate when Estelle went off to college in 1914. That same year the family fortunes also shifted. The livery business declined, and Murry had to sell his house to cover the debts. He bought a hardware store on the square and was even unhappier than he had been previously.

From his early years in Oxford, then, William was considered "quair," as one resident remembered him. He was always very bright but after the early years neither school nor Oxford society seemed to interest him much. After his mother the most important influence in his youth and the first to recognize his talent was a law student who had graduated from the University of Mississippi, Phil Stone. Influenced by Stone and by his reading of the Romantic poets, Faulkner began to experiment with his own verse. At this point his poetry was a blend of the luxuriant melancholy of the Romantics and the ironic pessimism of A. E. Housman.

He began to dress the part of the poet and dandy, buying twenty-five-dollar suits and fancy shoes. Around this time he picked up the derogatory nickname "Count" which eventually became even more pointedly sarcastic as "Count No 'Count" when he got older. Poetry may have seemed to him to be the only escape from the trauma of lost love. In 1918 Estelle had married the handsome and ambitious lawyer Cornell Franklin and gone off to live in Hawaii. Faulkner tried to enlist in the Air Force but was rejected because of his slight five-foot six-inch frame.

Always the storyteller, Faulkner devised a tale about his English birth, made himself a year younger (perhaps to help account for his lack of stature), and joined the R.A.F. in Canada. It was around this time that he put the "u" back in Faulkner, as well. As one soldier during the time put it, "In those years death itself exerted a curious magnetism on young men . . . and death became a romantic dream for the new generation of American writers." A romantic and a dreamer, Faulkner wanted the glory of war but he never did get to fight in Europe. He did go through flight training, and although there is no verifiable evidence to support his story, he said he flew upside down, hanging from his seat belt while attempting to drink from a crock of bourbon, executed an Immelman maneuver or two, crashed into an airport hangar, and ended up perched on the rafters. He also came back from his service in Canada with tall tales about leg injuries, metal plates in his head, and heroism in the sky. He returned to Oxford with a neatly trimmed moustache, a Piccadilly-tailored British uniform, a swagger stick, and a stockpile of stories in his imagination.

After the war, perhaps as an atypical gesture of conformity to please his parents, Faulkner entered Ole Miss as a special student. He traded the swagger stick for an umbrella, abandoned his pompadour for a middle part, took up smoking cigarettes from a long holder, and studied, according to his mood at the moment, Shakespeare, French, and Spanish. At the end of the first semester, he received an *A* in French, a *B* in Spanish, and a *D* in English. Not bad, considering he supposedly refused to take exams.

A number of odd jobs, especially odd for a future Nobel laureate, perhaps, followed: bank teller, painter, bookstore clerk, postmaster at the University of Mississippi post office. In particular, his work at the post office became the stuff of legend. As people remembered him, Faulkner sat in the back of the post office in a rocking chair with a writing arm attached and wrote continuously. When people came to the post office window, Faulkner would ignore them or come begrudgingly up to serve them. Faulkner's brother Jack thought the situation was ironic. "It never ceased to amaze us," Jack said, "that here was a man so little attracted to mail that he never read his own being solemnly appointed the custodian of that belonging to others. It was amazing that under his trusteeship any mail ever actually got delivered." Some mail didn't. Some things, according to legend, he just threw away. Others he found interesting enough to open up and read before he passed them along. Stories about his going to work unshaven, in sandals, denim pants, and an unbuttoned shirt made even some of his relations say, "He's not worth a Mississippi goddam."

His tenure as postmaster came to an end when a postal inspector came to the general delivery window and found Faulkner playing bridge with a few cronies. As Faulkner left the building, one of the bridge players asked, "Bill, don't you feel strange leaving this place for the last time this way? Next time we come here it'll be like everybody else. We'll have to treat the post office like a post office and not like a club." Faulkner walked on without speaking for some time. Finally he stopped, turned to his friend, and said, "I reckon I'll be at the beck and call of folks with money all my life, but thank God I won't ever again have to be at the beck and call of every son of a bitch who's got two cents to buy a stamp." Not even Faulkner was prescient enough at that time to guess that in August 1987 there would be a ceremony in Oxford to celebrate the U.S. Postal Service's issuing a commemorative Faulkner stamp.

Leaving stamps and letters behind, Faulkner went to New Orleans, where he met the established writer Sherwood Anderson. With Anderson's help, Faulkner launched his writing career. His first book, *The Marble Faun*, a book of poetry, had just been published in December 1924 with the promotional assistance of Phil Stone. During the time he was in New Orleans he worked intensely with a blend of energy, determinination, and ingenuity that would mark his entire career from that point. He worked so intensely that the former postmaster had no time at all to write letters. When his mother and friends in Mississippi didn't hear from him, they began to worry. Phil Stone eventually sent him a wire: "What's the matter do you have a mistress." Faulkner replied immediately: "Yes and she's 30,000 words long."

From New Orleans, Faulkner followed the expatriates to Europe, but after a six-month *wanderjahr* he returned to Oxford, Mississippi, for the publication of his first novel, *Soldiers' Pay*. Hearing that the book was immoral, his father refused to open it and continued to read his favorite Zane Grey novels. Phil Stone, Faulkner's close friend and early mentor, offered a copy to the University of Mississippi, but they would not accept the gift.

In 1927 his second novel, *Mosquitoes*, was published, but then his third novel, at first titled *Flags in the Dust* and later *Sartoris*, had a more difficult route to publication. At first rejected, it was published two years later in 1929, a few months before *The Sound and the Fury*. The next seven years were magical ones for Faulkner and memorable ones for American literature as a whole. During this period Faulkner wrote four of the greatest novels ever produced by an American writer: *The Sound and the Fury*, *As I Lay Dying*, *Light in August*, and *Absalom, Absalom!* In his own fury of explosive creativity, Faulkner accomplished what no other American writer had done before or has done since. Singlehandedly, he matched the golden period in American literature during the middle of the nineteenth century when Thoreau wrote *Walden*, Hawthorne *The Scarlet Letter*, Melville *Moby Dick*, and Whitman *Leaves of Grass*. Faulkner was a writer of tremendous energy and discipline. As he told a *New Yorker* reporter, "I write when the spirit moves me, and the spirit moves me every day."

In the same year, 1929, Faulkner married his childhood sweetheart, Estelle Oldham, now divorced from Cornell Franklin and living in Oxford with her two children. The ill-fated marriage began with a prophetically unenthusiastic approval from both families, a refusal by the Episcopal minister to marry divorced persons, a drive in a borrowed car, and a departure with borrowed money for a honeymoon in Pascagoula. The honeymoon clearly foreshadowed the strained relationship that was to be the story of the marriage. Faulkner, once consumed by a youthful love for Estelle, now had literary passions, too.

Both Faulkner and Estelle drank heavily. One story suggests that on the honeymoon Estelle attempted suicide. Although their marriage lasted for more than three decades, the stormy first weeks provided the pattern for their life together.

Pressed for money as he often was during his life, Faulkner began working at the university power plant from 6 P.M. to 6 A.M., shoveling coal and working on *As I Lay Dying*. His daughter Alabama, who was born in 1931, lived only nine days.

Tragedy and frustration seemed to run together in his life. Recognition of his writing talent came slowly but money came in even more sluggishly. In 1932, shortly after he finished *Light in August*, Faulkner was forced to make the first of his many trips to Hollywood as a scriptwriter. He didn't want to go, but his publishing company (Cape & Smith) was in bankruptcy and his magazine sales had dried up. Faulkner must have felt much the same as Melville had when he was writing *Moby Dick* and said, "Dollars damn me!" Faulkner was overdrawn at the bank by $500, and when he wrote a three-dollar check at McCall's sporting-goods store, the owner said she would prefer the cash. His angry response—"That signature will be worth more than three dollars"—didn't change her mind. He headed for MGM studios for the substantial salary of $500 a week.

In the next few years, as he worked on his masterpiece *Absalom, Absalom!* and grieved over the death of his brother Dean in a plane crash, Faulkner made a number of trips to Hollywood. The trips were all financially motivated until he met the twenty-eight-year-old secretary to filmmaker Howard Hawks, Meta Carpenter. Their affair was destined to last intermittently over the next fifteen years.

Faulkner said he was like an "orphan" in Hollywood, but things were never that simple with him. He loved Mississippi and told Estelle he would write only about the South, but like Quentin Compson he had deeply ambivalent feelings about his homeland. He hated Hollywood and often drank himself into a stupor while he was there, but Meta was there and for many years she was the love of his life. When he was in Mississippi he missed his passionate relationship with her. When he was in Hollywood he missed his home.

Faulkner's relationship with his wife continued to deteriorate and reached its public nadir on June 22, 1936, when the Memphis *Commercial Appeal* carried an ad which ran three days later in the *Oxford Eagle*: "I will not be responsible for any debt incurred or bills made, or notes or checks signed by Mrs. William Faulkner or Mrs. Estelle Oldham Faulkner." It was signed William Faulkner. The thought of losing his daughter Jill, however, seemed to stop him from asking for a divorce.

By 1937 Faulkner was beginning to become an unwilling tourist attraction. His face appeared on the cover of *Time* for January 23, 1939. He was becoming world famous, but in Oxford he was still an oddity. In addition, he was still in economic straits, partly because he had taken on the responsibility of supporting many members of his family. At one point in 1941 he was writing to thank a publisher for a loan and told him, "When I wired you I did not have the $15 to pay electricity bill with, keep my lights burning." Economic circumstances forced him to boil the pot or return to the salt mines, his expressions for writing stories for magazines or working in Hollywood.

In 1945 the critic Malcolm Cowley began work on *The Portable Faulkner*. At that time most of his books were out of print. "What a commentary," he wrote to his publisher. "In France, I am the father of a literary movement. In Europe I am considered the best modern American and among the first of all writers. In America, I eke out a hack's motion picture wages by winning second prize in a manufactured mystery story contest." Not until the sale of the movie rights for his novel *Intruder in the Dust* in 1948 did Faulkner begin to feel financially secure. And it was not until 1949, when he won the Nobel Prize for literature, that America could no longer ignore his stature as a writer.

Although at the awards ceremony in Stockholm Faulkner stood too far from the microphone, spoke too fast, and confused his listeners with his southern accent, his speech will be remembered as one of the most moving ever given at such an occasion. He finished his brief statement by saying, "I believe that man will not merely endure: he will prevail. He is immortal, not because he alone among creatures has an inexhaustible voice, but because he has a soul, a spirit capable of compassion and endurance."

He had become the great American novelist of the twentieth century, but even a Pulitzer Prize and a National Book Award in 1954 and other assorted honors could not lessen the controversy of his involvement in the civil rights movement after the Supreme Court's decision in the same year. He wrote a series of letters to the Memphis *Commercial Appeal* in favor of integration and was accused of ignorance, cowardice, and treachery in print and by anonymous phone callers. To many he was seen as a southern moderate or, worse, as a southern apologist. Somehow he seemed to alienate both sides. To the activists he was a gradualist. To the rednecks he was a traitor. Like his fictional creation Quentin Compson, he was caught between his love for and hatred of the South. He wished to defend his homeland, but he was sickened by the racism he saw around him.

When the opportunity arose to serve as writer-in-residence at the University of Virginia in Charlottesville, he took it. He seemed to like everything about Virginia—being near his daughter Jill, the fox hunts, the aristocratic sensibility of old-world Virginians, his classes, even the UVA football games. Faulkner, who so often called himself a Mississippi farmer, must have been appropriately amused when "Bullet Bill" Dudley, interviewing him at halftime of a Virginia football game, introduced him as "Mr. William Faulkner, the winner of the Mobile Prize for literature."

In the last few years of his life, Faulkner, who had adopted so many personas—wounded flyer, bohemian poet, working farmer—now played the most satisfying role of his life, the acclaimed writer-sage. He had come a long way, from being Count No 'Count to being an honored personage as respected as the Old Colonel himself.

In 1961 he finished *The Reivers*, his nineteenth novel, a comic tale that he may have viewed as his *The Tempest*, like Shakespeare's work of love and farewell. On July 6, 1962, he died unexpectedly at Wright's Sanitarium in Byhalia, the hospital he had often been taken to in order to recover from his alcoholic binges. That same year he was awarded the Pulitzer Prize posthumously for *The Reivers*.

His name, his life story, and his characters are tangible presences in the town. A line from his Nobel Prize speech about man's ability to endure, to prevail, is inscribed over the entrance to the library. His words seem to echo across the campus. Everyone in Oxford has a Faulkner story or knows someone else who has one. When I was in Columbus, Mississippi, someone told me to stop in Tupelo and ask about the tornado. Everybody, I was told, has a tornado story. Faulkner is the tornado that hit Oxford.

The eye of the storm, serene and still, is and perhaps always will be Rowan Oak. The only breezes seem to blow softly from the past. The only voices seem to be those of ghosts. This may be fitting, for even when Faulkner bought the house over half a century ago it supposedly came with its own ghost story. Rowan Oak was originally the old Shegog mansion. Colonel Shegog bought the land from a Chickasaw Indian who received it as a grant from the U.S. government. According to the legend (one probably created by Faulkner himself), the beautiful Judith Shegog, the colonel's daughter, fell in love with a deceitful Yankee prisoner during the Civil War. He was supposed to return to Oxford after the war but never did, and she committed suicide. According to Faulkner, Judith's ghost roamed among the magnolias.

It's Faulkner's ghost that roams now, or at least that is what Howard Bahr, the present curator of Rowan Oak, would have me believe. Bahr, tall and slim, at least six-feet two-inches and not more than 135 pounds, but with hawklike features and ascetic good looks that bring Faulkner to mind, has worked at Rowan Oak since 1976. He came to the house as a student assistant under Professor James Webb, then chairperson of the English Department, a man Bahr speaks of in reverential tones. It was his labor of love, according to Bahr, to convince the University of Mississippi to buy Rowan Oak from Faulkner's daughter, Jill, in 1972.

When Webb died in 1984, Bahr took over as curator, and he seems ideally suited for the task, like a monk accustomed to the pattern of the monastery. Sitting in front of his rolltop desk in the hallway off the kitchen, Bahr is rarely without a pipe in his mouth or hand. For him Rowan Oak is a monument to the past, and Bahr likes living in times gone by. His only concession to the modern world has been the new truck he bought last year. Otherwise he doesn't have much use for things modern.

While I am with him, he answers the phone. "Hey, Miss Pat, how are you, dear?" he asks. With all women he uses the genteel southern formula, placing Miss before the first name. He is a member of the local Masonic lodge with its old fraternal order and roots in eighteenth-century England. He doesn't play tennis or golf. For recreation he engages in Civil War reenactments. He is a solitary figure, standing behind a screen of past as tangible, it seems, as the curtains at Rowan Oak.

He feels more at home in the rooms at Rowan Oak than he does in his apartment in downtown Oxford. His hate list is not long but it's definite: billboards, condominiums, new boutiques on the square, young intellectuals in the English Department at Ole Miss—"They're all dynamic and ambitious, Marxists and atheists, deconstructionists and new constructionists," he says. He doesn't seem to like the brand-new national landmark sign outside Rowan Oak either, but he appears to take pleasure in the fact that some fool had to pay nearly $1,000 for it.

He doesn't give tours, unless he is asked by someone who comes in and wants to do more than browse. Usually, he's there at the rolltop desk, ready to answer questions, or in back brewing some tea on the hot plate in the kitchen. He offers me a cup and shows me the 1961 Oxford telephone directory, where Faulkner is listed as "William Falkner 719 Garfield Avenue" because Garfield Road was to be extended past Rowan Oak. It never was. He smiles and says,

Statue of Confederate soldier on the square in Oxford,
Mississippi

"So the town got the wrong address and misspelled his name besides. That seems about right."

The telephone numbers Faulkner penciled onto the wall in the pantry are still there. We walk past the dining room cart, which holds a bottle of Captain Morgan's Spiced Rum, and stand on the wide-board wooden floors looking out the six-foot-high front windows. The sun, angling through the cedars, makes squares of light at our feet as Howard takes off his wire-rimmed glasses, rubs his eyes, and tells me about his life. The perfect southern gentleman, he adds "sir" to all his responses until I begin to wonder if I've aged dramatically since the trip began.

He was born in Meridian and traveled all over the state with his stepfather, who worked for the Illinois Central Railroad. After high school and a stint in the navy, Bahr began working for the railroad himself as a yard clerk. Carrying a pistol, he patrolled the darkened yard, on the lookout for hobos. He speaks dreamily of running over one hundred loads of bananas in the good weeks on the railroad. But things changed. Fewer bananas and more modernization. He left.

In 1973 he came to Ole Miss to major in English and history. Like Faulkner he seems wedded to this place. In 1984 he contemplated leaving. He had just returned from his twenty-year high school reunion in Belleville, Illinois, where he had spent his senior year when his father was transferred with the railroad. At the reunion he met his high school sweetheart, recently divorced and now the mother of two. They talked of getting married, even got engaged. He traveled back and forth from Oxford to Illinois a few times. Like Faulkner meeting Estelle after her divorce from Cornell Franklin, Howard sensed a second chance. But he had to choose between Oxford and the concrete and asphalt world of Belleville, Illinois, where, because of the divorce agreement, the children had to remain.

He chose Mississippi. He chose the past. "Two things I've never had," he says, "common sense and ambition." But the world of Rowan Oak seems to be truly his. It is quiet, pastoral— ordered and clear. "I can't imagine myself thirty days from now," he admits, "let alone thirty years from now." But to see him thirty years

Howard Bahr, curator of Rowan Oak, in front of the barn

before, in a columned mansion on a dirt road leading toward the past, is not so difficult to imagine.

It's not the past but the present that is the province of Lyn Gilliam. I speak with him as he cleans one of the rooms in the Oliver-Britt House, the one and only bed-and-breakfast in Oxford. Lyn is a twenty-four-year-old black man, but he isn't interested in talking about racial matters. One in a family of ten children, Lyn is interested in becoming a chef in a country inn, and his dream is to own one.

Lyn is small and spare, and it is difficult to see him as the father of two children, one of them four years old. He's lived in Oxford all of his life and still lives with his parents off Martin Luther King Street in the projects. The woman who is the mother of his children has her own apartment in another section of town. She is a seamstress at the local pajama factory. They both take care of the kids. He visits her every day.

They plan to get married, but their living arrangement is not unusual, he says. "Lots of my friends have kids but aren't ready to get married or live together." He stares at his hands, picks at a callous on his knuckle, touches his chin, scratches his head. His hands constantly move as he talks about the things he has to do before marriage, mainly pay for his 1982 Delta 88 and get more experience as a cook. He takes the dust broom he's been using on the furniture, brushes off his Air Jordans, and puts a Smokey Robinson tape in the boom box which sits on an antique desk in the corner of the room.

Looking down once again to examine his hands, he tells me he lives only in the present. What happened years ago does not affect him. "I get by," he says. "I don't have a desire to live anywhere else in the world. Some people say this is Faulkner's town; but I don't get excited when I hear his name. I don't say 'wham' or anything. For me it's just something in the history books. Faulkner was prejudiced. He used the word 'nigger,' but that don't bother me none. That's in the past. I'm here now. That's someone else's lifetime. I can't do nothing about it."

Some feel something should be done, though, about the racial imbalances in the town, that no black man or woman holds a

Faulkner's kitchen

position of real power, that for all practical purposes many of the clubs are still segregated. I meet two brothers in the Hoka, two black men who grew up in Oxford and now live in San Francisco and Chicago. They are home to visit their mother. One of them, William Fox, the president of Fovaco Enterprises in Chicago, says, "This is a closed society. There are no blacks in decision-making positions. Helping blacks? Ole Miss is a joke. Even the Center for the Study of Southern Culture is a token. That's what we've had for years, token programs and token results." His brother says, "When we walked into these clubs, it recalled the past. All I could say was here we go again. This is 1988, half this town is black, but it's the same damn thing. All white people. I helped build this town but it hasn't changed."

Barry Hannah, a novelist who lives in Oxford, agrees: "If I were black, I wouldn't be here. There's little to make black intellectuals feel comfortable here. Blacks on the faculty feel cut off. Intentionally or not, there are two distinct cultures in Mississippi." With a smile he adds, "Mississippi's not a bad place for a white person to live."

Finally, though, for Hannah, Oxford is a wonderful mixture of people and energies, a "United Nations with catfish on its breath." It's a place where the past is alive and vibrant.

Bill Appleton, the sixty-four-year-old former caretaker for St. Peter's Cemetery where the Faulkner family is buried, has a booming voice, a volcanic laugh, and a love for the past that proves Hannah's point. Appleton meets me in front of his modest brick house on the outskirts of town. A mouth full of peanuts doesn't stop him from roaring "Hello," a cannon boom that sprays like shell fire in my direction.

Appleton is big and bulbous, an archetypal "good ol' boy." His speech reminds me of Willie Morris's description of the breed, speaking "the grammar of dirt farmers and Negroes, using 'ain'ts' and reckless verb forms with such a natural instinct that the right ones would have sounded high-blown and phony, and pushing the country talk to such limits that making it as flamboyant as possible became an end in itself."

The first thing he says to me when we arrive at the cemetery is

Michael and William Fox in Oxford

"Ain't shit been done here since I left." He spent six years as caretaker at the cemetery after twenty-six years as a police officer. Clearly, the cemetery is his love. He lifts a wide, thick hand into the air and points a finger shaped like a tulip bulb toward the hillside, saying, "You looking at history." This cemetery is his textbook, his classroom, and he maneuvers across the landscape and through his stories with the agility of a practiced lecturer. Once again I am reminded of Willie Morris's description of just such a place in *North Toward Home*: "We took also to spending long hours in the cemetery, the coolest place in town and in some ways the most sensible. Death in a small town is a different proposition than death in a large city; in a small town one associated death with landmarks, with the places people had lived or the places they spent most of their time, so that I connected certain graves with specific houses, or stores. One day when I was ten or eleven, I made a count of all the houses on my street as I walked home, and to my horror discovered that someone I had known or knew about had died at one time or another in more than half of them. Death in a small town deeply affected the whole community."

His jowls shaking in the breeze, Bill Appleton talks and laughs and points ceaselessly as we wend our way toward Faulkner's grave near the shade of an oak tree. "Look at them acorns," Appleton says, punctuating each sentence by spitting a sharp, straight line of saliva. "Faulkner said he wanted acorns falling on his grave when he died. You could sell them in New York City for a fortune. One day my niggers was out there working in the grass, and they saw a Jap putting Hershey kisses and a bottle of whisky on his grave. Can you imagine what this guy would have paid for a few acorns? He told them it was ritual. Shit, man, Faulkner didn't need that whisky, but he wanted a picture with the whisky by the grave. My niggers sat out there beating the ground laughing." He uses the word "nigger" without any malice and would be offended if any-one thought so. He has been accused, as Faulkner was, of liking blacks too much. But the old language dies hard and it lingers in his speech.

He makes it clear that he talks to me, despite my northern accent, because I lived in Georgia for six years. "You ain't no

Yankee, bud," he says. He rubs his palm against his rough, un-shaven cheek, a thumb and forefinger lingering over one of the moles that rise from his skin like granite outcroppings. He has a story for every grave and knows where everyone in Lafayette County is buried, from Captain William Delay, who fought through three wars, to Chief Toby Tubby of the Chickasaws.

When he wishes to make a point, to make sure I'm attending to his story, he taps my shoulder with his index finger. When he finishes, he slaps me on the back, as if to congratulate me on my ability to concentrate. He shows me a broken vault that some college students vandalized, pulling the women's bones out and stealing a wedding ring. Then he points out his own tombstone: "Virgle E. Appleton/March 5, 1925." He's had two heart attacks and he wants to be ready.

On our way out he takes me by the arm and leads me to a far corner of the cemetery, a parcel of land technically in the county. There he points to a plain marble marker that reads "Pete 1970–1983." His mouth opens in a wide laugh, but the angles of his face quickly jiggle back into a serious expression. He removes his National Rifle Association baseball cap, and his eyes beneath his sunglasses nar-row. "This here's where the third smartest dog in the world is buried. There was Rin Tin Tin and Lassie. Then there was Pete."

Pete was Willie Morris's dog, and Appleton buried him in friendship. As he describes the scene when he brought Morris out to show him the grave, Appleton's voice gets clogged with emotion. Tears well up in his eyes. He changes the subject, begins to talk about World War II, the bullet holes in his chin, D-Day, the Second Armored Divison. He laughs again, remembering Berlin at the end of the war and selling American goods to the Russians. He sold his pants for $600, and walked back to his division in his underwear. "If I could do one thing before I leave this here old earth," he says, "I'd go back to Berlin and see that Sherman tank. It's still there."

He has two grown children, but he has married for a second time and has an eight-year-old daughter. He tells me about her but seems to have more to say about the war and this cemetery he turns back to look at one more time. "You're looking at history here," he says.

I stop in Square Books on my way back to my room, look at Frederick Karl's recent biography of Faulkner, eat a bowl of soup, and get an invitation to dinner from the mayor of Taylor, Mississippi, a town of about 200 people roughly eight miles south of Oxford. The mayor, Jane Rule Burdine, happens to be ladling out soup on the second floor of Square Books, between biographies and southern fiction. She's in her early forties, has big blue discs for eyes and blonde hair that reflects like sparks off her silver earrings. She's a photographer and pours soup only in her spare time to assist Richard Howorth, the owner of Square Books, during the holiday season.

Jane's house, out in the flat land around Taylor, is a columned "high yellow" country place with about seventy acres of cotton land behind it. Jane has also invited Jimmy Phillips, a blues singer and recent emigré from Nashville, to dinner. He's a Mississippi native, but like many of the artists, writers, and musicians in the area, Oxford and the country nearby are the only places in the state he would consider living. "Things don't change drastically in Oxford," he says. "It's a place to return to to get energy." In the background, as he speaks, his album *They Don't Make the Blues Like They Used To* rises to meet his voice in sweet, liquid tones.

Jane's conversation is peppered with distinctive phrases—"Ah, they did it on the sperm of the moment" or "Listen, I'll tell you the real skinny on that." She gets paid forty-eight dollars a month to be mayor and knows what it will take to succeed: "If I can get cable TV for these folks out here, I'll be mayor for life."

As Jane takes us on a tour of the house, she explains her most recent photographic project. She had been photographing people and places in Tunica County, Mississippi. It's the poorest county in the entire nation. Most people live in cement block apartments with no windows. Their lives, as her photographs strikingly show, are without light or hope. She wants to document what happens to a group of people when the government says it is going to make things better but never asks what the people want or need. "Every now and again Tunica loses its place as the poorest county in the United States," she says. "It trades places in the competition with a leper colony in Hawaii."

We walk onto the second-floor front porch and study the copper tub sitting there. In the tub is a copper pig, reading a copper book. When I get close enough to see some of the words cut into the book, I realize it is "pig pornography." And I realize there is another side to the mayor of Taylor. There are three bedrooms on the second floor, the first two filled with antiques and family photographs. The third is packed with costumes: a genuine three-piece pimp suit, clown sneakers, huge fuzzy feet, masks, hats, beads, assorted dresses, suits. An accordion and a trumpet stand in the hall next to a writing desk. She is a connoisseur of garage sales and thrift shops, a hoarder of Halloween costumes and Mardi Gras outfits, still a little girl who loves to dress up. Most parties at her house, whether they are on Valentine's Day or New Year's Eve, turn into costume parties. It might not be unusual to find William Styron in a wig or Barry Hannah in a pig mask sipping bourbon around the butcher block table in her enormous country kitchen.

This "costume room" has a few other idiosyncrasies. The books stacked upon the night tables are all rare, antique jokes. The thickest is *The Complete Guide to Bust Culture* by A. F. Niemoeller. Niemoeller is also the author of *Superfluous Hair and Its Removal*. Next to it are *The Hussy Handbook*, *Too Many Women*, *The Gentle Art of Smoking*, *When to Drop Your Date*, and *Ten Secrets of Bowling*. Some are even more daring—the protagonist of *The Gay Cockade* is Jimmie Handy, a book placed suggestively next to *Professional Lover*, *The Bedroom Company*, and *Jane Lends a Hand*.

It's in the costume room that Jane tells her "cow story." One cold spring day a few years ago she had gone on a picnic with Willie Morris. They went to the Greenville cemetery to eat amidst the porcelain heads that had been shot off by vandals, and disappointed by the destruction they headed off, ending up on the cold, rainy levee. There they sat in her car on a long stretch of earthen mound and gazed out the windows at the Mississippi and Delta along it. That's when they saw a local farmer, her brother's friend, kissing a cow. "It wasn't just a friendly kiss, either," Jane says. "This was true love." Faulkner's story of Ike Snopes doesn't seem that exaggerated now: "He [Ike] sets the basket before her [the cow]. She begins to eat. The shifting shimmer of incessant leaves gives to her the quality of illusion as insubstantial as the prone negative of his late hurrying...one blond touch stipulates and affirms both weight and mass out of the flowing shadow-maze." Jimmy Phillips, who has heard Jane's story before, says, "Mississippians may be conservative in politics, but they're liberal about love."

As I leave, the mayor of Taylor gives me a railroad spike, the equivalent in this town of a key to the city. It's a spike, she tells me, from the station where Temple Drake of *Sanctuary* jumped off the train to go to the general store. If I had forgotten, I'm reminded once again that this is Yoknapatawpha County. People here, like avid soap opera fans, make little distinction between people made of words and those of flesh and blood. Temple Drake is real, and Faulkner is part of everything you touch.

As I drive back to Oxford I glimpse a homemade sign in the door frame of someone's house: "If your hart ant in dixxie get your ass out."

In "Mississippi" Faulkner wrote that the state was his "native land; he was born of it and his bones will sleep in it; loving it even while hating some of it." This sentence could well serve as an introduction to Willie Morris, a man who has made a career of his Mississippi heritage. He has pondered it, analyzed it, and written lovingly and evocatively about his past and his connection to Mississippi. After many years as editor of *Harper's* magazine and resident of New York City, what he calls "the Cave," he has returned, it seems for good, to his birthplace.

He has the face of a southern sheriff and the heart of a poet. In a sense, he is as much the split personality as Sam Clemens was. Morris is nostalgic raconteur and teasing practical joker. He is hermit and gregarious party-goer. He lived in the northern megalopolis for much of his writing career, but the southern country boy was always the truest part of his character.

When I meet him outside Square Books, the day is heading toward dusk, toward what Joseph Blotner called the "Faulknerian time of day: twilight." Morris is wearing Reeboks and baggy flannel pants. One sleeve of his sweater is rolled up and his shirt hangs out. He smiles, tells me it's his birthday, and asks to stop at a local package store so that he can buy a bottle of white wine and a fifth of Jack Daniel's. He plans to celebrate as he takes me on a tour of Yoknapatawpha.

Morris hasn't been an easy man to reach. His telephone number is unlisted, but even though I've managed to find it out, he doesn't answer the phone. His friend Larry Wells, president of Yoknapatawpha Press and husband of Dean Faulkner Wells, tells me to leave him a note on his car, a small gray Dodge parked next to one of the faculty houses on campus. Morris typically stays out to three or four each morning and doesn't get up until after one in the afternoon. He's not unsociable. He just comes alive when most people are finishing their day.

If Faulkner is Mississippi's Homer, then Morris is its Orwell. He has written scores of essays on the land, the people, and the history of Mississippi, and recently a number of articles on Oxford itself, a town which "lurks forever now in my heart." His writing about Mississippi, like Orwell's about Burma, is always autobiographical. There is no way to separate the speaker and the place. For Morris, it is the landscape of the South and places like Oxford that give the acoustical range to his voice. Other than William Faulkner, Eudora Welty, or Walker Percy, I can't imagine a better tour guide through a Mississippi town.

He seems able to comment on any aspect of Oxford, from its history to its significant gossip. Morris, obviously happy to leave big-city life behind, feeling that he "served his time," is pleased with Oxford's status as the third-smallest town in the United States that is the site of a historic capstone university. He seems a bit jealous of Orono, Maine, and Vermillion, South Dakota.

As we drive through the campus he points out a few Ole Miss beauties, whom he calls "lingering goldfish," those with an exam to take, a paper to write, or an end-of-term party to attend before they head home. His eyes scan the buildings and he says, "The last battle of the Civil War occurred here in 1962." He opens the bottle of Soave Bolla and pours a big yellow cup half full, takes a drink, and points toward the uppermost part of the columns of the Lyceum, where bullets have taken chunks out of the wood. We stop in front of the old law school, Ventress Hall, bend our heads out the car window to see the steeple that Faulkner once painted.

To paint such a place took as much courage as writing *The Sound and the Fury*, and the process must have been as complicated. Near the Lyceum is the library, with its inscription from Faulkner's Nobel Prize acceptance speech: "I believe that man will not merely endure . . . he will prevail." Close by is the Ole Miss football stadium, the Hemingway stadium, perhaps an irony that goes unnoticed by most of the 40,000 fans that gather there for each game. Morris tells me of two French scholars that he was chaperoning a few years ago. When they asked him about the name of the stadium, he told them that the university offered to name it after Faulkner, but Faulkner said, "No, name it after Hemingway. He needs it worse than I do." "Who knows," Morris says with an innocent look, "that story may have found its way into a French literary journal by now."

As we drive across campus, back toward Rowan Oak, past a group of black students and white students tossing a football and a blond-haired woman leaning casually against a bare dogwood tree conversing with a tall young black man, I think about the fact that twenty-five years ago it was the Freedom Summer of 1964. Then, hundreds of northerners faced the violence, poverty, and racism that made Mississippi seem to be a symbol of all that was wrong with our culture. A couple of years before President Kennedy had sent over 20,000 troops to quell the riots caused by one black man having the audacity to register to take classes at Ole Miss. For these reasons and others, Willie Morris feels that Mississippi has a darker past than New York or Ohio or even the neighboring Alabama and Louisiana. However, maybe even more than most other southern states, as Morris says, Mississippi holds fast to "much of its communal origins, its sense of continuity, of the enduring past and the flow of the generations—an awareness, if you will, of human history."

We leave the football stadium and the practice field, with the predominantly black team running laps, behind us and continue past the power plant, where Faulkner wrote *As I Lay Dying*. As Faulkner described the job in the plant it was back-breaking but allowed him time to write: "I shoveled coal from the bunker into a wheelbarrow and wheeled it and dumped it where the fireman could put it into the boiler. About 11 o'clock the people would be

Bill Appleton in St. Peter's Cemetery

going to bed, and so it did not take so much steam. Then we could rest, the fireman and I. He would sit in a chair and doze. I had invented a table out of a wheelbarrow in the coal bunker, just beyond a wall from where a dynamo ran. It made a deep, constant humming noise. There was no more work to do until about 4 A.M., when we would have to clean the fires and get up steam again." It was in *As I Lay Dying* that Faulkner first named his apocryphal county "Yoknapatawpha" after the Indian *Yockeney-Patafa*, a Chickasaw word meaning "water runs slow through flat land." As we drive toward Rowan Oak I'm sure I hear the humming from the power plant, the same buzzing sound Faulkner heard a half-century ago.

We park the car outside Rowan Oak and say hello to the departing Howard Bahr. Morris turns to me, saying, "Howard claims he felt Faulkner's ghost a while back. He's kind of ghostly himself, though. And he's still alive!" We stand in front of the house, near the biggest muscadine vine I've ever seen, as thick as a boa constrictor. Morris, replenished cup in hand, tells me about Dean Faulkner Wells's daughter's wedding on the grounds, how Ron Shapiro and he spent the night before the ceremony planting plastic bowls of orange juice laced with rum in the shrubs so that they could have something proper to drink the next day.

Willie Morris has a long history of practical jokes to his credit. In *North Toward Home* he describes himself as a fourth grader in Yazoo City, Mississippi. One Christmastime when his feelings against his dictatorial teacher Miss Abbott were running particularly strong, he went out and searched for the biggest, foulest dog turd he could find, took it home in a paper sack, and gift-wrapped it in a box with beautiful red paper. Then he put it successively in larger boxes, more elaborately wrapped in green-and-white paper with ribbons. He mailed it to Miss Abbott and felt good for days.

His sense of humor may be a bit more refined but it's still very much a part of his character. On our way out of Rowan Oak he wonders if we should go to "Coontown," but says, "We'd better not; there'd be a lot of traffic. I hear the New York Philharmonic is playing at a juke joint out that way." As we pass through the town on our way into the country, he spies a local photographer he thinks I might wish to speak with. "He's colorful," Willie says, "especially when he dips into the corn gourd."

In a mile or so, Oxford disappears and the backwoods take over. We stop near a country cemetery on a lonely hill. The gravestones are poured concrete. The names and dates were cut into the wet cement. I stand by the grave of Mrs. Epsie Mathis, died 1971, her name cut in neat child-like letters. Morris disappears into the woods for a few minutes. The wine had caught up with him. As we drive along the country road he annotates the scene: the swamp bottom at Hurricane Creek is where some come during the summer, cane poles in hand, standing between the cypress trees, trying to spear catfish. Out in Sardis Reservoir is the Indian mound from "The Bear." From another hill you can see Lafayette County. His eyes seem, at that moment, to reflect Faulkner's words in *The Town*: "And now, looking back and down, you see all Yoknapatawpha in the dying last of day beneath you. . . . on to where Frenchman's Bend lay beyond the southeastern horizon, cradle of Varners and ant-heap for the northwest crawl of Snopes."

On our way back to town to meet Dean Faulkner Wells, the daughter of Faulkner's beloved brother Dean who died in a plane crash, Morris's conversation is brilliant and amusing, stories about Walker Percy, T. Harry Williams, John Steinbeck, James Jones, Gene Hackman, the history of Abbeville, Mississippi, Ruth and Jimmie's Sporting Goods and Cafe, and a range of other subjects. Our last stop before we get to Dean's house is St. Peter's Cemetery. Like Appleton, Morris knows the cemetery as a scholar knows a difficult text. But it's getting late and we stop before only one grave a few yards from Faulkner's. The tombstone reads "Junie Hovious"; the dates are blank. The tombstone sits there waiting for Hovious, but the grave will probably never be used. Morris tells me the story: Junie, a famous former running back for Ole Miss, was awakened in the middle of the night by some noises. He got out his shotgun, went downstairs, and blew his wife's head off. A few years later Junie remarried, but his space is still there next to his first wife, right near Faulkner's grave, the macabre story buried next to the man who often created such tales.

† † †

Dean Faulkner Wells and her husband Larry live in Maud Faulkner's old place, the house in which Faulkner wrote part of *Absalom, Absalom!* Her father died a few months before she was born, and William Faulkner became her surrogate father. She still refers to him as "Pappy." She has doleful eyes and a soft tremor in her voice. She sounds like Katherine Hepburn and even has a similar smile and short brown hair. As we sit down to drink, of course, a glass of bourbon, Dean tells us about a call she received this morning from the *National Enquirer*, saying that they wished to do an article on her book about ghost stories from Rowan Oak. She is skeptical, though, and looks uneasily at Morris. "C'mon, Willie," she says, "I know you made the call." Although Willie denies it, Dean doesn't seem reassured.

She'll probably never give the copy of *Ghost Stories* to the *National Enquirer*, but she gives me a copy of *The Great American Writers' Cookbook* as a Christmas gift. It's published by Yoknapatawpha Press. William Faulkner's recipe, appropriately enough, is "Pappy's Hot Toddy," a concoction of Heaven Hill bourbon, lemon, and sugar. Faulkner prepared this to cure his family's ailments. The Jack Daniel's was reserved for his own ailments. My favorite in the whole book, however, is John Cheever's: "The only time I ever go into a kitchen is when I'm being chased out the back door." I guess we appreciate those lines the most that describe our own situations.

The next morning, heading away from Oxford back toward Milledgeville, Georgia, Flannery O'Connor's town, I recall Willie Morris standing near the barn at Rowan Oak, staring off into Bailey's Woods, talking about Faulkner as if he might at any moment walk through the front doors of the main house and greet us. Morris described Lafayette County, roughly a square of about twenty-five miles on each side. He talked of the murky, sluggish Tallahatchie to the north of the county, with its swamps and black-bottom land, flowing into Toby Tubby Creek, named for the Chickasaw chief. He described the Yocona River to the south, the city to the west, and Pontotoc to the east.

He seemed to be describing another time, some past, horse-drawn age, that is now lost to us forever. I saw men sitting on the benches in the courthouse square, chewing tobacco, exchanging gossip. I saw a town where the only strangers were young and beautiful and strong, carrying books and Frisbees. I saw the past amid the impoverished red earth and the forlorn hills, in the faces of Joe Christmas and Quentin Compson. I saw the house Morris pointed out near Rowan Oak, a brick house with white columns he called a Snopes place. I remembered the tall woman, with cool distant eyes, her arm ebony against the white columns, as she ushered two white children into the house. She reminded me of Dilsey, who was "to be the future, to stand about the fallen ruins of the family like a ruined chimney, gaunt, patient, indomitable."

As I drive toward Georgia on the Pontotoc Road, I look in my rearview mirror and see a Mack truck with a rebel flag covering its grill following me out of town. I recall Willie Morris's favorite Flannery O'Connor story: she went to the doctor for a physical, and he told her she was very sick. "Take it easy," he said. "Don't do any work." "No writing?" she asked. "No, you can do writing. Just don't do work."

I glance down at a Xeroxed page from *Current Biography* that has fallen from a folder. The page lists Willie Morris's birthday— November 29, 1934. I realize we weren't celebrating his birthday the other day and maybe he made the Flannery O'Connor story up, but it's a good story and it doesn't matter whether it's true or not. I push my foot down on the gas pedal. That rebel flag is getting dangerously close.

4

A Good Writer Is Hard
to Find:
O'Connor's Georgia

Going to Milledgeville, Georgia, after Oxford,
Mississippi, is like sipping tea after drinking
bourbon.
> Hitchhiker in Barnesville, Georgia

Not as I'd pictured her, enthroned on high,
fiercely Promethean with eagles, say, or lions on
the headstones . . . Flannery lies unadorned except
by name who breathed in fire and fed us on flame.
> Maxine Kumin,
> "Visiting Flannery O'Connor's Grave"

You have to keep going in deeper.
> Flannery O'Connor, in an interview

FLANNERY O'CONNOR ONCE SAID, "The South is traditionally hostile to outsiders, except on her own terms. She is traditionally against intruders, foreigners from Chicago or New Jersey, all those who come from afar with moral energy that increases in direct proportion to the distance from home." I'm not sure about my moral energy increasing in Georgia, but I sense a tangible xenophobia soon after I get to Milledgeville.

I enter the town, which is the old state capital, on Route 22, shortly after passing Plentitude Baptist Church. According to the signs along the way, Milledgeville is the present capital of Baldwin County basketball, the home of Concord Fabrics factory, and the site of one of the state's biggest homes for juvenile delinquents. It is also the location of the state mental hospital, an institution that gave rise to the regional idiom "gone to Milledgeville," a phrase that every long-time Georgia resident associates with "gone crazy."

The back roads in Milledgeville are open country roads, often lined with tall Georgia pines. Today there is a light blue southern sky, dotted with cottony cumulus clouds. The clear line of blacktop is interrupted only occasionally by winding dirt roads to the right or the left, like jagged, bloody scars in the earth.

As in many other towns of this size (about 15,000 people) in the South, at least one of the entrances into town runs the impoverished gauntlet, past unpainted shacks on cinder blocks. Many southern towns have routed traffic around such realities by creating highway extensions that lead directly to interstates or, as they have in Milledgeville, they allow the commercial district— the motels and malls—to blossom along the primary thoroughfare into the business district. In this case, that's the old Milledgeville-to-Eatonton road, now Route 441. The road, with its gas stations and stores, is barely distinguishable from a major artery of Phoenix, Arizona, or Norman, Oklahoma. As one resident of Milledgeville said to me, "Greed was once the driving force here; now commerce rules." Its minions, ugliness and anonymity, make Route 441 an unpoetic proof of the power of commerce.

The town itself might well have taken its motto from O'Connor's "The Partridge Festival": "Beauty is Our Money Crop." What she said in that story is still true of the town: "The houses were the most picturesque types of run-down antebellum." Milledgeville prides itself on having been Georgia's capital from 1803 to 1868, and the bureau of tourism and trade lists about thirty homes and buildings that qualify as historic spots. The Gordon-Cline-O'Connor house, in all its rambling and disheveled magnificence, makes the list for the historic tour, as does the Flannery O'Connor Room in the library at Georgia College. The old governor's mansion, a monumental piece of Greek Revival architecture; the small but handsome Sacred Heart Catholic Church, with its Gothic arched windows; the old state capitol building, now classrooms for Georgia Military College; and the Memory Hill Cemetery, where Flannery O'Connor is buried, all make the historic district tour. There are houses with cantilevered balconies, two-story clapboard places with gingerbread trim, and enough wainscotting and white columns to renew one's belief in the Confederacy. However, the place where Flannery O'Connor spent a good many years of her writing life, Andalusia, the family farm, is noticeably absent from the list.

The fact that Andalusia is missing from the historic tour of homes is the first clue I encounter in the strange case of Milledgeville and Flannery O'Connor. O'Connor may not be Georgia's most popular writer—that distinction perhaps goes to Margaret Mitchell—but she certainly is Georgia's most important and most profound writer. Unlike Oxford, Mississippi, which essentially ignored Faulkner until after he died, Milledgeville appears to ignore O'Connor even after her death, as if it had forgotten her presence or could afford only a perfunctory acknowledgment of its most famous citizen. It's as if some of the townsfolk still have not gotten used to her dark humor, her savage insights into the people and place she knew so well. She never named her Yoknapatawpha as Faulkner did, but her leathery, taciturn country people, the pentecostal churches, the prideful college-educated youth, and the blind elderly ladies are all part of her anonymous landscape, Milledgeville and the country surrounding it.

My first stop is the Milledgeville Bureau of Tourism and Trade on West Hancock Street in the center of town. The place has a sterile elegance, as if history and commerce worked like twin demons within the same decorator. There is a poster-map of Milledgeville on one wall but no notations for Andalusia, or even more surprisingly, none for Flannery O'Connor.

A few weeks before I came to Milledgeville, I wrote to the Bureau of Tourism, asking them to send me any information they could. Among the usual maps and brochures, they included a packet of cards titled "In Pursuit of Milledgeville Trivia." There are nine cards and twenty-seven questions in all: questions about the old governor's mansion, about the shoreline of nearby Lake Sinclair, about Sherman's march to the sea, and about murder, horse stealing, highway robbery, and counterfeiting in antebellum Milledgeville. There's even a question about Oliver Hardy, the famous comedian, who lived for a few years in the town. But there are no questions about Flannery O'Connor. It seems odd to me that the Bureau of Tourism, the most likely group to promote her name on maps and brochures, fails to do so.

A woman in her early thirties, the director of tourism, looks up from her desk when I wonder aloud about the omission. She peers at me, similar to the way I imagine Mrs. McIntyre staring fixedly at Mr. Guizac's legs lying flat on the ground in O'Connor's "The Displaced Person." Her stare seems to say I'm not worth saving, probably barely worth speaking to, but she does: "How did you get those trivia cards?" she demands. "They're only supposed to be sent to business groups." I hesitate, feeling as if I've been stopped by the flashing lights of a police car, and although I may be uncertain about the nature of the crime, I must be guilty of something. I answer her questions feebly and quickly ask my own: "Why isn't there any mention of Flannery O'Connor anywhere around here? It seems to me she's the most famous person from this area."

She looks at me as if I'd uttered some foul language. Once again

I feel myself slipping into O'Connor's fiction, remembering Bailey in "A Good Man Is Hard to Find" saying something after his mother recognized the Misfit, using words that shocked the sharp-tongued children and even made the murderer blush. "We keep a low profile on O'Connor," she says. "I wouldn't want to do anything against Mrs. O'Connor." She doesn't explain to me exactly how honoring Flannery O'Connor's name by mentioning it on a poster or map would alienate Regina O'Connor, Flannery's ninety-four-year-old mother, but this young woman, like Mrs. Freeman in "Good Country People," appears to have only two expressions that she uses for all her human dealings, forward and reverse. She's in forward gear now, and I suspect she rarely goes in reverse. O'Connor's description of Mrs. Freeman seems appropriate here: "Her forward expression was steady and driving like the advance of a heavy truck. Her eyes never swerved to left or right but turned as the story turned as if they followed a yellow line down the center of it. She seldom used the other expression because it was not often necessary for her to retract a statement, but when she did, her face came to a complete stop, there was an almost imperceptible movement of her black eyes during which they seemed to be receding, and then the observer would see that Mrs. Freeman, though she might stand there as real as several grain sacks thrown on top of each other, was no longer there in spirit."

Neither, it seems, is the director of tourism. She's long gone, leaving just her dark, vacant eyes behind. The only words of wisdom she's willing to offer are directions to the O'Connor Memorial Room at Georgia College library. Jan Fennel, the director of the library, has to open the room especially for me. Most buildings on campus are quiet or shut down for term break. The room itself is small, but it's filled with handsome antiques. Locked glass bookcases line the walls, and photographs of Flannery O'Connor are placed around the room. All the furniture, memorabilia, manuscripts, and books were donated by Regina O'Connor. The photographs of Flannery as a child or in her early twenties, before the ravages of lupus, the disease that eventually took her life, show that she was an attractive young woman. One photograph of O'Connor as a young child reading a picture book has two statues of peacocks in front of it. Jan Fennel and I stand looking at the bright-eyed, healthy little girl in the photograph. I realize that I have already lived longer than O'Connor did, and for a moment I'm lost in my own amazement at how much she was able to accomplish in such a short time, with death, like a dark inevitability, waiting just beyond her writing desk. I recall Robert Coles's comparison of O'Connor's vision of the South to Frost's New England, saying they both used "American regionalism in the service of a vision that glances toward Heaven and Hell." So many images in her stories—Mrs. May, grotesque in face paste and hair curlers, coming to shoo away the neighbor's scrub bull; Mr. Head gaping at the "artificial Negro"; the Misfit shooting the grandmother; Tom T. Shiftlet racing the storm into Mobile; Hazel Motes burning out his eyes; Mrs. Turpin gazing into the enraged face of Mary Grace—linger like comic nightmares.

As if she's reading my thoughts, Jan Fennel turns to me and says, "I love her letters; her fiction doesn't appeal to me." But although it might not appeal to her, Fennel wishes to preserve every scrap of it, the ideas O'Connor wrote down on the back of song books, the jottings she made on the ends of newsprint. She looks around the room, her eyes stopping once again on the photograph of Flannery the child, and apparently speaking to it, says, "People in Milledgeville don't recognize the importance of O'Connor. The world does, but Milledgeville doesn't. People have tried to accomplish things here, create an O'Connor Writing Center for instance, make Andalusia part of the college, preserve it like Thomas Wolfe's house, but invariably they get their hands slapped. Or they're ignored. And they give up."

There is considerable speculation in Milledgeville, some of it whispered, about the town's unwillingness to honor O'Connor's name more forcefully. Some attribute it to general ignorance. Others say it's a mall mentality, the sort of attitude that places two statues of Lewis Grizzard, selling for sixty dollars apiece, in a more prominent place in the local bookstore than the scant copies of O'Connor's stories that are available. Some say that Regina O'Connor doesn't want to admit that "her sheltered daughter could have written such stuff."

† † †

Like Scarlett O'Hara, I decide to wait for tomorrow to figure out why the town seems so willing to forget O'Connor. Before I head out of the center of town toward the Holiday Inn, I walk across the street to the antebellum governor's mansion. It stands in all its columned grandeur next to the Cline-O'Connor house, where Flannery spent part of her life and where her mother now lives. The woman who gives the tour offers what appears to be a series of memorized speeches about one ballroom after another. When she mentions the yearly ball sponsored by the Daughters of the Confederacy, attended by women in hooped gowns and men in southern uniforms, she seems pleased with her memories, but I have difficulty understanding her place in such an affair. She is a tall black woman in her early fifties. She may be aware that the Milledgeville slave code, which consisted of a number of ordinances from 1808 to 1865, made little distinction between free blacks and slaves. Freedoms for both groups were limited, curfews were enforced, and assembly was restricted. In the early nineteenth century, for instance, the town's spring-keeper was permitted to inflict "reasonable corporal punishment" on any black found washing in or abusing the spring, according to historian James Bonner. In 1843 the town passed an ordinance making it illegal for blacks to smoke cigars in public. Social dancing among blacks was discouraged, and the balls that they were allowed to have during the Christmas season had to be in the daytime. Somehow this part of Georgia history, of Milledgeville's story, she seems to have forgotten. Instead she talks of Governor Brown, a nineteenth-century politician whom she calls "the most famous Georgian." When I mention Flannery O'Connor she says, "I've heard his name but haven't read any of his books."

It's getting dark. The sky is a purpling streak worthy of a place in one of O'Connor's stories. As I drive along the commercial drag that runs out of town, the tongue of purple in the sky recedes into the widening mouth of darkness, but enough light remains for me to see the entrance to Andalusia across 441 from the Holiday Inn. There are a number of "Warning: Keep Out" signs clearly visible and a short way up the winding dirt road to the farm is a locked gate.

The coffee shop in the Holiday Inn directly faces Andalusia. Of course, there's no sign to suggest that O'Connor ever lived there. It's just another dirt road and another country farm set back among the rolling hills which are a vulnerable stone's throw away from the arm of commerce. I wonder how many Manley Pointers or Ruby Turpins have stopped here on the way to Macon or Atlanta or Augusta and gazed blankly across the highway at the 500-acre farm.

The Holiday Inn is typical for the breed, not any more or less garish than the rest. The decor in my room is early 1960s, all faded yellows and avocado greens. The window looks out on the parking lot, and the television offers a choice of adult movies— *Island of One Thousand Delights, Supergirls,* and *Coming Together.* I can only guess what O'Connor would have made of all this, but I can readily see Tom T. Shiftlet and Hazel Motes sharing such a room. If O'Connor had lived a few years longer, this very Holiday Inn might have found its way into one of her stories, as an image like Joy-Hulga's wooden leg or the piece of statuary Mr. Head stares at in wide-eyed wonder. In an essay, O'Connor once wrote, "The novelist with Christian concerns will find in modern life distortions which are repugnant to him, and his problem will be to make these appear as distortions to an audience which is used to seeing them as natural; and he may well be forced to take ever more violent means to get his vision across to this hostile audience. When you can assume that your audience holds the same beliefs you do, you can relax a little and use more normal means of talking to it; when you have to assume that it does not, then you have to make your vision apparent by shock—to the hard of hearing you shout, and for the almost-blind you draw large and startling figures."

I imagine this motel, staring like an ugly expression across the road from Andalusia, filled in its peak season with the almost-blind and the hard of hearing. Dimly at the top of the path into Andalusia is O'Connor, drawing her large and startling figures, shouting above the roar of traffic going north and south. But no one notices. Especially not the townspeople who pass by each morning and night on their way to and from work. Their eyes are fixed straight ahead and the car radios are turned just loud enough to drown out the sound of St. Cyril's instructions to the catechu-

Andalusia, Flannery O'Connor's home

mens, whispering, it seems, from the hillside: "The dragon sits by the side of the road, watching those who pass. Beware lest he devour you."

O'Connor's fiction is always concerned with the dragon, in its many shapes. In her life, as in her stories, she had the courage to confront monsters, the strength to have faith despite great suffering, the ability to laugh no matter the terror and to continue writing whatever her physical limitations. She wrote virtually on her death bed. In the final months of her illness when she was in Piedmont Hospital in Atlanta, she hid unfinished copies of her stories under her pillow, afraid the doctors wouldn't permit her to continue writing. At the very end she was wrestling with the same problem she had started with—"The problem of the novelist who wishes to write about a man's encounter with . . . God is how he shall make experience—which is both natural and supernatural—understandable, and credible, to his reader."

She was born on March 25, 1925, in Savannah, Georgia, and baptized at the Cathedral of St. John the Baptist as Mary Flannery O'Connor. These two apparently modest facts may be at the core of her artistic sensibility. Living in Georgia and being a Catholic were never far from the rhetorical heart of her work. She was always a Catholic writer in the Protestant South. She was always a southern writer judged mainly by northeastern intellectuals. Like all southern writers who worked and lived in the South in the second half of the twentieth century, she had to be conscious of Faulkner's presence. As she once said, nobody wants to be caught on the tracks when the Dixie Limited comes barreling through. Like all southern writers of the time, she had to find her own track to follow.

That track may have begun with her Catholic grandparents. Patrick O'Connor, Flannery's paternal great-grandfather, left Ireland in the middle of the nineteenth century and opened a livery stable in Savannah. Her father, Edward Francis O'Connor, served as a lieutenant in World War I and married Regina Cline in 1922. Flannery's maternal great-grandfather, Peter Cline, left Ireland for America in 1845 and became a teacher in Augusta, Georgia. His son Peter became a successful businessman in the late nineteenth century in Georgia. He owned a number of dry-goods stores and acquired a substantial amount of property around Milledgeville. In 1888 he was elected the town's first Catholic mayor.

Soon after he married Regina Cline, Edward O'Connor became a successful real estate broker, opening the Dixie Realty and Dixie Construction Companies. While her father prospered in business in Savannah, Mary Flannery attended St. Vincent's Grammar School. In the late 1930s Edward O'Connor's business and health began to decline. To solve his business problems he took a job in Atlanta with the Federal Housing Administration. For his deteriorating health there was no such easy cure. Initially diagnosed as arthritis, his illness, it was finally determined, was lupus erythematosus, an incurable disease in which the body's immune system attacks its own vital tissues.

The family was not happy in Atlanta and moved within the year to Milledgeville, where Flannery had spent part of each summer as a child. Shortly after their move to Milledgeville, Edward O'Connor's failing health forced him to retire. He died of lupus on February 1, 1941, two months before his daughter's six-teenth birthday. Less than ten years later, Flannery would also be diagnosed as having lupus. Illness and the presence of death would shadow her life and everything she wrote as an adult.

During her final two years in high school, O'Connor became more serious about her writing. She contributed book reviews and poetry to the *Peabody Palladium*, the school newspaper. She attracted notice in other ways, too. Always a bird lover, and noted in later years for her special affection for peacocks, she sewed clothes for her bantam hen in a home economics course. Many thought this unusual, but it was in character for O'Connor. As a first grader in Savannah, she had taught a frizzled chicken to walk backwards, an achievement that caught the attention of Pathé News, a New York newsreel company. She became a minor celebrity when they sent a cameraman to film her and her unusual pet. Her later well-documented love for peacocks (at one time there were over forty at Andalusia and her self-portrait is with a peacock) may be a fitting symbol for one of O'Connor's major themes—the centrality of pride in human affairs. She once said, "The first product of self-knowledge is humility, and this is not a virtue conspicuous in any national character."

In the summer of 1942 she began studying at Georgia State College for Women, which was a few blocks from her house on West Greene Street. It was during this time that she may have sensed her vocation as a writer. She began to sign all her work as Flannery, even though her family and friends continued to call her Mary Flannery. Throughout her college years she lived in the Greene Street household with her mother, two unmarried aunts, a female lodger, and uncles who visited occasionally. They inspired her, it seems, to write and illustrate comic portraits such as the one titled "My Relitives." She also began to write stories and poems for the college literary magazine, and for class assignments she handed in unusual essays such as "The Domestic Bliss of Samuel Taylor Coleridge" and "The Bookkeeper's Chaucer."

Many people think of Flannery O'Connor as an Emily Bronte, whose keen imagination leapt wildly over the ivy-covered walls enclosing the rectory where she lived. Both, the theory goes, never left their little villages but poured their tormented souls into their fictions. Both died young, never having physically escaped their staid environments. As far as O'Connor is concerned, though, this hardly approaches a half-truth. In 1945 she was awarded a scholarship in journalism to the University of Iowa Graduate School. She left to study, but the letters she wrote every day to her mother back in Milledgeville and her visits home indicate that she was not a Joy-Hulga who thinks, ". . . had it not been for this condition [her heart trouble], she would be far from these red hills and good country people." As Sally Fitzgerald, O'Connor's friend and biographer, has pointed out, ". . . she was by no means a complete misfit in Milledgeville." While she was away she even read the Milledgeville newspaper regularly.

But, like many southern writers before her and since, her ambivalence about the area seemed to make a journey into the wider world desirable, and perhaps necessary. Her first story acceptance ("The Geranium" in *Accent*) came while she was still in graduate school in Iowa. In 1947 she completed her master's thesis, *The Geranium: A Collection of Short Stories*, and she won the Rinehart-Iowa fiction prize competition for a first novel. The novel, *Wise Blood*, was eventually published by Harcourt, Brace in 1952.

After graduate school O'Connor went to Yaddo in Saratoga Springs, New York, a philanthropic foundation and artists' colony granting writers a situation that allowed them time and space to work freely. There she met Robert Lowell and Malcolm Cowley, among other writers and critics. After Yaddo she moved for a time to New York City, where she lived in a room "that smelled like an unopened Bible" at the 38th St. YWCA. She met Robert and Sally Fitzgerald, who were to become her lifelong friends, and in 1949 she went to live with them in their country home in Ridgefield, Connecticut.

The following year she found out that, like her father, she had lupus. She was hospitalized, and her mother telephoned the Fitzgeralds to say she was dying. But because of her will to live, her need to write, and the injections of ACTH, a newly developed cortisone derivative, O'Connor lived another thirteen years. After the lupus was diagnosed, she temporarily lost much of her hair, and her face swelled because of the cortisone, but she continued to work on her first novel even while she was in the hospital. When she was released from the hospital, she moved in with her mother at Andalusia so that she could take the room on the first floor because she was too weak to climb the stairs. Although she hoped to live once again in the Northeast, she very soon came to accept the limitations her illness created. Sally Fitzgerald has said, "Her acceptance was more graceful than merely stoic. She has written that 'vocation implies limitation,' and it can only be supposed that she regarded the circumscription of her life as a necessary aspect of her vocation as a writer and as an individual. She knew that her literary gift made special demands on her, and I think that she saw the restrictions on her life in the same light."

In 1952 the publication of *Wise Blood* appeared to be a first act that dramatically foreshadowed what was to happen in the rest of her career. According to Sally Fitzgerald, the novel received mixed reviews and provoked outrage among some Milledgeville residents. The book was powerful and shocking, not a story that provided easy answers or comforting characters. She would be linked to what was called the grotesque school in southern fiction. Eventually she would be placed among the best Catholic storytellers, would be seen in the tradition of the Southwest humorists, and would be associated with Hawthorne and Poe. But rarely during her lifetime would she be understood and fully appreciated, especially in her own hometown, and never would she become a popular writer. In the first six weeks after the publication of *Wise Blood*, she earned $1.35 net in royalties. Later about her own town O'Connor wrote: "Everybody here shakes my hand but nobody reads my stories. Which is just as well." O'Connor was tough-minded and often witheringly laconic, but by all accounts she was absolutely without self-pity. And always, even when she was suffering, she was very funny. When one of her interviewers asked her about crank letters she responded, "Some old lady said that my book left a bad taste in her mouth. I wrote back to her and said, 'You weren't supposed to eat it.'" But O'Connor always wrote back. And as she once said, "Manners are of such great consequence to the novelist that any kind will do. Bad manners are better than no manners at all, and because we are losing our customary manners, we are probably overly conscious of them; this seems to be a condition that produces writers." Of course, she's referring to the sort of social rituals that a novelist can observe and use, but it can also be applied to a social decorum that is part of southern culture.

She continued to write her stories whether they became best-sellers or not, whether they were understood at home or abroad. By 1954 she was using a cane to walk because of a deteriorating bone condition caused by her medicine, but she published *A Good Man Is Hard to Find and Other Stories* in that year. It sold relatively well (4,000 copies in three printings), but although she was not becoming wealthy from her writing, she began to decline the occasional offers of screenwriting that would come her way. In 1957, however, a television version of "The Life You Save May Be Your Own" was produced by CBS, starring Gene Kelly as Tom T. Shiftlet. A few months before the production, which she had nothing to do with, O'Connor wrote a prophetic letter: "I have just sold the television rights to 'The Life You Save May Be Your Own' to what I understand is called General Electric Playhouse. All I know about television is hearsay but somebody told me that this production was conducted by Ronald Regan (?). I don't know if this means RR will be Mr. Shiftlet or not. A staggering thought. Mr. Shiftlet and the idiot daughter will no doubt go off in a

Chrysler and live happily ever after. Anyway, on account of this, I am buying my mother a new refrigerator. While they make hash out of my story, she and me will make ice in the new refrigerator." Depending on one's political bias, Ronald Reagan might seem a far better choice than most to play the part of Shiftlet. It wasn't until after the television show aired that O'Connor saw how fully and disappointingly right she had been. But her "kinfolks" thought the show was "a great improvement over the original story," and the town, O'Connor said, felt "I have arrived at last."

During those years her illness limited her movement and her energy. Without fail, however, she left the morning hours for her writing. In a letter to Robert Lowell she showed her spirit: "I am making out fine in spite of conflicting stories . . . I have enough energy to write with and that is all I have any business doing anyhow. I can with one eye squinted take it all as a blessing. What you have to measure out, you come to observe more closely, or so I tell myself."

By 1960 she had published her second novel, *The Violent Bear It Away*, and in the last few years of her life she produced some of the most striking stories of her generation—among them "Greenleaf," "Everything That Rises Must Converge," and right before her death, "Revelation." Two months before she died she signed a contract for her new book of stories, choosing the title *Everything That Rises Must Converge*. On August 2, 1964, she slipped into a coma and a few minutes before midnight on August 3 she died of kidney failure. The next day she was buried next to her father in Memory Hill Cemetery in Milledgeville.

I spend the evening with people who knew O'Connor and who know Milledgeville. Mary Barbara Tate is a woman in her early sixties who lives in one of those damp, rambling Victorian houses so common in the town. We sit in a room off the main hall, the five of us—Mrs. Bates; Lyne, her middle-aged son; Manfred, a snuffling, bounding Doberman that is the size of a small truck; John Lawrence, a photographer who has to click as he ducks Manfred's ham-like paws; and me.

Mary Barbara grew up in Toomsboro, a town of about seven hundred people, twenty miles south of Milledgeville. The town figures prominently in "A Good Man Is Hard to Find." It becomes the place where a series of violent shocks occur. But for Mrs. Tate it was an idyllic place, "a storybook town to grow up in."

Her son Lyne squints at this, a grimace that seems half nervous twitch and half disapproval. Throughout the conversation his face twists itself into odd shapes, his cheeks rising and falling, his lips curling up and to the side, his eyes closing, his mouth opening wide and silent. Clearly, these spasms are beyond his control but he seems to make the most of them, to use them as a comment on his mother's conversation.

Like Alice I feel myself slipping down into the rabbit's hole, but there's no tea party, just O'Connor's world, just Milledgeville. This mother-son relationship seems straight out of O'Connor's fiction. He sits on one side of the long room, she on the other. John and I are in between them. Manfred prowls among us. Sharp looks pass between mother and son. She ignores his sarcastic remarks, but she ignores his mild ones too. He blinks and talks over her words until I feel as if I'm at a tennis match where each contestant is serving at the same time. The entire situation doesn't seem very different from the scenes with Mrs. May and her sons in "Greenleaf," Joy-Hulga and Mrs. Hopewell in "Good Country People," Bailey and his mother in "A Good Man Is Hard to Find," or Julian and his in "Everything That Rises Must Converge."

However, Mary Barbara Tate does not resemble the elderly ladies in O'Connor's stories. A former professor of English at Georgia College, she is soft-spoken and articulate. She was one of the members of the reading group that met with Flannery O'Connor at Andalusia. Mrs. Tate knows O'Connor's fiction and appreciates it. But she also knows that she's in a minority in the area. "A lot of people around here," she says, "don't even know that O'Connor existed. There's no devotion to literature in these parts."

As if to prove her point she tells her favorite O'Connor story. It happened around the time Stanley Hyman, the literary critic, came to Milledgeville to do research. He was the first, according to Tate, to come to town to write about O'Connor. Mrs. O'Connor met him and liked him a great deal, but took Mrs. Tate aside during one of Hyman's visits and asked her, "Have you noticed his hands?" Mrs. Tate hadn't, but before she could manufacture a reply, Mrs. O'Connor said, "He never worked a day in his life." To this Mrs. Tate suggested, "Well, he's a writer, though." Flannery's mother closed the conversation with, "Well, he must work on a typewriter then!" Like Willie Morris's story about Flannery O'Connor's doctor who told her she was too sick to work but doing writing was fine, this story reflects the local consensus about the writing profession. As one resident said to me, "Georgia in general doesn't seem to value its writers very highly. In the South there's a strict hierarchy. For instance, Georgia is certain it's better than states like Alabama and Mississippi, but Mississippi genuinely respects its literary figures."

Tate believes that O'Connor would never have come back willingly to Georgia, "except for visits, that is." She begins to talk about the state of the cultural and literary life in the area. "There is a writer behind every pecan tree in this county," Lyne says, breaking into the conversation. O'Connor may have agreed. She once said, "Everywhere I go I'm asked if I think the universities stifle writers. My opinion is that they don't stifle enough. There's many a best-seller that could have been prevented by a good teacher."

Manfred taps his chin, which weighs about the same as a blacksmith's anvil, twice against my thigh. Lyne whistles him away and says about O'Connor, "I'd rather read Franz Kafka. And I don't even like Kafka." Then in what appears to be a smooth non sequitur he starts talking about the Milledgeville city limits. "You can find most of the names from O'Connor's stories—the Shiftlets and Hopewells—still in the phone book. But the place isn't the same. We actually have a Mexican restaurant staffed by Mexicans. They arrested a prostitute downtown last month, and there's a striptease bar on the outskirts of town." Although Lyne seems to relish the irony of prostitution, even if that means *one* prostitute, in Milledgeville, it may be less unusual than he thinks. In *Milledgeville: Georgia's Antebellum Capital* James Bonner writes: "Perhaps the greatest blot on the town's early reputation was its propensity for harboring bordellos. A census made in 1828 by the town marshall listed fifteen white prostitutes out of a total of 346 white females of all ages; this was ten percent of all women in the town between the ages of fifteen and forty."

It's getting late, so I thank Lyne and his mother and drive out past Andalusia to see if Milledgeville really does have dancing girls. About two miles beyond Andalusia is a country road that intersects on the right. There are two signs a little before the road, one for a Baptist church and another for "Dreamers," which boasts six exotic dancers and welcomes visiting fishermen. The bar itself is another mile or so down the road in the middle of the country, and even though there are a few houses in sight, it seems to stand naked and alone and strange among the pines. Judging from the parking lot, one would have to assume that Dreamers was hosting a convention for pickup truck owners. Inside, the place has a stale, smoky smell. The atmosphere is not exciting. Everything about the bar seems to say bored decadence. The dancers are sleepy-eyed, and although they are naked except for G-strings, they seem asexual. In one corner two men lazily play pool. At the bar three men sit with topless dancers. A woman in her late twenties, who has the look of someone who will age a quarter of a century in the next few years, dances unenthusiastically, blank-eyed and expressionless before a half-dozen men in cowboy hats and baseball caps who seem more interested in their beers than they do in her. I have the urge to say, "Everyone named Tom T. Shiftlet raise his hand." I am convinced at that moment every hand in the room would go up. But before I can test my theory a man with a scraggly beard and a brown cowboy hat comes up to me, saying the cover charge is two dollars. Given the price of things in general, that seems inexpensive, but he sees my hesitation and says, "They take it all off, buddy. I mean everything." I can tell that he is sure this will sway me, but as I take another quick glance around the room, I decide two dollars is way too much. I can't even calculate how much he'd have to pay me to stay. When I say no thanks, he shrugs and looks away, raising his eyes in despair over my lack of culture or libido.

There's enough left of the evening once Dreamers retreats into my rearview mirror like a fading nightmare to visit one more Milledgeville resident who has been there since O'Connor's time. Jack Thornton has lived most of his seventy-two years in Millegeville or the surrounding area. He lives with his wife in a sprawling brick home on the crest of a hill overlooking the town. He has forty acres between himself and the road, and if it weren't for the faint sound of cars in the distance the illusion of absolute isolation would be complete. Tall, slim, and handsome, Thorton appears to be much younger than he is. Only the gray hair and lines half-hidden behind his glasses betray his true age.

Thornton doesn't have much to say about O'Connor's writing, but a gleam comes into his eyes when he speaks about local affairs or his connection to the past. He remembers O'Connor, who was a few years his junior. "She'd come down to visit my aunt," he says. "But she was kind of homely I thought at the time, so I took off down the river when she showed up. I'd come back after she and her momma left. Her writing shocks the old biddies in this town, but it doesn't shock me. I just don't like it much."

But he does like, or at least he wants to talk about, *Paris Trout*, the novel that won the 1988 National Book Award. Pete Dexter, the journalist who wrote the novel, was a friend of Thornton's son. A few years before the book was published Dexter returned to Milledgeville from his home in California to spend some time doing research on the novel. According to Thornton, *Paris Trout* is not so much based on the story of a murder in Milledgeville as it is "an actual record of *exactly* what happened." His reaction is not an unusual one. Many people in Milledgeville feel the same way. Even a scholar and former resident of the town, David Payne, who now teaches at the University of Georgia in Athens, feels that *Paris Trout* is "accurate to the point I feel uneasy."

Payne, as a literary scholar, felt uneasy about the aesthetic rightness of using so literally the journalistic facts of the case. He felt uneasy about Dexter, a journalist for the *Sacramento Bee*, not deviating from the actual story. Payne seemed to wonder about what he thought were necessary distinctions between journalism and fiction. The townspeople in Milledgeville also felt uneasy but perhaps for less philosophical reasons. *Paris Trout* describes not only a murder and a murderer; it depicts an entire town as well. Cotton Point, Georgia, in *Paris Trout* is certainly a pseudonym for Milledgeville, and one of the central characters in the novel is the town itself.

It is a story, according to Payne, "too powerful to have been invented." Jack Thornton agrees and smiles over the fact that "The biggest game in town the year the novel came out was guessing which character stood for whom in the area." But, as Thornton points out, everybody in town knew. It wasn't too hard to guess. Thornton smiles again and gives me what he calls the "*Reader's Digest* condensed version":

Paris Trout is based upon the story of Marion Stembridge, a man who owned a grocery store and ran a loan-sharking operation that preyed upon the black community in Milledgeville. In the novel, Trout is a well-to-do businessman in Cotton Point, a cold and brutal man who kills a teenage black girl and seriously wounds her foster mother in his rage over an unpaid car loan. Trout believes there are two sets of rules, the one lawyers write down and the one people actually live by. The rule he lives by, and by implication most of the town accepts silently, is that blacks are less than human and should be treated accordingly. Trout is reminiscent both of Faulkner's Percy Grimm and of his Popeye, in his violent racism and sexual perversion. In 1860 more than one half of the residents of Baldwin County were black, and as one historian pointed out, "The value of slave property in both the town and the county exceeded the combined value of all real estate." One hundred years later some in Milledgeville were still treating blacks as if they were property.

Paris Trout, like O'Connor's Manley Pointer, is an astonishing personification of evil, of the chilling emptiness that perhaps is at its heart. Trout murders a young girl, an act that seems inconsequential to him because she is black. He rapes his wife with a bottle of mineral water, forces unwanted food down her throat, and holds her gasping for breath under the water in the bathtub. He feels no guilt; he is merely exercising his power. In the end he goes on a murder spree, killing his laywer, his wife's lawyer, his mother, and himself.

However, before the final murder spree, Trout had been convicted of killing Rosie Sayers, the young black woman. His conviction comes as a surprise to just about everyone, although not because anyone thought him innocent. He is given an absurdly short sentence, which he never has to serve because after his appeals run out he bribes a local judge to free him on a writ of habeas corpus. Nothing is done to bring him back to jail. Many in the town feel an injustice has been done, but none are appalled enough to do anything about it.

These murders occurred in Milledgeville in 1953, shortly after O'Connor returned home to stay because of her illness. Rosie Sayers, Harry Seagraves (Trout's attorney), and Carl Bonner (Mrs. Trout's divorce attorney) were Milledgeville residents: Emma Johnekin, Marion Ennis, and Stephen T. "Pete" Bivins. Marion Stembridge, who in the novel may seem too evil to be true, was actually as twisted as Dexter portrays him. Along his route to self-destruction, Trout's madness, like Stembridge's, takes many forms, from sociopathy to psychosis to paranoia to simple, elemental greed. In the course of the story he begins to think he is being poisoned and to fear he will be shot. He places sheets of glass all over the bedroom floor so that he can detect intruders from the smudge prints. He places sheets of lead under his bed so that he can't be shot from a floor below. And, maybe strangest of all, he fills five Belgian safes with bottles of his own urine, marked "To be used in the event of death for evidence I have been poisoned."

From beginning to end Paris Trout remains a hypnotizing moral cipher, not unlike some of O'Connor's characters. And the novel *Paris Trout* has intersecting lines of horror and grotesque comedy that are O'Connor's trademark. Even some of the images recall her unusual metaphors. Early in the novel, a young girl returns home to find her mother's friend standing inside the family shack: "He was holding a knife in his teeth. It resembled a smile."

Paris Trout has been compared to Faulkner's work, but for me the novel seems fixed in O'Connor's country. It is a story concerned with what happens when polite society converges with a moral emptiness. This is not the South of Atticus Finch from *To Kill a Mockingbird* but rather the South of Harry Seagraves, who says, "We are all flawed people, some more than others." Like the grandmother in "A Good Man Is Hard to Find" who is so desperate to seem the lady or Mr. Turpin in "Revelation" who so clearly senses her own superiority, the characters in *Paris Trout* see life in terms of the safe social order of the Kiwanis Club and the Rotary. What the townspeople in the story and the readers of the novel come to understand is that Paris Trout, as horrific a character as he is, may reflect the community as a whole. According to Jack

Thornton, some people in the area thought the town was guilty, that racism allowed the murders to happen. For some, Stembridge, like Trout, mirrored the bigotry, complacency, and cowardly defense of the status quo that may be the dark soul of such towns.

The Stembridge story was so compelling that Dexter's novel was not the first fictional account. In 1961 O'Connor's story "The Partridge Festival" appeared in *The Critic*, as far away from the eyes of Milledgeville as O'Connor could place it. The story is not one of her best, a realization she came to herself, calling it "lightweight" and keeping it out of a proposed collection. She rewrote the story, giving it close to a dozen concealing revisions, disguising the actual event. Where O'Connor masked the facts, Dexter seemed obsessed by them.

O'Connor's image of Marion Stembridge is a man she calls Singleton. Rather than being the frightening picture of evil that Dexter portrays in the person of Trout, Singleton borders on the ridiculous as O'Connor describes him in the mental hospital: "Two burly attendants entered with Singleton spider-like between them. He was holding his feet high up off the floor so that the attendants had to carry him. . . . He had on a hospital gown of the type that opens and ties up the back and his feet were stuck in black shoes from which the laces had been removed. On his head was a black hat, not the kind countrymen wear, but a black derby worn by a gunman in the movies." O'Connor has Singleton briefly escape his attendants, dash madly around the room, and expose himself to a young woman. He is clownish where Trout is frightening. The motivations for Trout's murders are dark and they are many, but Singleton seems to kill because he was locked up in a mock jail with a goat during the Partridge Festival. Like Dexter's story, O'Connor's raises question about the town's guilt. Finally, though, O'Connor's two main characters, aspiring writers, are merely self-deluded and prideful. They think they have the answers, they think they know Singleton, but they don't.

According to some, the town's version of the murder was more interesting than the murder itself. As one man said to me, "In Milledgeville you have a compulsive group of storytellers and a limitless source of stories, but you also have a complex sort of possessiveness, an ownership of the gossip, of the stories, whether they're Pete Dexter's or Flannery O'Connor's."

Jack Thornton was in the local Piggly Wiggly when the murders described at the conclusion of *Paris Trout* occurred. For people who lived in the town at that time it was like Kennedy's assassination: everyone remembers exactly where he was and what he was doing when the murders took place. That sort of violence is extraordinary in Milledgeville, Thornton suggests, but resistance to change certainly is not. In many respects Milledgeville is the same place it always was.

The town was literally carved from the wilderness. In the late eighteenth century the lands that now make up Baldwin County were all part of Indian territory. As in Mississippi and most other parts of America, the whites in Georgia, by sheer weight of numbers, drowned the Indians under a wave of civilization.

Milledgeville became Georgia's fourth capital, and one of the few in America to be laid out and designated specifically as a seat of government. Like most of Georgia at the time it was on the outer edge of white culture. From its beginnings with a royal charter in 1732, Georgia was planned as a frontier outpost that would protect England's holdings against the onslaught of Spain or France. The old notion that Georgia was a den of murderers and thieves, that England opened its jails and shipped the lowlife to the colony, is not true, according to Walker Percy's cousin, the historian Phinizy Spalding: "The first transport to Georgia was made up primarily of small businessmen, tradesmen, and unemployed laborers mainly from the London area. Perhaps fewer than a dozen released debtors came to Georgia during the entire Trustee period."

But Georgia remained a frontier for a long time, as it expanded into Indian territory and became the empire state of the South, a title it can rightly claim. From its northern border in the rugged peaks of the Blue Ridge and the beginnings of the Appalachian Trail to its southern boundary in the Okefenokee Swamp and the lakes of northern Florida, the state runs about 350 miles. From the Chattahoochee River, which separates it from Alabama in the west, to the Savannah River, which runs along the South Carolina border and washes into the Atlantic, Georgia stretches 250 miles.

In between are more than 6 million people and nearly 58,000 square miles of pine forests, coastal plains, foothills, and mountains.

Milledgeville lies at the fall line of the Oconee River near the heart of the old plantation cotton belt. It is at the approximate geographic center of the state. But despite its status as former capital, its industrialization, and its promotion of Lake Sinclair as a middle-class playground, Milledgeville still appears to be a frontier outpost—much of Georgia, regardless of its Sunbelt reputation, does. It is a town between nowhere and everywhere else, moving in slow motion in search of a personality. As Georgia historian James Bonner pointed out, "After the removal of the capital, Milledgeville lapsed briefly into the role of an agricultural trade center and it was without distinguishing characteristics other than that afforded by the presence of the Georgia Lunatic Asylum." His description could fit today, it seems to me. After it lost its place as state capital, Milledgeville seems to have developed an identity crisis. The homes on Jefferson Street remained posh, but the nearby town business district deteriorated. The Milledgeville city council minutes for January 10, 1876, include a complaint from a group of women who were horrified by "a large party of goats which promenade the streets at night and often take lodging on our porches and piazzas which in the morning present . . . a filthy and disgusting appearance." They concluded by saying, "We cannot look upon it with Christian resignation." But live animals were not the only problem. There were apparently enough dead animals lying about to make the city council rule that the owners of these animals must take the carcasses and drag them to the mouth of Fishing Creek, where they could be dumped. Although I did notice a few stray cats, the problem no longer seemed a pressing one.

Bonner goes on to say that "Milledgeville remained inaccessible even after the building of the state's basic rail system." This too seems true today, even though it is a short distance to Atlanta and Macon and Augusta. It is part of its own triangle, one like the famous Bermuda zone, where things have a tendency to disappear. Bonner also says, "The poverty of good reading material was a characteristic of frontier communities." Things have not changed much.

† † †

Some things should never change. Once called Grey Quail Farm, Andalusia is a few miles outside of Milledgeville, right along the commercial strip, but it seems a world away. In 1947 Flannery's uncle Bernard Cline died, leaving Andalusia, five hundred acres of fields and one thousand acres of woods, to Regina O'Connor and Louise Cline. The timber land has been sold, but the five-hundred-acre farm remains in the family. The large white farmhouse is at the top of a hill that offers a view of a half-acre pond from its screened-in porch. A few years before my visit, the novelist Alice Walker described it as "...neatly kept, and there are, indeed, peacocks strutting about in the sun. Behind it there is an unpainted house where black people must have lived."

Although it's no longer as neatly kept as it was when Walker saw it, it is not in disrepair. The peacocks, though, are long gone. The only trace is a peacock feather or two lying on a table inside the house. The sharecroppers' cabins are still standing out back, although they haven't been used for many years. It's easy to imagine O'Connor sitting on the screened-in porch watching a Lucynell or a Mrs. Hopewell or a Mrs. Freeman living out some local drama. O'Connor's social scene focused on the poor white rural and small-town people, the ordinary working-class men and women. These are the people she seemed to know best. She described them honestly but surely with compassion as well. But as she was never self-pitying, she was never sentimental about her characters either. Alice Walker has said, "O'Connor's description of Southern white women leaves no whiff of magnolia hovering in the air."

On my way to Andalusia on my last morning in Milledgeville I stop at the public library in town to meet with Louise Florencourt, Flannery O'Connor's first cousin. A woman in her early sixties, Florencourt is a few years younger than Flannery would have been had she lived. Florencourt greets me outside the library. For a moment I feel as if I were looking at O'Connor herself. Florencourt has the same thin hair, curling up in fine wisps on the sides. She has the same oval face and almond-shaped eyes, magnified by the lenses of her glasses. She is a pretty woman and makes me think of Katherine Anne Porter's description of Flannery: "I am always astonished at Flannery's pictures which show nothing of her grace.

She was very slender with beautiful, smooth feet and ankles; she had fine, clear, rosy skin and beautiful eyes. I could wish I had some record of her as she appeared to me." Louise Florencourt appeared to be that physical record. Her smile sneaks into every muscle and line of her face and is centered in her eyes. The glasses make the smile larger but the lenses also reflect the narrow median in front of the library. In her glasses shines a reflection of the statue of a Confederate soldier standing on the edge of a manicured patch of cotton in the center of the median.

Florencourt, who was a member of the first class of Harvard University Law School to graduate women, is still a lawyer at heart. In her hand is a manila folder marked "Pearson" in red letters. The folder holds an outline for our conversation and an agenda for a tour of the town. She is prepared, and the smile that forms gentle creases in her face cannot mask the lawyer's circumspection. She has a rule: never speak about O'Connor's writing or personal life. She's willing to talk but not to answer questions. Milledgeville's silence on the subject of O'Connor may start with her and she may closely mirror Regina O'Connor's feelings on the subject. Although Sally Fitzgerald has been working for a number of years on a biography of O'Connor, there is still no detailed published account of her life, over a quarter of a century after her death. Even though she died within a few years of Faulkner and Hemingway, whose biographies must be weighed not in pounds but tons, there are only brief notes about O'Connor's life.

Florencourt was raised in Boston and worked as a lawyer in Washington, D.C. She spent many summers in Milledgeville playing with Flannery, but her New England origins are still visible. Her red hat is pulled primly down on her head, allowing only a few sprigs of gray-flecked hair to peek out. Her plaid coat and brown buckled shoes have a pilgrim look to them. She seems torn between her manila folder and her smile, a northerner in the South.

She ushers me into her brand new car, the first one she has owned in twenty-five years. Her 1965 Dodge Dart still sits behind the West Greene Street house, where she lives with Mrs. O'Connor, taking care of her as Mrs. O'Connor once took care of Flannery. Miss Florencourt can't bear the idea of parting with her old car, so

Louise Florencourt, Flannery O'Connor's first cousin

there it sits. Like so many characters in O'Connor's stories, she is a sensible woman, careful with her money, but she's also capable of sighing sadly over a trusted piece of machinery.

Once inside her car, she pushes the folder aside, her smile broadens, and she makes the first turn like someone who negotiated many a Boston rotary. Our first stop is Sacred Heart Catholic Church, a small church that seats about two hundred. Its most famous parishioner, Flannery O'Connor, has a hall between the rectory and the chapel named after her. Other than the O'Connor room at the library, the only other place named in her honor is O'Connor Drive in a subdivision out past Andalusia with homes in the $200,000 range that would have satisfied Mrs. Turpin's criteria for heaven.

We drive down Liberty Street, named for its proximity to the penitentiary and its potential as a route to freedom. Marble Hill Cemetery, across from the First Baptist Church, is nearby. A satellite dish in the side yard of the church keeps what appears to be a watchful and ironic eye on O'Connor's grave, this Catholic in the shadow of the Protestant South. The cemetery is one of the four original public squares built when Milledgeville was hewn out of the Indian territories. It is the oldest burying ground in the city, filled with politicians, soldiers, college presidents, slaves, and even Bill Miner, a notorious western outlaw. O'Connor's tombstone is simple, indistinguishable from the other stones. Cut into the Georgia marble are her name and dates—March 25, 1925, and August 3, 1964.

As we drive through the town, Florencourt does a running commentary about the sites. She says, "Everything is becoming commercial around here. Our great-grandparents' home is now a one-story office building—Andrews Insurance and Tugman Dentistry." Route 441 was a two-lane macadam road back in the early sixties, but the new road, unrolling like a magic carpet, has changed everything, it seems. "Bissy Bland's Hat Shop, Mrs. Benford's Ice Cream Parlor, the Green Frog Snack Shop—all gone. Everything's gone. The Piggly Wiggly in town used to be the Sanford House, where Regina and Flannery ate dinner every afternoon. Milledgeville was spared in Sherman's march to the sea. Some say he was moved by the beauty of the city. Others say he had an affair with a local woman and spared it for her. But the town has not been spared the march of commercialism. It's slower than Sherman's march but probably more destructive."

So far Andalusia has been spared, despite the Holiday Inn across the road from it. Once you walk up the road and get beyond the locked gate, it is a separate world, one in which Florencourt seems right at home. Even though she looks more like a modern-day nun who has discarded the habit than a farmer, she seems perfectly comfortable opening a corral gate and letting herself in to feed a few pieces of candy cane to Equinox and Flossy. Equinox, a donkey, is twenty-six years old and has been on the property since before O'Connor's death. Flossy, a hinny, is ten years old and, like most of the breed, an accident of nature, a rare mating between a stallion and a female donkey. It's the impractical opposite of a mule, a cross between a mare and a male donkey. A hinny is not much good for work or anything else, and Florencourt, perhaps for that reason, offers it a few extra pieces of candy. When I step closer to the fence, both animals bolt away, like many of the people I've met in Milledgeville, a bit shy of strangers.

PBS filmed its version of "The Displaced Person" on Andalusia, and it would be the perfect choice of location for any O'Connor story. I can see the peacock following Mrs. Shortley up the road to the hill. I can see Tom T. Shiftlet, the one-armed carpenter, negotiating over car and fiance. I can see Mrs. May bent over the bull, apparently "whispering some last discovery into the animal's ear." In response to someone's remarking about the truth of Thomas Wolfe's statement concerning not being able to go home again, O'Connor said, "Nonsense—that is the only place you can go." It is Georgia and Milledgeville that she wrote about, returning over and over, imaginatively, to the people she saw daily—practical, struggling, prideful characters. She sat there in Baldwin County, Georgia, as Robert Coles has said, "dying, burning with life, praying, reading, pouring out her soul's worries, reservations, deepest yearnings." When one former resident of Georgia wrote to her, saying that he had grown up with the characters she wrote about and that he loved her stories, her only response was, "poor man." Her characters are exaggerations. They are often large, startling figures. But the worst of them can be saved. Even a Mr. Head can feel the "action of mercy touch him," even he can understand that "it grew out of agony, which is not denied to any man and which is given in strange ways to children." None of O'Connor's characters are beneath her contempt or beyond her sympathy. Her view of the South, as Robert Coles has said, is "both protective and critical."

Before I leave Milledgeville, Louise Florencourt takes me back to the O'Connor-Cline house on West Greene Street to meet Regina O'Connor. The ninety-four-year-old Mrs. O'Connor is unable to get out of her bedroom chair and move around without help. She has lost much of her hearing and her voice trembles as she speaks, but she reminds me of an ancient queen, smiling royally and fingering the high ruffled collar of her red blouse. Then her hand rises, of its own accord, it seems, to her gray hair, which is pulled back into a meticulous bun. She fixes a stray strand behind her ear and looks at her hand, as if she were surprised to see an old friend. She shows me a new ring on her finger, proud not because it is beautiful but because of the bargain it was. At that moment she reminds me of one of the competent, practical country women in her daughter's stories. As delicate and frail as she is, it is possible to see even now the accuracy of Richard Gilman's description of her in 1960: ". . . a small, intense, enormously efficient woman, who, as she fussed strenuously and even tyrannically over Flannery, gave off an air of martyrdom which was the exact opposite of her daughter's quiet acceptance." She is still an indomitable figure, the matriarch of the town as well as the family. Mrs. O'Connor will not speak about her daughter, and anyone who is to meet her must respect that. But I can't help regretting all that silence and wonder what words she could use to cut into the unknown.

As I drive out of Milledgeville, the radio plays The Band's song about Stoneman's cavalry and the image in my rearview mirror is the sinkhole that has opened on the grounds of the Presbyterian Church, but the image in my mind is of Regina O'Connor, sitting in her bedroom, the light from a floor lamp reflecting off a painting of Jesus hanging behind her head as she watched me leave the room. The tableau could have been in one of Flannery O'Connor's stories, and it made me wonder whose line of vision, the mother of

Louise Florencourt feeding Flossy and Equinox at Andalusia

the long-dead author or the writer come back to see, was the least obstructed.

The sky is bone-white, and the road between Milledgeville and Eatonton stretches out like one of O'Connor's black serpents. The land returns to pine forests and muddy waters. The road snakes through hay fields and cow pastures, past pulp mills, alongside railroad tracks. A red-tailed hawk perches on a section of telephone line, the sun glinting through its feathers, striking the rose-colored edge of the highway with a prism of light.

Eatonton is about halfway to the Atlanta airport, and although there are no signs about Alice Walker, who lived here, there are plenty of reminders that this was once the home of Joel Chandler Harris. There is even a statue of Br'er Rabbit in front of the domed courthouse. But somehow it seems fitting that Alice Walker was a great admirer of O'Connor's work. O'Connor once said that the writer is initially set going by literature more than life, and for Alice Walker, it was Flannery O'Connor, more than Faulkner or Welty or other white southern writers, who helped set her going.

O'Connor realized that storytellers and readers need the redemptive act "that demands that what falls at least be offered the chance to be restored." She found the necessary knowledge in her community of the fall and the potential for redemption as well. "The materials of the fiction writer," she once remarked, "are the humblest. Fiction is about everything human and we are made out of dust and if you scorn getting yourself dusty, then you shouldn't try to write fiction. It's not a grand enough job for you." For Flannery O'Connor, it was grand enough, and she never scorned getting dusty. She was a woman of tremendous honesty but also of great faith. As she said, "People without hope do not write novels."

Two months before her death O'Connor wrote a note to an English professor in response to his question about the significance of the name of one of her characters: "Thank you for your note. I'm sorry I can't answer it more fully but I am in the hospital and not up to literary questions. . . . As for Mrs. May, I must have named her that

Regina O'Connor at home

because I knew some English teacher would write and ask me why. I think you folks sometimes strain the soup too thin." With that admonition in mind and the Atlanta airport in sight, I decide to turn my thoughts to Ernest Hemingway and Key West.

5

The Idea of Key West: Hemingway's Florida

Key West is the last resort.

An anonymous copywriter

It's a very, very dead place because it has died several times. It died as a resort of pirates, then as a house of smugglers and wreckers, then as a cigar manufacturer... then as a winter boomtown....

Robert Frost in a letter to a friend

Writing, at its best, is a lonely life. ... [The writer] grows in public stature as he sheds his loneliness. And often his work deteriorates.

Ernest Hemingway,
Nobel Prize Speech

THE FLIGHT from Norfolk to Miami has a brief layover in Charlotte, North Carolina, but the red earth and drainage ditches around the airport make the landscape indistinguishable from many other sprawling cities that have rooted in the clayey Sunbelt soil. The flight is smooth, and the only sounds are the reassuring hum of the engines, the hiss of the air conditioning, and an occasional exclamation in Spanish. Miami sits waiting in the sun.

The part of Miami I see from my rental car seems to have been in the sun too long. The palm trees are wilted, the satellite dishes stare blankly, the rusted cars that sputter by me are driven by leather-faced men. "The Geraldo Rivera Show" is on the radio, and the pink cadillacs and beautiful, sad-eyed women of "Miami Vice" seem far away. But within a few miles the land is perfectly flat, and the skyline, stretching forever and glinting off the rows of houses, is terra cotta.

Within half an hour. I reach U.S. 1 and dusk comes suddenly but in various tones, from a sooty black to a hazy lavender. It quickly gets too dark to see much besides the marinas and motels, Florida's equivalent of Vermont's inns or Georgia's Baptist churches. In Key Largo my image of Humphrey Bogart and Lauren Bacall is shattered by a succession of Winn-Dixies, Eckerds, and Domino's Pizzas. There is a steady stream of lights departing the Keys, even though it is the middle of the week. The hundred-mile drive is a blur of lights and drizzle. When I get to Key West the palm trees are swaying in the trade winds from the Atlantic, and Duval Street, the main business thoroughfare which runs the width of the island from the Gulf of Mexico to the Atlantic Ocean, is vibrating with people and lights and music.

Duval Street is where the Hemingway legend is marketed most ferociously on the little island. In late July there is a Hemingway Days celebration, a week-long party, a mini-Mardi Gras, complete with a Hemingway look-alike contest, a short story competition, a bullfish tournament, and boxing matches. During the rest of the year there are Hemingway posters, mugs, memorabilia. Sandwiches and drinks carry Papa's name. T-shirts with his bearded visage are a bigger industry than shrimping. There is no rest for Hemingway's perturbed spirit on Duval Street. His ghost is conjured up in a thousand different ways. One trip to Sloppy Joe's, Hemingway's favorite bar in the town, will initiate the innocent tourist to the mythology of the place. All the bouncers and bartenders wear Sloppy Joe's T-shirts with the bearded Hemingway emblazoned on the front. Photographs of the legend cover the walls, but the biggest and most telling picture is a mural opposite the entrance. The mural depicts Hemingway, with a Bacchanalian crown of grape leaves on his head, sitting at a table in the bar writing while Joe Russell, the original owner of Sloppy Joe's, and a host of others, stand around toasting the master. This may be a dramatically appropriate image for Hemingway's years in Key West, years in which he moved gradually but inexorably toward becoming a public figure surrounded by his groupies. He became his own best creation and the mural, perhaps unwittingly, suggests that.

According to James McLendon in *Papa: Hemingway in Key West*, the years between 1928 and 1940, those Hemingway spent in Key West, were the most important years of his life. "They were a time," McLendon says, "when the Machismo Myth was born—a myth that allowed Hemingway to move in an aura of self-created magnificence around the globe." During his Key West years, Hemingway, according to McLendon, had a small army of bookies, thugs, bartenders, soldiers of fortune, movie stars, athletes, sportsmen, hangers-on, and even a few genuine friends in his entourage. Hemingway transformed himself, with a little help from his friends, certainly, into "Papa" during these years. As McLendon said, "That there is a Hemingway Myth, a legend, a code of machismo, is as sure a thing in American literature as that there is a

A view of Petronia and Thomas Streets from the second
floor of "Blue Heaven"

Yoknapatawpha County, Mississippi. . . . [Hemingway's] life style is still played out by many who drift into the end-of-the-line city of Key West and by countless others who read his books, see his bearded face in old magazines, or pause over it on the back flaps of Scribner's Contemporary Classics series."

For many, Key West is figuratively and quite seriously the last stop. According to James Kirkwood, who lived there for years, "This is a crazy island. It's not Florida, or even America, but a country and a state of mind. It's the end of the line, even the world." Judging from the noise and crowds on Duval Street, I can only guess that the end-of-the-line town is having an end-of-the-world party, but it's late and perhaps I've been reading too much Hemingway. I'm betting the sun will rise again tomorrow morning. I head toward Victoria Lesser's house on Virginia Street.

I met Victoria Lesser two years ago when I was working on an article for the *Atlanta Journal and Constitution*. I was roaming around Key West looking for people who had known Hemingway, searching for places he had frequented. I was walking along Petronia Street in old town Key West when I came across a rundown, unpainted two-story building with a sign that read "Blue Heaven." I recalled that this was the place that had been a brothel and gambling house during Hemingway's time. During the 1930s Hemingway could be found there in the evenings in the side yard watching or refereeing boxing matches between local fighters.

It was the middle of the summer, humid enough to make me daydream about a cold shower and a silk shirt as I stared up at the Blue Heaven sign. A young woman walked out of one of the dilapidated doors, held up a shimmering swath of silk cloth, and checked the color in the sunlight. I never did get the silk shirt or cold shower I was imagining, but I did get to meet Victoria Lesser, the designer who creates the silk pajamas that Bill Cosby wears on and off his show. Although she had a number of other clients, I found out that designing pajamas for a man like Cosby, who has seven homes and enough pajamas in each that he can wear them once and send them out to be dry-cleaned, is a full-time and lucrative job.

When we moved from the street into her design studio on the bottom floor of Blue Heaven, from the rank smell and grey decay of

Thomas Street into the freshly painted art deco atmosphere of her office, I felt as if I were following Dorothy in *The Wizard of Oz* from a world of black and white to one of astonishing colors. The place had a Hollywood unreality to it, as the events of Lesser's life had a scripted American success story quality. That year she had shipped $250,000 worth of clothing from her Blue Heaven shop. A few years before she had made leather pocketbooks in New York City, selling them for fifteen dollars apiece. Twice divorced, with a young son to care for, a recent M.A. in psychology she wasn't sure what to do with, an ability to use a sewing machine, and an instinct for design, she took off for Key West. She had found out that OMO by Norma Kamali meant "On My Own" and that after Pauline's divorce from Hemingway, she had opened up a fabric shop in Key West. Victoria decided, "I could do that. And I did."

First she opened up "Solo Flight," a store that sold fine leather clothing, and then she began to design in silks. Her dramatic change in fortunes came when she met a clothing buyer for "The Bill Cosby Show" who liked her designs. Since then she's started making clothes for those who can afford to pay over $1,000 for a pair of pajamas or a blazer, Sophia Loren and the members of Aerosmith among them.

Victoria, who lives with her eighteen-year-old son Justin in an old frame house that she gutted and redesigned into an art deco masterpiece, complete with fifteen-by-twenty-foot swimming pool in a courtyard connected to the house by a series of French doors, gives me the top floor of her home as my Key West headquarters for the week. The diminutive Lesser, five-foot-one and about 100 pounds, has just returned from a city council meeting. Last year she moved out of Blue Heaven and bought a building in the heart of downtown. The top floor of the building is her studio, and the bottom she is renovating into a restaurant. Because of a zoning technicality she has been battling city hall for over six months. Tonight she won and will be allowed to increase the seating capacity in the potential restaurant. If no one leases the space, she'll just become a chef, she says. "But after putting half a million dollars into this venture, I better learn fast."

The next morning I head for Blue Heaven to see how things have changed in two years. Blue Heaven is on Petronia and

Thomas streets in the heart of what is called Bahama Village, Black Town, or Drug Alley, depending on who is giving directions. A few of the houses in the area have been painted, blues and pinks and oranges—like a West Indian explosion of personality. And there's the Caribbean House, a new bed-and-breakfast, perhaps the first one ever to appear in this section of town. But, generally, the area hasn't changed much. A line of men still sit near or lean against the walls of Johnson's grocery store across the street from Blue Heaven. There are Dixie cups strewn along the sidewalk, but most of the men drink out of bottles or cans wrapped neatly in brown paper bags. No one pays any attention as a rooster or two prances down the street. Cats stretch idly in the shade as men listen absently to the conversations around them.

Blue Heaven, too, has been painted, blue and yellow, reminding me of a house in a children's story. Like a neighborhood cat that has used up a good number of its nine lives, Blue Heaven, once beer joint, pool hall, gambling house, bordello, apartments, and design studio, will soon become an ice cream store and a grocery. "It will be something like a Bahamanian straw market," Corinne Crockett, the thirty-nine-year-old owner, tells me. Corinne is from Baxley, Georgia, and her husband, Bud, is from San Francisco. They met in Vidalia, Georgia, where Corinne worked as a technical researcher in a nuclear power plant. Bud, an engineer who does consultant work for nuclear plants, had bought a sixty-three-foot schooner four years before, hoping to sail away from engineering, but some financial reversals had forced him to work part of the year in order to sail the rest of it. Two years ago they got married and headed out on the schooner, dropped anchor in Key West, and stayed. A few months ago they bought Blue Heaven so that they could stay in Key West permanently and live on their boat. Like Thomas McGuane, who used to spend part of each year in Key West, they "wanted to live on the most scrambled edge of America, but they didn't want to disappear."

With Bud away in Georgia working on the power plant for a few months, Corinne lives on the boat with her two crew members, Shona Van Wyk and Robin Roberts. Her schooner, the *Cassiopeia*, stays docked in a slip in the downtown harbor, in the midst of a few dozen other boats that make up a community of sorts, a suburb of Drug Alley. Each day Corinne comes in to work on Blue Heaven. Today she takes a break from painting the door frames to give me a tour. She has brown eyes and a sailor's tan that matches her bronze earrings. Her clothing is bland—brown shorts, T-shirt and sandals, but her hands glow with green paint and her hair is streaked like a punk rocker. She waves an unbraceleted arm in front of her and tells me how she imagines the sawdust and paint cans will be transformed in a few months: "We want this place to fit into the neighborhood. To keep it funky. Most people in America can only see Hyatts and A&P's. Europeans don't have that problem. They seem to be able to allow the new and old to co-exist. Blue Heaven will keep the island flavor. I can see all the doors and shutters open, maybe some artists in residence, a basket weaver, a wood carver, a potter. All the doors and shutters will be open. . . ." She looks past me, as if she can see it all there, clearly.

As it was for Hemingway, Key West is Corinne's place to start over. The very fact that it's not like Los Angeles or Miami, that people live in the streets, the drama of daily life enacted for everyone to see, is what she loves about the old section of the town. "Hemingway took pleasure in these people," she says. "I can see the boxing and drinking, smell the sweat, hear the shouts. These people live out in the open. There aren't any masks here. Most of us live in air-conditioned houses and watch TV. These people live in the daylight."

The second floor of Blue Heaven has been made into a two-bedroom apartment, but it's a most unusual sort of apartment. It has one huge room, mostly bare, which serves as a kitchen, living room, and studio for the woman who rents it. There are three other rooms along the far wall but four doors that lead into them. Each door has a slot opening about two inches high and eight inches long. The slots, which are at eye level, were originally for the convenience of the prostitutes who used the cubicles. The wall between one cubicle and another was broken down, leaving one bedroom large enough for a single bed and another bedroom equally narrow but long enough for a table and a chair, as well. The third cubicle is now a bathroom. "People live in small spaces around here," Corinne tells me. "They learn to live within themselves."

In the courtyard just below the apartment, boxers fought and Hemingway refereed. Corinne wants to have open-air theater. From bordello to apartment, beer hall to ice cream parlor—"This probably would be too gentrified for Hemingway," she says.

On our way to see her schooner, we pass her friend's house on a side street near the marina, hidden behind bushes aflame with bougainvillea. The house, according to her, was owned by Henry Faulkner, who she says was one of William's nephews and a lover of Tennessee Williams. She recounts the rumors about armies of naked little boys and goats roaming through the house. A glance in the front windows shows huge ornate mirrors on the walls and plaster angels on the tables. I glance again, but the little boys and goats are not visible.

On the *Cassiopeia*, Corinne talks once more about the value of space. "You have to respect space," she says. She appreciates the lines from Gretel Ehrlich's essay about living in Wyoming: "Space has a spiritual equivalent and can heal what is divided and burdensome in us.... Space represents sanity, not a life purified, dull, or 'spaced out' but one that might accommodate intelligently any idea or situation." Corinne has a heightened sense of space, partly from the vistas of the ocean but mainly because there is so little space aboard the boat. Every inch becomes precious. Like Ehrlich she feels, "We fill up space as if it were a pie shell, with things whose opacity further obstructs our ability to see what is already there." For Corinne the confined community of boat people, the narrow margins of Key West itself, forces her to confront daily the edges of space.

The next morning I have breakfast in a place called the Deli. It's away from the main drag and obviously the "in" place to eat on the island. Everyone is deeply tanned and has the casual appearance of well-to-do Key Westers. I eat there because the food is good—thick, old-fashioned home fries, six pieces of rye toast, and two eggs for $1.80. It's the kind of place in which waitresses rarely smile—first, they are too busy shuttling eggs and pancakes and orange juice from kitchen to the tables, and second, they don't feel it's a job requirement. People come in for the food and the local paper. They get both and don't expect smiling conversation, too. The sour dispositions of the waitresses seem an integral part of the genuine character of the place, giving the customers even more confidence in the food.

I've always found the experience of eating alone in a restaurant a strange one. It's lonely but at the same time it permits a wonderful sort of eavesdropping. By yourself, you become invisible, a fly on the wall, and all the other tables become tiny stages—a Tennessee Williams play here, a Pinteresque drama there. Half the tables seem filled with homosexual lovers, holding hands and gazing into one another's eyes. Two men, looking longingly at one another over scrambled eggs and oatmeal, both have Sloppy Joe's T-shirts on, with Hemingway's stern, disapproving eyes looking out from one to the other. It's difficult to say what Hemingway would have made of all this—the considerable gay community in Key West, his image on so many chests, even all this oatmeal—but it's probable that he would not have liked it. As the owner of the restaurant said to me, "If Hemingway were alive, he'd like the cooking in my place, but he wouldn't be in Key West to taste it."

The other main group in the restaurant seems to be real estate entrepreneurs. Everyone is talking about variances and lots and interest rates. The biggest business in Key West is buying old houses, renovating them, and selling them to northerners for exorbitant profits.

"Can you believe it," one man says, "she bought the place for 250, didn't do a thing and sold it for 400 the next week."

"It's the goddam gays," his friend says, taking one furtive look around and lowering his voice, "they'll pay anything."

The longing looks and conversations about real estate stop abruptly as a man with thick, long hair twisted into uncombed knots and a heavy, matted beard that reaches down to an oil-stained shirt, swings open the front doors and makes a loud noise, a guttural, animal-like cry. Everyone looks up and the man growls again, turns and walks out, banging the door so that the glass rattles. Eyes are wide, mouths open, oatmeal suspended on spoons in mid-air. "What the hell is Key West coming to?" one man says. "Did I tell you what the McAllister place sold for?" asks his companion.

James Roberts ("Iron Baby") and Kermit Forbes ("Shine")
in front of Forbes's home

It's just a short walk back to Drug Alley, where I am to meet James Roberts, whom everyone knows as "Iron Baby," a man who sparred with Hemingway in the 1930s. But on my way I pass the Bottle Cap Lounge, and even though it's barely eight in the morning, I've been told that I will find Kermit Forbes, another of Hemingway's former sparring partners, there. And I do.

Kermit, who's known to everyone in Key West as "Shine" and to his former boxing fans as "The Battling Geech," reminds me of Hemingway's Santiago from *The Old Man and the Sea*. There are some significant differences, of course. Shine is black, and although he is seventy-two years old his skin has an elastic, youthful look. He is muscular, as if he could go ten rounds if it were necessary. Hemingway's Santiago was gaunt and wrinkled, with brown blotches of benevolent skin cancer on his face. Like Santiago, though, Shine's one good eye is cheerful and undefeated. The right eye is virtually closed, covered by scar tissue. Most people assume he was battered in the ring, but the truth is an angry woman threw lye in his face when he was in his early thirties. There's something gentle looking even about this half-closed right eye. His left eye is bright and seems to see everything, notice the smallest details. But it's his hands that remind me of Santiago's, thick and powerful. Resting on the bar in front of a glass of beer, those hands seem to have a character and memory of their own.

The bar is filled with men who are retired, out of work, or waiting for a night shift. Everyone is wearing a baseball cap and without one perched on my head I feel a bit like a man in a suit at a nudist colony. The bartender, a plump, orange-haired woman in her late twenties, has a baseball cap on, too. It says "Hemingway."

"You be good, Shine," she says as he leaves.

"I can't be anything but," he says and touches the brim of his Miami Dolphins cap.

In Oxford, Mississippi, Willie Morris acted as my tour guide. In Key West Shine takes on the job, and we start at his place on Fort Street, right next to the site of the old naval base. He was raised nearby in a house next to a cowyard and an almond grove. Both are gone now, but one almond tree remains and what used to be a barn is now his labyrinthine apartment with a number of corridors and tiny rooms and even more people—brothers-in-law, daughters, cousins, friends—than one would readily believe could fit into the angles and shadows of the place. Shine was brought up by a woman who babysat for him when he was an infant. His mother and father left one day, and the woman took care of him. As a boy he caught fish on the docks and sold them to the aquarium. He also made some money by cracking almonds and selling them in town, and climbing the trees and shaking down coconuts for sailors.

His early business career didn't last long, though. After the second grade he ran away from Key West and the woman who had taken charge of him. He jumped a freight train filled with pineapples, and traveled with two older boys, one called the king of the hobos and the other he remembers as Tunky Cash. They traveled together for a few weeks, or about until the smell of pineapple got out of their nostrils. Then he was on his own. He loaded ice onto freight cars, washed dishes, and did farm work. "I'd never seen a plow in my life, but I learned," he says. He meandered through Georgia and South Carolina, but his mind always went back to Key West. He thinks it's more than coincidence that he has ended up living right back in the dairy where he used to tend cows. As he tells me this, his story seems to have the perfect circularity of fiction, but the smell of cows still lingers faintly here, suggesting that there's not too much fiction in his story.

By the time he was a teenager and grown to his full five-feet six-inch sinewy frame, he had returned to Key West. As he tells this all now, he smiles, toothpick cantilevered from two gold teeth and thick African features animated with the memory. "The South is no place for a black man," he tells me. "I had to come back to Key West." As I look at him I understand. He has an earring in his left ear, silver bristles covering his face, white chef's pants, cracked sandals, and a T-shirt a suburban housewife would be ashamed to use as a rag, but in Key West he's a perfectly ordinary citizen.

When he returned to Key West he began boxing in his spare time. He started working in the upper keys on the railroad but returned every two weeks to fight at Blue Heaven. That's where he met Ernest Hemingway. He's told his story so many times I suspect it's taken on an element of myth: "I didn't know Ernest Hemingway from anybody else. I was down at Blue Heaven one night being a second for a friend of mine. Hemingway was refereeing the match and my man was losing. I threw in the towel. Hemingway threw it back to me. I threw in the towel again, and this time when he threw it back at me, I charged in the ring and took a poke at him. It just glanced off his chest, and my friend Iron Baby grabbed me and pulled me back. 'Do you know who you're trying to hit?' he asked me."

I'm certain Shine has not been reading Joseph Campbell, but his story has the sound of an archetypal meeting with the wise father. Shine went to Hemingway's house on Whitehead Street, a few blocks away, and apologized the next afternoon. Hemingway invited him to work out on his property. The first two hundred dollars Shine ever earned at any one time he earned a few weeks later at Hemingway's house by putting on an exhibition for Gene Tunney, Hemingway, and his friends. The spectators passed a hat and the boxers left with a windfall. As Shine remembers him, Hemingway was a huge man, even god-like. What Shine remembers is the mythic figure, the man who (before Sylvester Stallone was even born) used a giant tuna as a punching bag when a sparring partner couldn't be found, but with his Caribbean sense of balance and perspective Shine's also able to say, "I boxed a lot with Hemingway, you know, but I never hit him too hard. Never wanted to hurt him."

In 1942 Shine went into the Army and soon became the base middleweight champion in Macon, Georgia. When he returned to Key West he worked as a cook in the naval hospital for thirty-two years. Now, as he sits outside his squat house, smiling, his two gold teeth glinting flashes of sunlight, his meeting with Hemingway seems like Odysseus's encounter with Tiresias in the underworld. The pattern of departure, initiation, and return runs throughout his story. It was a magical meeting for him, one that seems to be the center of his life, a fulcrum for his memories and his storytelling.

His house is a museum of memories—bells and dolls and teddy bears. There are photos of Hemingway on the walls outside his front door, among the ceramic sculptures and baskets. Plants in children's football helmets hang like surreal growths from the almond tree outside his living room window. Christmas lights decorate the tree and twist like an intestine onto the tomato plants. The sign by the front door says "Shine's Ponderosa." He too,

I suppose, knows something about space. As we stand outside his front door, admiring the congestion of artwork on his walls, inside and out, three young couples ride by on scooters. They wave as they take the curve, but all I can see is a flash of Vuarnet shades and Bugle Boy shirts.

The tour of Key West Shine takes me on begins at the former Harlem Inn, which was in his day a "sporting house." He takes me through the historic red-light district, past what he calls "the house of all nations," named for the cultural diversity of the prostitutes. He takes me past every whorehouse he can recollect in Key West, and after half an hour I'm convinced he knows the location and story behind each establishment. If only he had more of an instinct toward marketing and promotion he could write a book about Key West. There are so many already—*Authors of Key West, Writers' Homes in Key West, The History of Key West, Fishing in Key West* and on and on—but *Whorehouses of Key West* might be a real addition to the scholarship.

We stop in front of 1016 Howell Street, in front of the debris, and gaze at the peeling white paint. "That was a famous place," he says. "They used to go upstairs and do their business, you know. But this place had a special story to it. They had only white whores there. One of them was a sailor's wife. He left her alone, he thought, at home. But she used to come down to trick when he was at sea. This was in the 1930s. One time he came home early and found out where she was. He went down there and cut her throat."

He says this, like a tour guide who blends his image with the scene, just as we pass a row of red hibiscus. Like most of us, Shine has a bit of the professor in him and enjoys lecturing on history, architecture, horticulture, or whatever subject is near at hand. He points out sea grape trees, and shows me the bent branches of a lime he climbed as a young man. We stop in front of a banyan tree and he says, "You don't see these up north." He's right. They look like trees Tolkien would have conjured up for one of his stories. Their roots strike like stalactites into the ground, shafting through the heavy, warm air and freezing into intricate patterns. He gives a disquisition on conch houses, just as the Conch Train, the primary tourist vehicle in town, rumbles by us, the voice from the train competing with Shine's.

Conch houses are an interesting topic of conversation on the island. Conchs are the native Key Westers, usually those with something of a Bahamanian heritage, but conch houses are not so easily definable. As Shine sees them, conch houses are fancy. They have balconies and intricate grillwork like houses in New Orleans. They have shutters and often lookout peaks, one to ward off winds and the other to help spot wrecks so that the residents could be the first out to salvage. But for others, conch houses are the rundown little places associated with poverty. The truth is they are simply the one-and-a-half-story wood frame houses with elaborate lattice-work often done by ships' carpenters who were forced ashore when their ships wrecked on the coral reef off Key West. The house might be the cramped, crumbling sort in Bahama Village or the sprawling, opulent variety near the southern tip of the island. When people use the word "conch" to describe houses in Key West, they seem to resemble Humpty Dumpty, using the word to mean what they choose it to mean—"neither more nor less."

Shine's tour is of the other Key West, down the side streets a tourist rarely sees. He takes me into the past through the disintegrating present—the remnants of the old pineapple factory, which flourished when the boats ran to Havana, and around the cemetery on Margaret Street, where he points like an art connoisseur to the unpainted shack with a four-foot-high wall of bottles (soda, wine, and beer) cemented together. "That's something to look at," he says.

Shine's Key West is not Duval Street or Mallory Square. It's not the restaurants or new hotels. It's not the convertibles or mini-vans that cruise the main streets. His Key West is bounded by the bicycle routes his old cronies take to the grocery store, by the neighborhood bars, the abandoned houses, and deserted factories. His Key West, still there in decaying bits and fragments, is the past, filled with loud laughter and heroic bouts with Hemingway. And in his friendship with other old-time Key Westers like James Roberts.

James Roberts is "Iron Baby," a heroic epithet like skywalker or pathfinder or deerslayer. It describes the man. His hands are like anvils and his chest as broad as a bulkhead. Half a century ago his fists must have hammered like iron into many an opponent. Like Shine, he was a champion in the Army, in the lightweight division at Fort Stuart, Georgia, during World War II.

On most mornings, the sixty-nine-year-old Iron Baby (whom I call Mr. Roberts because I feel too foolish using the word "baby" to describe him and can't abbreviate it to "Hey, Iron") can be found on Petronia Street near the crowing roosters who saunter between the old chairs lined along the brick pavement. The chairs are waiting to be occupied, and the Dixie cups strewn along the curb are waiting to be swept away. A new batch will replace them during the next twelve hours or so.

Iron Baby is about four inches taller than Shine and he has one more gold tooth than his friend. The extra gold tooth may be a sign of success in the business world. For close to thirty years he owned four different dry cleaners in Key West. Even now he works part-time at B&F Cleaners. "First boxing, then dry cleaning— that's all I know," he says.

I'm standing in front of the B&C Grocery Store on Petronia Street when Iron Baby pulls up on his dilapidated bicycle. It has no speeds and the tires are as thick as a back country bike's. Clearly, he's in no rush. He's wearing a shiny short-sleeved blue shirt, faded green slacks, and scuffed brown shoes that may soon become antiques. Style, like speed, is not an important part of his life. There are a number of older men sitting in front of the grocery, their bikes leaning against the wall. Skinny, back-alley dogs, the sort you would expect to find in an Apache village in the 1850s, walk casually by the men near the grocery and the cats sprawled in the alleys. A man with a cockatoo on his shoulder rides by on his bicycle. A chicken, followed by a line of three biddies, pauses in front of Floyd's Barber Shop across the street. The air, even this early in March, is as thick and slow-moving as a gelatinous stream. Everyone in Bahama Village seems to float along in it lazily and happily.

Iron Baby comes floating over to me, and we stand in the shade of a tree talking about chickens and dry cleaners and Hemingway. He has just come back from New York City, where his brother lives in Brooklyn. He can visit only for short periods because he is afraid

After a game, a table and chairs on an old Key West side street

to be on the streets there. This seems strange coming from a man who has lived his whole life on the streets of Drug Alley, an area once populated with prostitutes and now known for its crack addicts. But Iron Baby feels as safe as a stray cat—and as free. "We all feed the cats here," he says. "Cars stop to let the chickens by. These are our pets. But nobody owns them. People here in Key West all live together, always have, and have always let each other be."

He asks me to wait a moment while he goes home to get something he wants to show me. Within a few minutes he is back with a book bouncing in the bent metal basket on the front of his bike. It's a copy of *Hemingway in Key West*. He shows me his own photograph, a young James Roberts in a fighting pose. The years have not been as kind to him as they have to Shine, but something of that young fighter remains. The memory of his friendship with Hemingway, now a part of the local street mythology, certainly endures. That memory is as real for him as Hemingway's house, a few blocks away.

Hemingway's house, built in 1851 by Asa Tift, a wrecker and shipping tycoon who was one of the founders of Tifton, Georgia, is at 907 Whitehead Street. It's one of the few mansions in Key West and the first home Hemingway owned. This house has timbers of Georgia pine and the fence Hemingway had built around the place for privacy is made of Baltimore bricks. The house has one of the few basements in Key West because it's on one of the tallest peaks on the island—sixteen feet above sea level. The highest point on Key West is eighteen feet.

Hemingway's house is the preeminent tourist attraction in the town. Mrs. Dixon, the owner of the property and the woman who turned the house into a museum, charges five dollars per person for pilgrims to tour the grounds. There's a cadre of tour guides and people who sell books and shirts and memorabilia, but no one seems able to tell me how much it costs to run the house or how much it takes in each year. So I do some imaginative accounting based upon the number of people I estimate are there on the day I spend on the property. About $1 million seems right to me, and after I deduct the $1,000 a week Mrs. Dixon spends on cat food, the

The Hemingway house, Key West

cost of taxes and maintenance and staff salaries, I decide buying the home of a famous writer might not be such a bad investment.

There are four tour guides today ready, in rotation, to recount the legend of Papa. The guide for our group, Jerry, is a semi-retired real estate agent from Miami. He works himself enthusiastically through the house, occasionally wiping a bead of sweat from his brow or patting his bulging stomach as he recites the "facts." Legend and fact are one here, though. When someone on the tour says she read a biography of Hemingway that said he was an even six feet tall, Jerry dismisses her and the biographies by repeating, "He was six-feet-four, not an inch less." Later, when I leave the house I hear another tour guide say, "This is the doorway where Hemingway had to bend his six-foot five-inch bulk." The more tours, it seems, the larger he becomes.

In Key West it's the Hemingway legend that people buy and sell. Only one of Hemingway's novels and certainly not one of his best, *To Have and Have Not*, was set in the United States, specifically in Key West. But worshippers come seeking the man, his connection to the place, not his resonating description of the edge of America. It's an old-fashioned ghost hunt, and for many the logical place to start is his house.

Key West became Hemingway's permanent address in January 1930. It was his second wife Pauline who fell in love with what Jeffrey Meyers described as a "two-story white stone residence with a leaky roof and obsolete wiring on a fine lot on Whitehead Street, which her Uncle Gus purchased for eight thousand dollars and gave to her as a gift outright." With its beautifully landscaped grounds enclosed by wrought iron railings, it was one of the oldest houses on the island. The value of the house, like the Hemingway legend, has grown over the years. The property is assessed at over $2 million. It was the right place for Hemingway, who during his years in Key West wrote *A Farewell to Arms*, *Death in the Afternoon*, *Green Hills of Africa*, "The Short Happy Life of Francis Macomber," and the beginning of *For Whom the Bell Tolls*. Carlos Baker, Hemingway's first biographer, says that soon after Hemingway began living there he fell "into a work-and-fishing schedule precisely suited to his temperament. Except for an occasional night on the town, followed by what he referred to as 'gastric remorse,' he rose early and retired early. He liked to write in the mornings while he and the day were both fresh, spending most of the rest of his time in the open air talking with anyone whose face or occupation interested him, questioning them closely about their backgrounds, their families, and their professions." According to Baker, Hemingway said that with the big scar on his forehead, everyone mistook him for a northern bootlegger or drug smuggler, and nobody would believe he had written books. This, Hemingway took as a compliment, or so legend would have it.

One thing is certain, however, and that is that during the Key West years Hemingway began, as Oscar Wilde said of himself, to give his genius to his life and his talent to his writing. Hemingway began to listen less and speak more. He began to become his own most famous character. The public became most fascinated by the story in which he was the protagonist—the drinker, the lover, the fighter, the fearless hunter. Like many other American writers, Clemens, Frost, and Faulkner among them, he began to invent his past and live his present according to the outlines of the imagined plot.

In the Hemingway story, it's often difficult to separate reality from fiction, but dozens of critical works and at least four major biographies—by Carlos Baker, Jeffrey Meyers, Michael Reynolds, and Kenneth Lynn—have made the attempt.

He was born Ernest Miller Hemingway on July 21, 1899, in Oak Park, Illinois, an upper-class suburb of Chicago. His mother was a successful singing teacher and his father a respected doctor. Like Faulkner, Hemingway came from a proud military tradition, with two grandfathers having fought in the Civil War. And like Faulkner, the contemporary he most respected as "competition for the title" of great American writer of the twentieth century, he had a family with roots that were deep and often twisted. As Faulkner followed his father into alcoholism, Hemingway followed his into suicide. Faulkner's mother had an important influence on his life. Grace Hemingway had an even more complex influence on her son's life. His ambivalence about her eventually turned into hatred. But perhaps, as Faulkner did, he inherited, as Jeffrey Meyers says, "the temperament and artistic talent of his mother, the looks and sporting skills of his father."

For his first eighteen years, Hemingway lived the life of Tom Sawyer in the upper-middle-class white Protestant enclave of Oak Park, secure and protected but dreaming of adventure. Then for the next four decades he became what he had pretended to be. Even though Gertrude Stein called him 90 percent Rotarian and despite the fact that he never lost the anxiety of the guilt-ridden Protestant work ethic, he shocked America with his fiction and his life. Most of his life, it seems, was spent shattering what he saw as the brittle icons of middle-class America, revealing brutal truths about war, marriage, love, and honor. Like many other American writers before him, he was constantly reimagining his life story, often renaming himself. He never liked the name Ernest, which he associated with the staid values that Oscar Wilde mocked in his most famous play. So he gave himself other names through the years—Wemedge, Stein, Taty. Eventually the patriarchal "Papa" stuck fast, a name that grafted the man and the legend together.

Like Mark Twain and Stephen Crane, Hemingway started his career as a journalist. Hemingway's education as a writer, which began in his high school English classes, continued while he was a reporter for the *Kansas City Star*. The newspaper's handbook of style, emphasizing short paragraphs, crisp sentences, authenticity, precision, clarity, and immediacy, had a distinct influence on his prose style. It was a style that perfectly matched his emerging stoical philosophy, a code that emphasized honesty, courage, and restraint. No one will ever know exactly all the sources of the famous Hemingway code, the main precept of which was "grace under pressure," but Michael Reynolds sees the origins in his Oak Park upbringing. "After the war," Reynolds says, "young Hemingway entered the new age, taking with him the values formed in his first world, the one he had lost, the one he never wrote about."

Once again the story of his life runs a course parallel to Faulkner's. Both men wanted to go to war in search of romance and heroes. But like Faulkner who was rejected by the military because of his height and weight, Hemingway was rejected because of his defective vision. He volunteered as a Red Cross ambulance driver in 1918. In Milan, along with other drivers, Hemingway had himself fitted for a uniform that resembled the type worn by the American Expeditionary Force. He wanted to be part of the action. He wanted to be a hero. Around midnight on July 8, 1918, at Fossalta di Piave, he had his chance.

He was struck by fragments of a trench mortar, severely wounding his legs, but according to some accounts he managed to pick up an Italian soldier and carry him to the first-aid dugout. This he did with over two hundred pieces of shell fragments lodged in his legs. The soldier he carried was dead. Although there are several somewhat contradictory accounts, a few of them from Hemingway himself over the years, undeniably he showed great courage. At first, Hemingway's version of the event was fairly accurate, but soon his imaginative skills took over. Like Faulkner he began to embellish the story of his war experience. Hemingway, of course, had a much more solid reality to work with, but at the very time Faulkner was parading around Oxford Square in his R.A.F. uniform complete with pilot's wings he had never officially earned and a cane he had no real use for, Hemingway was making his experiences bigger, starting his legend. Machine gun fire and an aluminum kneecap, for instance, were later additions to his story.

While he was in an Italian hospital, Hemingway met one of the most influential women in his life, Agnes von Kurowsky, a nurse who tended to him. They fell in love and planned to get married. There are even reports that, like Frederick Henry and Catherine Barkley in A Farewell to Arms, they became lovers in his hospital bed. But when Hemingway returned to America to recuperate, she jilted him. Twice disillusioned, first in war and then in love, Hemingway returned home, like Harold Krebs in his story "Soldier's Home," to a place that no longer made any sense to him.

Shortly after he returned he met Hadley Richardson. She was no striking beauty, but she was attractive and had traits Hemingway admired even more than beauty. He said she fished like a man, understood boxing, and was a good drinker. In addition, she had just been left a trust fund of $3,000 a year. Agnes had been seven years older than Hemingway and Hadley was eight years older than he was, and they were married on September 3, 1921, a few months after they met.

Hadley's trust fund, plus $8,000 she inherited when her uncle died in 1921, allowed them to leave for Europe and live comfortably there. They were not rich, but there were not many financial pressures. For instance, on one trip to Germany they had four full days of room and board for $1.60. Even without Hemingway's income as a foreign correspondent for American newspapers, they had enough money to live in Paris, ski in Switzerland, travel in Italy, and follow the bullfight circuit in Spain.

During those years in Paris, Hemingway's career as a writer truly started. He wrote many fine short stories and published *The Sun Also Rises*, his first novel and one many of his readers still consider his best. It was during this time, as well, that his charismatic personality began to take on the shadings of legend. He was handsome. One person described him as a Clark Gable with biceps. He was strong, masculine, energetic. He was also a great conversationalist, witty and entertaining. His son Jack once said that his "enormous appetite for life flowed over everyone around him." Archibald MacLeish believed that Hemingway "could exhaust the oxygen in a room just by coming into it." For Allen Tate there was charm even in his malice.

And there was plenty of malice. In the foreshadowing of Faulkner's brutal fun at the expense of one of his mentors, Hemingway wrote *The Torrents of Spring*, a cruel satire of Sherwood Anderson's fiction. But Faulkner grew to regret his youthful carelessness; Hemingway never did. He could be vicious, paying back a real or imagined insult with venomous wit or, at times, his fists. Like the man in Landor's poem, pride, envy, and malice were often his graces. If he were out-boxed, he would make up excuses. If he encountered a worthy writer, he often found a way of belittling him.

In Paris he met many of the important writers of his time and formed many relationships, but few of them were to endure his own jealousies or competitiveness. He met Ezra Pound, Gertrude Stein, James Joyce, Wyndham Lewis, Ford Madox Ford, John Dos Passos, and F. Scott Fitzgerald. By the end of his life he had alienated nearly everyone on this list and many others too. But he never broke with Joyce or Pound. As he did with so many others, Pound saw Hemingway's genius and became, as one critic put it, "a midwife for new literary talent."

Right from the beginning Hemingway lived by his own dictum: "Prose is architecture, not interior decoration." He built his sentences along simple, strong lines. He wrote, as he said, on the principle of the iceberg, keeping seven-eighths under water for every part that shows. He wrote five simple sentences for every complex one. There were few similes, hardly any authorial intrusion, and a great emphasis on an objective rendering of experience. Like his character Wilson in "The Short Happy Life of Francis Macomber," Hemingway felt that it "Doesn't do to talk too much about all this. Talk the whole thing away." If Faulkner exploded onto the page, trying to say everything, get every nuance of experience, leaving nothing out, Hemingway's prose was an implosion, saying it as simply, directly, and straightforwardly as possible, leaving the reader to reach into the icy waters below. Finally, both were after truth and Faulkner may have agreed with Hemingway's statement about what was necessary in his profession: "The most essential gift for a good writer is a built-in, shock-proof, shit detector."

What Hemingway didn't have, at times, was an ability to pierce through the curtain of his own delusions. In a letter to Fitzgerald he wrote, "To me heaven would be a big bull ring with me holding two barrera seats and a trout stream outside that no one else was allowed to fish in and two lovely houses in the town; one where I would have my wife and children and be monogamous and love them truly and well and the other where I would have my nine beautiful mistresses on nine different floors." His fantasies began to clash with his responsibilities, and as he became successful and famous, his marriage to Hadley fell apart. The eight-year-difference between Hemingway and Hadley became a wider gulf as she got older and after their son John was born.

He divorced Hadley in January 1927 and married Pauline Pfeiffer in May of the same year. Hemingway was following a pattern by now. Pauline was older than he was (although she was younger than Hadley) and she was an heiress (much wealthier than Hadley). There has been much speculation about Hemingway's relationships with women, but one pattern seems clear. As a young man he was invariably drawn to older women. As an older man he seemed obsessed by younger ones. Faulkner theorized that Hemingway's problem with women was that he felt he had to marry them all. Fitzgerald believed that Hemingway needed a new woman for each big book. For *The Sun Also Rises* he had Hadley, for *A Farewell to Arms* Pauline, for *For Whom the Bell Tolls* Martha, and for *The Old Man and the Sea* Mary. But Jeffrey Meyers's theory may be the most convincing: "Hemingway was a romantic at heart. Every time he fell in love with a woman, he sincerely believed that he had to marry her and would remain married to her forever." Unlike notorious womanizers like Irwin Shaw, Hemingway was generally true to his wives until he fell in love with another woman and left his present wife to marry her.

Hemingway was a man who was never satisfied with his wives, his children, or his life. His life seemed to be a continual test of his courage—in the boxing ring, in the bullring, in war, on the hunt. Big and clumsy, he had bad eyesight and a bad temper, drank heavily, and frequently behaved recklessly. And he paid the price with accidents and illnesses. As John Dos Passos said, "I never knew an athletic, vigorous man who spent so much time in bed as Ernest did." One of his biographers devotes an entire appendix to his accidents and illnesses: boxing injuries and football accidents, concussions and war wounds, groin pulls and accidental shootings, broken bones and cuts. He was clawed by a lion, pulled a skylight down on his head, shot himself in the leg while gaffing a shark. The list is awe inspiring. Even the most uneducated amateur psychologist would have to wonder about death wishes in such a case.

Hemingway was also a master escape artist. When a marriage became intolerable, he left. When someone bested him, he insulted him and found another friend. When a country harbored bad memories or proof of his irresponsibility, he sought other climes. In 1928 he left Paris and Hadley behind and headed for Key West. Carlos Baker suggests that it was Dos Passos's description of his "dreamlike crossing of the keys" that first excited Hemingway's imagination. After his divorce from Hadley, Key West was the kind of dilapidated Eden he needed. It was, as Dos Passos had said, faintly New England in appearance, but a New England down-at-the-heel, with a population that had shrunk from 26,000 to 10,000 in the years following the war. Jeffrey Meyers described the Key

West Hemingway probably encountered then: "The maritime atmosphere of the seedy unpretentious town, with weathered clapboard houses and open balconies, was a mixture of Nantucket and New Orleans. The pace was slow moving, with many bicycles and few cars. It was then an exotic, almost foreign locale. Spanish was spoken everywhere, the rollers of big cigars were prospering and there were many Cuban tourists. The place was far from urban distractions, but had two tennis courts at the Navy yard, good cock fights, thriving whore houses and an endless supply of smuggled Prohibition whiskey in several fine saloons." Kenneth Lynn, another of Hemingway's biographers, said Key West was the perfect place for the writer "to start renewing his acquaintance with American life."

Key West was a decompression chamber of sorts, allowing him to readjust to American culture, partly because the island was American and foreign at the same time, part of the United States but separate from it. It was close to Miami but even closer to Cuba. According to Carlos Baker, Hemingway needed to shed the complexity of Europe and the guilt over his unfaithfulness to Hadley. He longed to return to the simplicity of America, but he could never return to the middle-class values of Oak Park.

In some respects Key West hasn't changed all that much in sixty years. The population has swelled back to 30,000 or so, but the place still has the same blend of lazy freedom and rank decay once you're off Duval Street or the other tourist avenues. Key West today, in a sense, treats Hemingway the way he started to treat himself in the early 1930s—as a public hero. Once he left Paris he cut himself off from cosmopolitan, intellectual culture and educated companions. Outside of writing he turned his energies exclusively to marlin fishing and boating and drinking with his friends—Joe Russell, Jim Sullivan, Captain Bra Saunders, and Charles Thompson. To a certain extent, the new atmosphere, as many writers have pointed out, encouraged him to boast and swagger. He became the center of attention, a great writer among ordinary men. He was then a living legend. It took only a few entrepreneurs to make him the main tourist attraction later on. For some, like Edmund Wilson, he became "his own worst invented character."

Others saw the best of Hemingway emerge in his relations with the people of Key West. The warm side of his personality seemed to come out most naturally among non-literary people. Jim Sullivan, a construction worker from Brooklyn, who ran a machine shop on the island, thought Hemingway was a silent, deep man who spoke slowly and thoughtfully. Charles Thompson loved hunting and fishing and just about every night went fishing for barracuda and red snapper with Hemingway. After fishing they would head for the bars along Duval Street, particularly Sloppy Joe's, where the roar of rumba music and the brawls of sailors were commonplace. Hemingway felt most comfortable among ordinary people, perhaps because there was no intellectual competition and hero worship was his for the asking.

Mario Menocal, one of Hemingway's close friends during his Cuban years, made a similar point about the public image of the writer: "[He] engaged in creating and perpetuating the Hemingway *persona*, and engaged in promoting and selling his works. . . . No one was more conscious than Ernest of the figure and the image he possessed in the American press and reading public. . . . He deliberately set out to keep the legend and the image alive in the form he wanted it."

Some critics believe that during his lifetime the Hemingway legend became so prominent that it replaced reality, and that in expending so much energy on his legend, he never again had the strength to match some of his early stories and novels like *The Sun Also Rises* and *A Farewell to Arms*. Jeffrey Meyers concluded that Hemingway had been "dazzled by the rich, turned into a celebrity, created a legend that made his life better known than his works."

In Key West his reputation, his charismatic persona, seem far more important to most people than his writing. It's Hemingway the Byronic hero most people associate with Key West, not Hemingway the writer. Key West finds its way into only one of his novels, *To Have and Have Not*. He describes the "frame houses with narrow yards, light coming from shuttered windows; conch town, where all was starched, well-shuttered, virtue, failure, grits and boiled grunts, under-nourishment, prejudice, righteousness, inter-breeding and the comforts of religion . . . the brightly lit main street with the three drugstores, the music store, the five Jew stores, the three poolrooms, two barbershops, five beer joints, three ice cream parlors, the five poor and one good restaurants, two magazine and paper places, four dentists' offices upstairs, the big dime store, a hotel on the corner with taxis opposite; and across, behind the hotel, to the street that led to jungle town, the big unpainted frame houses with lights and girls in the doorway, the mechanical piano going and a sailor sitting in the street." This was Hemingway's Key West, and there's a mild irony in the fact that the mythic persona he created has been carefully appropriated by modern mythmakers from Madison Avenue to create another Key West, one he probably would not have been comfortable in, a colony for painters, writers, sculptors, the lost, the runaways, the touring—a place where Perrier flows more readily than beer, where posh hotels rim the coastline, and T-shirts with his legendary mien are more common than the fruit fly.

It was during his Key West years, 1928–36, that Hemingway became the most public of American writers. Dorothy Parker's *New Yorker* profile was the spark, perhaps, that started the blaze in 1929. Parker claimed she wanted to describe the "real" Hemingway, not the figure of newspapers and magazines, but she wound up writing about his service in the Italian army (he was in the Red Cross), his seven woundings (there was one), his leaving home to become a prizefighter (he became a newspaper writer), and his status as a foreign correspondent before the war (not unless Kansas City had been annexed by France). But as literary scholar John Raeburn points out, it was not all Parker's fault: "There was something compelling in Hemingway's personality that encouraged myth-making and defeated even scrupulous efforts to tell the truth, and by the time of Parker's profile one could hardly disentangle the truth from the hyperbolic fantasies."

Hemingway's desire to live in Key West, a place *Vogue* magazine at the time described as an island where "food and wine were cheap, swimming and fishing year-round activities, and life in general simple and unsophisticated," may have been less because of an inclination to escape than it was an impulse to remain in the perfect arena for the heroic legend to perform. It may have been the perfect spot for the "photogenic Hemingway," as Phillip Young called him, to confuse the record further "by glamorizing it." In 1936 John Peale Bishop said Hemingway had turned into a composite of his photographs over the previous decade. He saw Hemingway constantly posing for the world—the handsome, brave hunter, smiling over a dead lion or standing next to a giant marlin on the docks of Key West.

Eventually Hemingway grew out of Key West. He went off to the Spanish Civil War, divorced Pauline, and married Martha Gellhorn. Within a few years came another war, World War II, and another wife, Mary Welsh. As Jeffrey Meyers pointedly phrased it, Mary was to "endure" for seventeen years as Mrs. Hemingway, until his death in 1961. His third wife Martha, who lasted seven years in his "orbit," said she didn't know how Mary lasted with him, living "a slave's life with a brute for a slave owner," a man who "was progressively more insane every year. . . . the biggest liar since Munchausen."

After World War II and his marriage to Mary there was no good writing left, except for *The Old Man and the Sea*. All that remained was the writer's legend he had shaped like a character in one of his stories. It's easy enough to understand, then, that in the 1950s *Look* magazine's Photoquiz, featuring the faces of Douglas MacArthur, W. C. Fields, Cary Grant, Marlon Brando, and President Eisenhower, only one author was pictured—Ernest Hemingway. By the fifties he had become a star. And what Hemingway once wrote of Teddy Roosevelt may have been better written about himself: "All the legends that he started in his life live on and prosper, unhampered now by his existence."

After he married Mary, Hemingway once again changed his residences, Wyoming to Idaho and Key West to Cuba. Always a serious drinker, he became even more a problem drinker as he got older. Clearly in the grain of American writers—Jack London, Sinclair Lewis, Ring Lardner, Eugene O'Neill, and others—he was an alcoholic. His writing and his health deteriorated. According to his younger brother Leicester, Hemingway would drink about seventeen Scotch and sodas a day on a typical Key West afternoon. Colonel Buck Lanham said that during World War II Hemingway drank gallons of hard liquor in a week, mostly martinis mixed at the rate of fifteen to one.

His drinking unquestionably contributed to his temperament. Truman Capote once described him by saying, "There was a mean man." And Capote's estimate doesn't seem far off the mark. Hemingway's own handyman Toby Bruce said he could be as mean as "a striped-ass ape," and the photographer Robert Capa said, "Papa can be more severe than God on a rough day when the whole human race is misbehaving."

In the last decade of his life he was a cultural presence envied and admired, but illness, accidents, emotional upheavals, and alcoholism stalked him through these years. During this time he was more famous for his African safaris, plane crashes, and concussions than he was for his writing. The less he wrote the more competitive he became about his own work. Fighting and writing had always been linked in his mind. In a letter he wrote to Faulkner in 1947 he said, "You should always write your best against dead writers... and beat them one by one. Why do you want to fight Dostoyevsky in your first fight? Beat Turgenieff— which we both did soundly... then De Maupassant.... Then try to take Stendhal.... You and I both beat Flaubert who is our most respected, honored master." But toward his contemporaries, those he felt still offered him ongoing competition, Hemingway was virulent, nearly pathological in his attacks. At one time or another he denounced most of them—Fitzgerald, Dos Passos, Faulkner, Wolfe, Lewis. His repulsively negative response to James Jones's *From Here to Eternity*, the great World War II novel that Hemingway hadn't been able to create, makes the point. In a letter to Scribners, he says: "Probably I should re-read it again to give you a truer answer. But I do not have to eat an entire bowl of scabs to know they are scabs; nor suck a boil to know it is a boil; nor swim through a river of snot to know it is snot. I hope he kills himself as soon as it does not damage his or your sales. If you give him a literary tea you might ask him to drain a bucket of snot and then suck the pus out of a dead nigger's ear."

Naturally, many of Hemingway's contemporaries struck back. Wyndham Lewis in *Men Without Art* wrote: "Hemingway invariably invokes a dull-witted, bovine, monosyllabic simpleton, a lethargic and stuttering dummy... a super-innocent, queerly-sensitive village-idiot of a few words and fewer ideas." Others, like Max Eastman, accused him of having "a literary style, you might say, of wearing false hair on the chest." Not even his parents appreciated his work. In 1924, the copies of *In Our Time* he had sent to his family were returned to him without explanation. In 1926, after the publication of *The Sun Also Rises*, his mother wrote to him in Europe: "What is the matter? Have you ceased to be interested in loyalty, nobility, honor and fineness in life...surely you have other words in your vocabulary besides 'damn' and 'bitch'—Every page fills me with a sick loathing—if I should pick up a book by any other writer with such words in it, I should read no more—but pitch it in the fire." Perhaps Hemingway felt he had a reason to be defensive.

His literary reputation after World War II began to deteriorate, but in 1952 he staged a comeback with *The Old Man and the Sea*, which one critic called a "*Moby Dick* for the masses." Aside from this slim volume, however, he was most famous in his later years for his African safaris, his deep-sea fishing excursions, and his hunting expeditions in the American West. In those years he was reported dead by the media more than once. The news media gave a great deal of space, for instance, to his second African plane crash in as many days. Jeffrey Meyers described Hemingway's injuries: "His skull was fractured, two discs of his spine were cracked, his right arm and shoulder were dislocated, his liver, right kidney and spleen were ruptured, his sphincter muscle was paralyzed by compressed vertebrae on the iliac nerve, his arms, face and head were burned by flames of the plane." If he weren't dead, as the *New York Daily Mirror* announced, he had come precariously close.

The discrepancy between his image as a twentieth-century Byron and the sad facts of his life became clear toward the end. He became paranoid, fearing everyone from his wife to the FBI. He became desperately afraid of security leaks. He wouldn't talk in front of his servants and was afraid to go out of the house. In the Mayo Clinic in 1960 he received twelve electro-shock treatments, which probably made his mental illness even worse. Sadly, the man who had tested his courage constantly in sport and war now shrunk from flickering shadows. On July 2, 1961, nineteen days short of his sixty-second birthday and six days short of the forty-third anniversary of his wounding in Italy, he put a twelve-gauge

Boss shotgun he had bought in Abercrombie and Fitch into his mouth and pulled the trigger.

In "The Idea of Order at Key West" Wallace Stevens wrote of "The maker's rage to order words of the sea . . . and of ourselves and of our origins,/In ghostlier demarcations, keener sounds." The same rage to explain and understand is still with us, but Hemingway remains a fascinating, troubling enigma. He is part hero, strong and brave and true. He is consummate artist, passionate, meticulous, and immersed in his work. He is part mythomaniac, part bully, part drunkard, part sad and insecure man. But there is something brash, expansive, self-promoting, and finally American about him. His work was always much more a popular and critical success in his own country than in any other. He left his imprint on America, and he left his mark clearly on Key West and on many who search for themselves and their origins, crossing the ghostly demarcations of legend and lore to come to the end of the road in America.

A number of writers have ended up in Key West for reasons similar to Hemingway's. For some of them it's like sliding into a far corner and placing your back against the wall. You make a stand where there's no place left to run. This afternoon the sunshine is as thick as melted butter, but I'm sitting in one of the few shady spots in Portside, a little bar off Mallory Square. Sitting across from me at an outdoor table is a distinguished man in his early fifties. He has a neatly trimmed gray beard that stays decorously away from the button-down collar of his pin-striped shirt. His tan pants look as if they were dry-cleaned just before he sat down. The Cross pen in his shirt pocket shines like a war medal. His name is Jack London. In college he roomed with Scott Fitzgerald. But I'm sitting directly across from coincidence, not a ghost.

Among other things, though, this Jack London is a writer. A few years ago Harper and Row published *Greater Nowheres: A Journey Through the Australian Bush*, a book he co-authored with Dave Finklestein. How he ended up living in Key West (he actually lives now in Summerland Key, which is twenty-five miles north) and how he came to write a travel book are parts of a long story, but he gives me the abridged version. He grew up in an Italian neighborhood in Boston and was a child of the sixties. Actually he was probably more influenced by the fifties, by Jack Kerouac and the image of Dean Moriarty. When he was in college he took a tip from a journalism professor, invested in some stocks, made a few thousand dollars and drove all over the country. When he returned, he opened up a business with a "pal from Harvard Business School"—a restaurant with high prices, a French chef, and lousy food. His partner (he says "paht nuh") took care of the money end, and they did so well that the bartenders got rich stealing everything they had. He sold his share of the place.

He got divorced, got in his car, and ended up in Key West. He started writing articles for *Nautical Quarterly* and *Sports Afield*. He also started "rescuing old houses." He became one of the new breed of wreckers in Key West, finding the wrecks—on land—and fixing them up, eventually selling them for huge profits. It was more lucrative than finding Spanish treasure. Eventually, like Hemingway, he found a dual residence. A home in Ireland and another in Key West. Then he grew out of Key West. "This is a completely phony town," he tells me. "I finally realized that. Beneath the veneer there's nothing but impermanence. Drifters, malcontents, people who are escaping things end up here, believing they can start over. This is a place where fantasies are lived out." He lived out his fantasies in the Keys, and then he met up with Dave Finklestein, his co-author.

As he is telling me his story the bar manager comes up and gives us two beers "on the house." Jack and he exchange a few words, and London turns to me, "They know me in this town. I'm the Hemingway around here now." Of course, my suspicion is that he's being honored, as Hemingway often was perhaps, for something other than his writing skills. But I have another suspicion that he may think he really *is* Hemingway, or at least as grand a figure.

He gets animated as he begins to talk about his relationship with Dave Finklestein and the nature of writing. "Dave knew— *knows*—how to work the system," London tells me. "He belongs to a group called 'Outdoor Writers of America,' a self-admiration society. They're a bunch of hacks and whores. That's what Dave really knew how to do—how to sell himself and get paid for it. He discovered how to get free airline tickets. He was a master at groveling, but he'd get to fly to exotic locales and stay in fancy hotels with his girlfriend. When he got there—Tahiti or Switzerland—he'd spend a few hours listening to these hotel managers' stories. Like a prostitute faking orgasm. Dave always had a fancy card, placing him as contributing editor of some impressive-sounding but really inconsequential publication."

London doesn't say too much about the fact that he got free airline tickets and accommodations during his year-long jaunt through Australia, but he does say quite a bit about the reason for his break with Finklestein. It was a simple case of robbery, as London tells it. Finklestein asked him to join the Outdoor Writers of America, but when London refused, Finklestein entered a story they had written in a contest the group sponsored. It won the $1,000 first prize, but when London asked for his half, Finklestein said that since London wasn't a member, he didn't get any money.

I can't get past the feeling that these are two pros arguing over a trick, but London genuinely feels some righteous outrage. The whole business has soured his taste for ever collaborating again. "It's like two men trying to make love to the same woman at the same time," he says. For that matter, he seems to have a sour taste about writing in general. "You have to make an investment in a book. Maybe three years. And what do you get out of it at the end? I can make an awful lot of money in a year. Why spend it writing?" This is not a scion of Hemingway I'm speaking with—an investment banker maybe, but not Hemingway.

Before I leave he wants to make sure that I know there is a marked difference between his sections of *Greater Nowheres* and Finklestein's: "All you have to do is read a few chapters. He's a reporter, straight facts. I'm a writer. I'm more interested in narrative, in storytelling. You have to invent characters and situations to write a good travel book. You have to capture a character with a few key phrases. Get the essence of the personality and the situation."

As I sit here with him, listening and jotting down notes, I wonder if I'm supposed to be inventing a character. Is he suggesting, after all, that I *invent* him? He continues to talk, but my thoughts have turned to the recent controversy over Janet Malcolm's *New Yorker* article "The Journalist and the Murderer." With the first two sentences of her essay she caught most writers' attention: "Every journalist who is not too stupid or too full of himself to notice what is going on knows that what he does is morally indefensible. He is a kind of confidence man, preying on people's vanity, ignorance, or loneliness, gaining their trust and betraying them without remorse." There is a pattern in the journalistic encounter, Malcolm suggests, of deception, betrayal, and revelation. The whole process, she says, is one of seduction. Many non-fiction writers responded defensively, often furiously, to what they considered an overgeneralization, or at least a misinterpretation of an honorable encounter. Although Malcolm's description of what really occurs between journalist and subject shocked many people, Joan Didion had said much the same thing more than a decade ago: "Writers are always selling somebody out." Didion was warning her subjects that, as she said, her presence ran counter to their best interests. What both Didion and Malcolm wrote makes sense to me in that every non-fiction writer has to get at the truth through the screen of his own perceptions. Although fiction only has to *seem* true and journalism has to *be* true, the line between "seem" and "be" is often hard to see. But journalists should be honor-bound to open their eyes at least, to quote honestly, to witness as accurately as they can what happened, and not to invent people or their words. If the subject has to be betrayed, it should be because of the writer's compulsion to respect his version of truth, to depict the world as he truly perceives it, and not because he's writing fiction in the guise of journalism.

I'm brought back to the present when London asks, "Why does it take two conchs to eat a raccoon?"

"Um, I don't know." I'm not sure if this is a joke or a trick question. Do they eat raccoons?

"It takes one to eat it and one to watch the road."

I smile, wonder for a minute if my ethical daydream had been too critical of Jack London, and then realize that perhaps it had not been critical enough. But how confusing it must be to be a travel writer with the burden of such a name. Could Leo Tolstoy write crime reports for the *Washington Post*?

† † †

I'm still wondering about Jack London and the new Key West as I walk down Greene Street past the Historic Key West Shipwreck Museum, a beautiful two-story brick building, the museum on the first floor and meeting rooms for the city council on the second. The museum has just opened, and Ray Maloney, the thirty-seven-year-old founder and director, stands alone near the entrance, sunglasses resting atop his head, on his thinning sandy hair. Every few seconds his calloused fingers touch a scant moustache, and his small eyes scan the street for customers. I'm the first one of the day.

Ray is a seventh-generation conch, a man who unintentionally returned to the profession of his ancestors and the original settlers of Key West. Ray is a wrecker, a treasure hunter, but it was only after he became one that he found out that he was diving for the same treasure that his direct ancestors dived for. It all began with his father's shrimp farm.

His father, Raymond, Sr., had a shrimp farm back in the early 1970s on Marathon Key, a little north of Key West. Raising shrimp is a bit like raising catfish, and he tried to mass-produce them. He would take the egg-bearing females from shrimp trawlers, feed them algae and trout pellets, and get them through the larval stage in nine days. He studied what they did in Ecuador and other countries and followed their example. The problem was that land prices were too high and it never became cost-effective to get an acre body of water. Eventually he closed down the project, but not before something happened that changed the course of his son's life. Ray, Jr., was working the farm one day when he was about eighteen years old. A few motorcyclists came by, kicking up dirt and rocks. And some gold coins, as well. Obviously, some eighteenth- or nineteenth-century pirate had intended to get back to where he had buried some treasure but hadn't gotten the chance. It started a mini-gold rush around the shrimp farm. Not much beyond those first few gold coins was ever found, but it started young Ray's treasure hunting.

"You can't be in it for the money, though," Ray tells me as he takes me through his museum. "You have to love adventure and love history." Ray never loved history in school, never loved school for that matter, but he always loved exploring. The research he did to help him with his own searches became the kind of history that made sense to him, the kind of history that he could see and touch, actually pick up in his workingman's hands. He started out by picking a likely spot and working it with a metal detector. Within a few years he began to dive. Several islands had deep channels, and he found some "relics." Spurred on by small successes, he started to look for shipwrecks. He became a real historian, searching the maritime records and library accounts. By the time he began a new search he would know the whole story of the wreck.

With his brother Steve, he built a forty-two-foot fiberglass cabin-cruiser. It took them two and a half years, and as soon as they finished it they began "prospecting." In August 1985 Ray made his great discovery. He found the *Isaac Allerton*, a packet ship named after one of the Mayflower pilgrims, a boat built in 1836 and last seen in 1857, the year it sank off the coast of Key West. In May of 1986 he began working on the wreck and found out from his researches that his relatives had salvaged parts of the same vessel nearly 150 years before. They had gotten about half of the ship salvaged, but some of it was simply too deep for them. Over the years the *Isaac Allerton* had been forgotten like so many other wrecks along the coral reef outside Key West.

The ship was in thirty feet of water. The upper decks, which his ancestors had salvaged, were at about ten feet. It had taken 150 years, some coincidence, and a magnetometer for Ray to continue the job. A magnetometer, an instrument that costs about $15,000, reads the earth's magnetic field. Iron distorts the magnetic field in an area, and a magnetometer reads the variation and points it out on a graph. The small console, containing jet fuel, sensors, and spinning protons, is towed from a boat at the end of a two-hundred-foot cable. Wreckers like Ray call it a "fish."

With the help of his fish, Ray reeled in quite a bit of treasure, which he preserves in the museum he designed in a building he renovated. The *Isaac Allerton*, a packet ship that sailed from New York to New Orleans bringing goods to Western travellers, had a wealth of treasures, if little gold or silver. Ray recovered brass candlesticks, ivory toothbrushes, china, coffee grinders, bottles of champagne, and the bones of livestock. There were adjustable, wraparound Ben Franklin sunglasses, telescopes, clay pipes, and some of the first plastic buttons ever made. He found bottles of

Mexican Mustang Liniment, which supposedly cured everything from leprosy to dizziness. He recovered pieces of Massachusetts marble that were on their way to the customs house in New Orleans. He even brought up some silk gloves that were intended for can-can dancers in the French Quarter.

Ray sees himself as a preserver, not a profiteer. He has to pay the historical society $55,000 a year to rent the building for his museum. He's not gotten rich, like Mel Fisher with his famous discoveries of Spanish gold and silver, but he feels that he's preserved some valuable Key West history, a past that is disappearing before his eyes. The Law of Salvage and Finds gave all parties with legitimate claims the opportunity to contest a find, but in 1987 Congress passed the Abandoned Shipwreck Bill, which gave the government rights up to three miles out, and there have been propositions to impose a two-hundred-mile restriction. That would virtually do away with salvaging in the area. "Hopefully I'm going to get out and find some more wrecks before the government makes it a felony," Ray says. "I guess they want us all to sit home and watch television and play video games all day long. There's no more sense of adventure in this world, but there's a lot of stuff out there in the water. They're still wrecking—a dive boat went out the other day and sunk in seventy feet of water. They can't find it, and it's just one of thousands of boats out there. It's all a time capsule waiting for someone to open it up."

The whole idea of Key West has changed for Ray Maloney. He remembers that in 1970 his brother had a brand new Plymouth Roadrunner that he would drag race down Duval Street. By the time he would pass Sloppy Joe's he would be doing one hundred miles per hour. "Can you believe that?" he asks me. "You can't go over fifteen miles an hour with all the traffic now." Not long ago the Key West Ray remembers was a sleepy little town which erupted every now and again with a sailor's brawl. But in 1973 the naval base closed down, and all the ships were pulled out. For Ray, Key West had always been a small town, where everyone knew everyone else, but it was never Main Street America because it was a seaport and "a seaport has all kinds." As he tells me, "A lot of small towns don't accept outsiders. Key West has never been that way. It's always had a port atmosphere. It's a place for migratory birds."

After all this talk about Key West's past, Ray thinks it would be a good idea for me to visit his mother and father and grandmother in their home on Whalton Street out toward the ocean side of the island. Their house is a modest ranch but property values have gone up so much they could never afford to buy it at current prices. Raymond, Sr., Ray's sixty-three-year-old father, greets me at the door. His grandmother, Hazel Kiefer, is sitting in the living room. Eighty-eight years old, Hazel can well remember when Flagler came in on the first train to Key West. She was in convent school on the island and stood in the specially made bleachers in her white uniform and waved an American flag. That was another time, and for Hazel and Raymond that was another Key West. The Maloneys are true conchs, their families deriving from both America and the Bahamas. Raymond remembers the other Key West vividly. He knew Bra Saunders and hung around with Joe Russell, Jr., the son of Hemingway's fishing and drinking companion, Sloppy Joe. "Joe Grunts is what we called him," Raymond remembers. "I'm not sure why. But we all had nicknames, and that was his. I remember Hemingway giving boxing lessons to the kids on the island. I remember knowing every face I saw when I went out. This used to be the friendliest place in the world. We were isolated, and maybe we had to be friendly, but now I can go out for a whole day and never see a person I know. How can that be?"

Raymond's wife comes in to join the conversation, and the talk stays in the past, circling around and around two topics—what once was and young Ray's museum. They get indignant when the conversation turns to the tourist trade. "Mallory Square is not a Key West tradition," Mrs. Maloney says. "My son's museum is tradition. The people who do juggling acts down there don't pay a cent, but my son pays plenty to keep Key West history alive. Captain Tony defends those hippies, but who'll defend the old Key West?" Mr. Maloney chimes in, "The old conchs are either dead or gone. All the good people have gone somewhere else. When the newspapers say that the new mayor Captain Tony *is* Key West it puts hell in me. How long has he been here? He's not Key West."

From tourists and politics, it seems natural somehow that the conversation turns to hurricanes, another destructive force on the island. And the Maloneys seem to love to talk about hurricanes. One mentions the time there were two hurricanes in one week. Raymond scoffs at any danger, saying, "Being on Key West in a hurricane is like being on a ship four miles long and two miles wide." His wife adds proudly, "This house will take two-hundred-mile-per-hour winds." Hazel recalls a house she lived in on the island when she was a young girl. The house was on piles, and when the storm came her father got everyone out of the house and cut holes in the floors so that the house wouldn't float away. "Those times was different," Raymond cuts in. "Some of those wreckers weren't afraid of anything. They'd go out in a fifty-foot schooner in a full hurricane. They don't make men like that anymore." The three of them get dreamy-eyed then excited when they talk about the storms, the rain coming with such force it seemed to cut to the bone. The way they see things, Key West can handle a hurricane better than any of the other islands in the chain off of Miami. All the other Keys have roads and bridges connecting and acting like dams, leaving the water no place to go but over them. Key West, with its open southern end, allows the water to flow naturally around it. Suddenly the sky grows a bit dark and the wind changes from a whisper to a howl. As the voice of the wind becomes another part of our conversation I remember Zora Neale Hurston's description of the 1935 hurricane in her masterpiece *Their Eyes Were Watching God*:

> Through the screaming wind they heard things crashing and things hurtling and dashing with unbelievable velocity. A baby rabbit, terror ridden, squirmed through a hole in the floor and squatted off there in the shadows against the wall, seeming to know that nobody wanted its flesh at such a time. And the lake got madder and madder with only its dikes between them and him. . . . The wind came back with triple fury, and put out the light for the last time. They sat in company with the others in other shanties, their eyes straining against crude walls and their souls asking if He meant to measure their puny might against His. They seemed to be staring at the dark, but their eyes were watching God.

The Maloneys have the same sort of eyes, only after the storm, years and years after the wind, the sort of eyes that wait and watch.

"Nothing can kill this place," says Raymond, "not even the DDT they sprayed twenty years ago to do away with the insects on the island. It wound up killing the birds and a lot of other things, but we're still here."

"I saw a butterfly the other day," says Mrs. Maloney.

"I saw a lizard last week," Mrs. Kiefer adds.

DDT has a half-life of fifty years or more, but they don't seem very concerned, as if it were just another one of those changes conchs in Key West would have to accept. Like many historians, perhaps, they are fatalists. Like many who are fascinated by the past, they realize that beauty and horror often are part of the same story.

Florida's history and the story of Key West are a mixture of romance and violence. Elizabeth Bishop called it "The state with the prettiest name,/the one state that floats in brackish water." It is, as its name implies, a land of flowers and tropical beauty but its roots are soaked in blood.

Sebastian Cabot may have discovered Florida and the northernmost Keys in 1498, and Columbus may even have seen the southernmost Keys in 1492, but generally Juan Ponce de León is credited with discovering Florida and its coral islands in 1513. He named the Keys "Los Martires," The Martyrs, because they looked to him like men suffering, and he named Key West "Caya Hueso," Bone Island, because of the scattered bones on the island, probably from an Indian battle. The Keys were heavily forested, and in the dense tangle of jungle in the interior were bear, panther, and deer. The Spaniards who first saw the islands reported that the Indians along the beaches were seven feet tall—ancestors of these sailors could well be working as tour guides today at the Hemingway House in Key West.

In 1513 Ponce de León was a robust adventurer of fifty who was eager to promote and strengthen his own image. He received a royal patent to explore and colonize "Bimini," the Indian word for the land northwest of the Bahamas. Ponce de León, who had been a companion of Columbus on his second voyage, had listened to the Indians' stories about gold and the fountain of youth. But Ponce de León was a practical man, a soldier and entrepreneur, not all that much unlike many who drifted into Key West in the 1960s and 1970s, and he was seeking gold, not the chimera of perpetual youth. He was no dreamy-eyed romantic but a hardened and often vicious military man. Like other conquistadors, he fought ruthlessly. For example, he used greyhounds trained to tear their quarry, usually American Indians, to pieces. When he was attacked by Indians, he fought back strenuously, often viciously. In the land of the Acuera Indians he cut off the noses of fifty Indians and then killed them. An object lesson worthy of a David Lynch film.

According to Gloria Jahoda in her book on Florida, "The history of white—and thus, ultimately, of black—America began in Florida, and it began in blood." The Spaniards explored and colonized on the Florida mainland and into the *cayos*, the Spanish word for small islands that was later Anglicized into "Keys." When de Soto came ashore in the mid-sixteenth century, he came with a full complement of priests and chalices, but he came with muskets and powder as well. A bishop in Mexico wrote to Philip of Spain that de Soto tormented and killed the Indians, pushing them like animals. "When one became tired or fainted," the bishop wrote, "they cut off his head at the neck, in order not to free those in front from the chain that bound them, and the body fell to one side and the head to the other." According to some eyewitnesses, de Soto had his men cut the lips and nostrils off some Indians, sending them back to their tribes as mutilated and bloody examples of the power of Christianity.

After the French and Indian War in 1763, Florida became a British possession. By the time the British got there most of the native tribes, the Tunucuas and the Calusas, were gone, victims of syphilis, diphtheria, and the violence of the white man. A new group of Indians, attempting to escape British expansion in the northern territories, came south. They were actually Creek Indians, whom their tribesmen called "wanderers," or Seminoles. Seminoles intermarried with runaway slaves. Olive-skinned Spaniards mixed with blue-eyed Britishers, and by the late eighteenth century Florida was becoming a melting pot.

With the end of the American Revolution came the end of

British Florida. In 1783 it was ceded back to Spain. Fifteen thousand English moved to the West Indies, leaving most of the plantations to Indians, robbers, and the fast-growing tropical jungle. A combination of Andrew Jackson's vicious military expeditions into Florida after Indians and an offer of $5 million from President Monroe convinced Spain to part with its colony. During 1835–42 the United States engaged in the ruinous Seminole Wars, costing the government the lives of 1,500 soldiers, countless and uncounted Indians, and more than $40 million in expenditures and property damage.

Florida was admitted to statehood in 1845 with a constitution that gave the vote to white males over twenty-one. The great cotton and sugar cane plantations required cheap labor, and slavery was a simple fact of life. Blacks were treated typically. Even in Key West in 1840 the seventy-six free blacks and ninety-six slaves were forbidden to appear on the streets after sundown without written permission, either from the mayor for free blacks or from the masters for slaves. Violators were whipped or forced to work on the streets.

In his 1912 history of Key West, Jefferson Browne talks about the black population of the island. His view of slavery seems similar to Thomas Nelson Page's nostalgic view of the good old plantation days. Browne writes: "The general prosperity had something to do with it also, as well-to-do Southern families could not manage with less than six to ten household servants. And such servants! Capable, respectful, neat, trustworthy, affectionate, and honest where money was concerned; is it cause for marvel that family servants were held in the most affectionate regard? And woe betide the outsider who interfered with one of them! The institution of slavery took savages from Africa, and made them a most docile, capable, respectful, honest and religious people. The contrast between what this institution produced, and what the period since 1865 has brought forth, is a study for the ethnologist." Not very subtly hidden between exclamation points and Victorian rhetoric lurks a racist mentality worthy of a Vardaman.

From Reconstruction on, however, Key West always seemed different from Florida and the rest of the South. The Federal Writers Project Guide of the 1930s argues that the isolation and proximity to the West Indies gave Key West its "characteristics of friendliness and leisure, and tempered it with the Latin approach to life; the inhabitants are congenial and curious, ready with smile and conversation in a community where it is normal for everyone to know everyone else." From the beginning in Key West there was a relaxed atmosphere—even, it seems, about who owned it. In 1815 the Spanish governor gave title to the island to Lieutenant Juan Salas for his services to the crown. But Salas was more interested in women, gambling, and drinking, and he headed for Cuba. Salas was a good businessman, so good in fact that he was able to sell the island twice, first for a $600 sloop that he used to travel back and forth between Cuba and Florida, and second to John Simonton, a New Jersey trader, for $2,000. Before Simonton got a look at his new property, the previous owner of the sloop sold the island to a third man, General John Geddes, former governor of South Carolina. Simonton also sold shares in the island. Although Geddes probably had better claim to the island, Simonton had more powerful friends in Washington, and in 1822 he was awarded clear title to the island. One of the main avenues in Key West is Simonton Street. Neither Salas nor Geddes is remembered.

In the same year the United States sent a fleet of ships to rout the pirates in the Keys. Soon after, families from New England, Virginia, and South Carolina came down to work as salvagers. Many British returned, as well, from the Bahamas. Wrecking became big business or at least *the* business. Some said ships were lured to destruction by fake flares and beacons. Whether caused by fate or human manipulation, during years of severe storms salvage receipts often reached $1.5 million. The population grew until it reached 22,000 by the early twentieth century when Henry Flagler's railroad connected the keys to the mainland.

In the sixteenth century conquistadors came looking for gold. In the twentieth century retirees came looking for sun. But the adventurers may not be all that different. As John McPhee describes the nineteenth-century pilgrims in *Oranges*: "Florida was the only wilderness that attracted middle-aged pioneers. The young ones were already on their way west toward California. ...Florida, even then, appealed to aging doctors, retired brokers, and consumptives."

The new Florida, particularly Key West, may appeal to an even wilder breed. The new Key West may be embodied by Tony Tarracino, known locally as Captain Tony, the former owner of Captain Tony's Saloon, the site of the original Sloppy Joe's Bar. Tarracino is also the controversial new mayor of Key West.

Despite how the Maloneys feel about Captain Tony, when I sit down with him on a bench outside the bar that he no longer owns (but that still bears his name), I feel as if I am talking to the ghost of Key West past as much as I am conversing with its present. It seems more than a coincidence that a few minutes before as I strolled down Duval Street and passed Kennedy's Gallery, I noticed that the front window displayed a photograph of Hemingway alongside a drawing of Captain Tony. Two Key West icons, side by side and only a few doors down from Jimmy Buffett's Margaritaville.

Tony Tarracino symbolizes Key West, old and new. He is both raunchy individualist and tireless media manipulator. He's a crusader for the voiceless and a loud self-promoter. The bar we sit in front of was once his; it's still a monument to his fame in Key West. Now, late in the afternoon, it is filled with couples from Ohio and Indiana in plaid shorts snapping photos of one another. When Tarracino owned it, the place was rougher, closer to what it was like when Hemingway sat on a stool, exchanging stories with Sloppy Joe. In *To Have and Have Not* Hemingway described it as Freddy's place: "Men in dungarees, some bareheaded, others in caps, old service hats in cardboard helmets, crowded the bar three deep, and the loud-speaking nickel-in-the-slot phonograph was playing 'Isle of Capri.' As they pulled up a man came hurtling out of the open door, another man on top, holding the other's hair in both hands, banged his head up and down on the cement, making a sickening noise. No one at the bar was paying any attention."

Now, of course, everyone "pays attention," tourists desperately seeking some local color. They watch each other, like spectators at a bullfight secretly waiting for a goring, hoping for a brawl or at least a drunken sailor.

Tarracino is what they get, but they don't seem disappointed. When he enters the room, it's like Buffalo Bill's coming to town with his Wild West Show. Tarracino, like Buffalo Bill, had the adventures and now has become a showman. The seventy-three-year-old Tarracino, recently elected mayor after running about half a dozen times before, was born in Elizabeth, New Jersey. As he tells the story, his father was a bootlegger and his mother's family were puppeteers. He grew up in an Italian ghetto and has always considered himself a peasant and a hustler. He was too small to fight in his tough neighborhood, so he learned to talk fast instead. But his background was not one filled exclusively with violence and fear. "I was in love with my eighth grade teacher," he once said. "She told me I should drop out of school because there was nothing for me there. 'You belong to the world,' she said. 'Go see it.' Whenever I think of her it's like smoking a joint." He left school and gambled to pay the bills. Eventually he took a number of odd jobs to support his first wife and their children. Gambling raised his standard of living, he says, making it difficult to be satisfied with ordinary employment and wages.

In 1948, after a horse-betting scam went sour, and as he put it, "I got the shit beat out of me by a couple of boys," he pulled himself out of a dumpster at the Newark Airport and drove to Miami with a blonde in a pink Cadillac. He ended up at Hialeah Park, lost all his money, and hopped a milk truck to Key West. When he arrived on the island it was like a frontier town—"strip joints, gin mills, hookers everywhere, beds above bars, crap tables." He entered the town at four in the morning, and ironically the first place he stopped was the bar he was eventually to buy—the original Sloppy Joe's on Greene Street.

He got a job cutting the heads off shrimp. Then he worked on a shrimp boat, and after a few years he bought his own thirty-six-foot charter boat, the *Greyhound*. In the late 1950s he got involved with mercenaries and was put on trial in Miami. He wasn't convicted, and he returned to Key West and began running guns to Cuba to help the Castro revolution. After Castro gained power, Tarracino used the same boat to help refugees escape the island.

In 1963 he bought the original Sloppy Joe's from Morgan Bird, who had run it as a gay bar. Because the navy had put Bird's bar off limits he wasn't making any money. Tony was able to buy it for $35,000. Immediately, he changed the name to Captain Tony's and broadened the clientele. In the sixties young drifters moved in and his place became a hangout for the likes of Jimmy Buffett and Jerry

Jeff Walker. "At night I became king of the hippies," he says to me and smiles, the bags under his eyes ballooning out with the memory. "I'd let the kids sleep on the tables. In the morning I'd bring in ten pounds of bologna. The respectable people tried to kick me out of town. There just weren't enough respectable people, I guess. Pritim Singh, the man who recently bought the Truman Annex in Key West for $17 million and is building a beautiful new housing complex here, was one of the hippies back then. I suppose he learned how to make money somewhere along the line."

I can imagine the bar back then, and it seems as if Jerry Jeff Walker's songs would have fit the atmosphere exactly. I can hear "London Homesick Blues" shaking the juke box— "When you're down on your luck and you ain't got a buck ..."—and the rising pitch of Jerry Jeff Walker's and Gary P. Nunn's twangs shattering the night. But right now a milky sun pours out of the late afternoon sky and no music comes from the bar, just murmurs of conversation. Captain Tony looks like an artist on a Paris side street; his white hair is thick, combed to the side, somewhere between unruly and styled. His goatee is also white. His expression and manner are animated. Everything about him seems to shout: "I'll tire you out with my energy." Only the craggy face, the sagging bags under his eyes, and the hearing aid give away his true age. He's a man, after all, with a fifty-three-year-old son, a son he invites over each week to play with his four-year-old brother. His present wife, Marty, is forty-one. He's been married three times and has, he tells me, thirteen children by five women.

As we sit in front of the bar and I listen to his story, he performs for all the passersby. And for me, as well. Language is part of the show. "Fuck" and "shit" are stanchions of his rhetoric. "I know what writers say when they come down here," he says as he waves to someone walking across the street. "'I've got to get back with the fucking story. I'll go down and see that old fucker Captain Tony. He's always good for a few tales.' And I am." A few college students walk by and the mayor waves to them, saying, "If you go to jail, call me." Another group of college students goes by and Tony yells, "Keep out of jail, fellas. Big cockroaches. We've got *very* big cockroaches down here."

He turns back to me and says, "We have a few people here that think we're going to turn this island into another Naples or a Palm Beach. They're down on the college kids. They forget they had sex in rumble seats. I have faith in kids, and I do things my way. I don't give a shit what other people think. As long as I like the guy in the mirror, that's all that counts. You can't fool him."

But it's clear to me and most of the people who pass by that this is a gentle spirit, not an angry revolutionary. If Gimple the Fool had a PR man, he might have awakened, a la Kafka, as Tony Tarracino. Steinbeck once said that Hemingway was an incredibly vain man, and some might take the same view of Tony Tarracino, but despite his self-portrait as a wild man, gun runner, gambler, lover, he has an old-fashioned sweetness about him, something of the old neighborhood, an Italian generosity and warmheartedness. His watery gulf-blue eyes grow even more gentle when he speaks to children. For his own kids he says he lived by one rule: "Give a lot of love. I hung in there with my kids no matter what. If you show affection, that's the key. Give your wife a kiss, a pat on the ass. Show love. And show compassion. Growing up in the Depression I was born with it. Compassion comes from fucking up. The more you've fucked up, the better you can understand and sympathize with others."

Another group of college students, this one from Notre Dame, stops in front of us and Tony says to them, "You mean to tell me you're twenty-two and you're *still* going to school? How dumb can you guys be?" His hands move in the air, like a Michelangelo from Newark sculpting invisible images. He looks at me and says, "Key West is a town with the biggest heart in the world."

For the next hour I have a center-stage seat for a great street theater. Sometimes he performs just for me, telling me about his five-pack-a-day cigarette habit: "Three doctors told me to quit. Now they're all dead." He smokes five or six cigarettes while we talk.

A few elderly women pass by: "Have a great day, *girls!*" He winks at them and whispers to me, "They love it."

A middle-aged man comes up, shakes the mayor's hand and says, "You're doing a great job." Tony replies, "I'll make you chief of police." He pauses for a beat. "You'll be the first one to get shot." Ah, vaudeville.

As I'm about to leave, he dashes off to get another match from his new Astro van (I expected a Chevy with fish tails) and comes back with a poster which he autographs for my teenage son. The poster has a black-and-white drawing of Captain Tony with one of his pithy quotations: "All you need in life is a tremendous sex drive and a great ego. Brains don't mean a shit." He tells me to remind my son that people from New Jersey have distinctive accents. Then he writes, "To Shane, Read and Loin."

But as he walks me down the street it's not jokes he has in mind. He talks about the AIDS crisis in Key West, a community with a large gay population. He also talks about the fact that the island has one of the highest multiple sclerosis rates in the world. No one knows why and no one in the area wants to publicize the news. His eyes grow narrow and his voice loses its barker's edge. For a moment he doesn't seem to know what to say, as if he's Harry Morgan in *To Have and Have Not*: "'A man,' said Morgan, very slowly, 'Ain't got no hasn't got any can't really isn't any way out...No matter how a man alone ain't got no bloody fucking chance.'"

The next day as I drive back on U.S. 1, I pass a road sign that says this highway ends in Fort Kent, Maine. It's hard to imagine this strip of tar reaching like a dark vein to the wintry ground in Maine, for all I see is the sun beating on marshlands and dwarf palms. Key West is the only place in the continental United States that has not experienced a frost. Fort Kent probably has frosts on cool August mornings. Passing through this tropical heat and seeing only faded paint and a scruffy Caribbean atmosphere, I find it hard to imagine any community where men don't have long hair and earrings or women don't have deep brown skin and cool blue eyes. Like Wallace Stevens, I see Key West as "the summer without end."

In a few hours the crowds on Duval Street will migrate like lemmings toward Mallory Dock to watch the sun set. They'll drift out of the Sunglass Emporium and Shell Jewelers and the Hog Breath Saloon, and gather on the dock to watch a man who balances shopping carts on his teeth and another who trains cats to perform like lions. There will be jugglers, comedians, lonely palm readers, pretzel vendors, lemonade stands, escape artists, and enough VCR cameras to make you wish you had stock in Curtis Mathes.

In a few miles the tourists on Mallory Dock seem far away, a surreal image disappearing against the changing landscape. The inlets on the ocean side are like scattered jewels glistening in the sunlight. The water on the gulf side shimmers shades of green. Dos Passos described the crossing of the keys as "dream-like," and it still is despite the KOAs and supermarkets. Sailboats drift by at a leisurely pace, looking like clouds in a blue-green sky. Pelicans stand sentinel on the bridge railings. Tall marsh grass and sea oats bend in the breeze.

I skirt the Everglades on my way back to Miami. The oyster-shaped island of Key West is 100 miles southwest. Now the road drifts through miles of farmland, trailer parks, past rusting pickup trucks and migrant farm workers. Even with the air-conditioning on, the heat penetrates the car. Hundreds of black migrant workers picking beans move in slow motion in a sun-bleached field. Older women in wide-brimmed hats and turbans bend alongside hatless men in the blistering sun.

I reach Miami about nine at night. With hours before my early morning flight I go to see *Revenge*, starring Kevin Costner and Anthony Quinn, because it was written by Jim Harrison, a Key West writer. Superficially, the movie is in the Hemingway vein, concerned with honor and filled with violence, but it's actually pretty silly and only slightly more interesting than roaming the mall, where it is playing. After the movie ends, I still have a few hours to wait before my plane departs and decide to take a nap in the rental car. About two in the morning my cramped sleep is broken by a thousand-watt light and a loud, "Get out of the car. Keep your hands above your head!" This is like a rerun of a bad episode of "Miami Vice," but once I shake the cobwebs I'm more embarrassed than terrified. My explanation— "plane, nap, etc." —seems more foolish than the plot of *Revenge* when I consider that I'm in a mall parking lot about three miles from the airport in the middle of the night. When the police officer tells me it's a high drug-traffic area, I say, "I've gotten enough sleep anyway. I think I'll be on my way." But being at the airport is even worse than being rousted as a suspected drug pusher. An airport between three and six in the morning could qualify for one of the lowest levels in Dante's hell. A few men and women vacuum the floors, drifting back and forth like zombies in a "B" horror movie. Some of the chairs are occupied by sleeping men, and a few of the less inhibited lie stretched out on the floor, heads resting on jackets or garment bags. It's lonelier and even less inviting than a Greyhound bus station, certainly one of the loneliest and least inviting locations on earth. Like malls, airports seem built around the word "dislocation." They belong to that species of non-place that makes all of us feel like strangers in a strange land.

By six-thirty I'm sitting on the plane listening to the roar of the engines and once again I'm reminded of something Steinbeck wrote about his travels: "The sound of a jet, an engine warming up, even the clopping of shod hooves on pavement brings on the ancient shudder, the dry mouth and vacant eye, the hot palms and the churn of stomach high up under the rib cage." Whether my dry mouth and dazed expression are from lack of sleep or wanderlust, in the engine's rising hum I hear Steinbeck's voice and see Salinas in the distance.

6

A Strip Angled against the Pacific: Steinbeck's California

Steinbeck's entire body of fiction . . . represents a singleminded attempt to come to grips with the idea of America.

Louis Owens,
John Steinbeck's Re-Vision of America

The truth about a country can be learned only from its common people.

Steinbeck,
in a conversation with Martin Bidwell

The Salinas Valley was the world.

Steinbeck, *East of Eden*

THAT STRIP OF CALIFORNIA running about thirty miles west to east from Monterey to Salinas and fifty miles south to King City, that curving union of ocean and cliff, mountain and valley, farm land and ranch, is Steinbeck's. It was his Yoknapatawpha, covering more area geographically but much the same territory in terms of the human heart. In *Tortilla Flat* and *Cannery Row* he immortalized Monterey, in *East of Eden* Salinas, in *Of Mice and Men* the Soledad area, and in *The Grapes of Wrath* all of California, the very dream of California itself. The valley and hills, the canneries and ranches, the farm workers and bindle stiffs came to represent all of America. As he wrote in *Travels With Charley*, after having taken his final look at his beloved valley from Fremont's Peak, "I remembered how once, in that part of youth that is deeply concerned with death, I wanted to be buried on this peak where without eyes I could see everything I knew and loved, for in those days there was no world beyond the mountains." In his best fiction he made his readers feel the same way, that the migrant camps in *The Grapes of Wrath* were the world or that the rolling hills of *The Red Pony* were a landscape that everyone should know well. The *paisanos* of *Tortilla Flat*, the bums of *Of Mice and Men*, or the Okies of *The Grapes of Wrath* may seem like exaggerations to some readers, but for many, Steinbeck is able to do what only great writers are capable of, in the words of Steven Millhauser, to make them feel that they are experiencing nothing less than the real world itself, a world that has been lost through habit or inattention or complacency.

Steinbeck's imagined country has not disappeared, despite the tourist traps in Carmel and Monterey, despite his deification in Salinas (a town that probably would have been more inclined to lynch him forty years ago), and despite the various economic and social changes the last quarter of a century has brought. The land is still very much Steinbeck's—one has only to look beyond the hotels and restaurants and fancy stores to find Tom Joad or Lenny and George.

When Steinbeck was a child growing up in Salinas, he thought of San Francisco as "the City." Later, when he was a young writer and others had become the lost generation in Paris, he was in San Francisco, as he said, climbing its hills, working on its docks, sleeping in its parks, and marching in its revolts. More than London or Paris or Rome and more than any other city in America, even New York where he spent many years, San Francisco was always his city. His last written description of it makes this clear: "San Francisco put on a show for me. . . . The afternoon sun painted her white and gold—rising on her hills like a noble city in a happy dream. . . . this gold and white acropolis rising wave on wave against the blue of the Pacific sky was a stunning thing, a painted thing like a picture of a medieval Italian city which can never have existed. . . . She leaves a mark."

I lived in Berkeley nearly twenty years ago and traveled across the Bay Bridge into San Francisco each day. I knew what Steinbeck meant: the city left its mark on me as well. In all my travels around America I have never found a more beautiful one.

In order to see out of the window near my seat on the plane, I have to crane my neck over a Chinese man who bears a remarkable resemblance to the old Chinaman in *Cannery Row*, whose face was "lean and brown and corded as jerky and his old eyes were brown even the whites were brown and deep set so that they looked out of holes." I take his presence next to me as an omen, although of what I'm not sure because he does not utter a word the whole flight and sleeps most of the time, even through dinner. The sky is a crystalline blue, and the earth below has lost the human density of the East Coast. The western landscape seems prehistoric, pock-marked and burnt-orange. I almost expect dinosaurs to rear their heads. It's a land of huge, lonely spaces, and for a moment I picture the pioneers, Okies, beatniks, and other wayfarers streaming in one long line across it. Like Kerouac in *On the Road*, I see "all that road going, all the people dreaming in the immensity of it." West seems the right direction to be heading. It always has in America. Down there somewhere is Route 66, what Steinbeck called "the mother road, the road of flight."

Beyond the bleak sand flats and the snow-capped Rockies, San Francisco appears suddenly, like an answer to any traveler's question. It is the reason for going. On my drive down to Salinas I have time only to glance at the city and agree with Steinbeck: it is a stunning thing.

Past Los Gatos, where Steinbeck lived for a number of years and where he wrote *The Grapes of Wrath*, the landscape begins to change. The mountain road rolls into the valley. Castroville appears out of nowhere, baked in the sun. The signs change to Spanish—"Welcome Amigos" and "Budweiser—Es Para Usted." Gnarled, wind-swept oaks are frozen into the high yellow grass and occasionally dot a landscape filled with fields of lettuce, broccoli, strawberries, and artichokes. Irrigation pipes, which appear to have been laid by some crazed geometrician, twist and glint in the sun.

As Steinbeck said, Salinas Valley is "a long narrow swale between two ranges of mountains." The town of Salinas stretches along the heart of the valley, between the sun-bleached Gabilans to the east and the lush Santa Lucias to the west. Steinbeck remembered the Gabilans as "light gay mountains full of sun and loveliness and a kind of invitation" and the Santa Lucias as "dark and brooding—unfriendly and dangerous." According to one of his critics, Louis Owens, this perception of Steinbeck's fits perfectly with the major theme of his books. Steinbeck, like F. Scott Fitzgerald, wrote about the failed America myth, about the dream gone sour. Even Steinbeck's greatest book, *The Grapes of Wrath*, according to Owens, is a journey away from a belief in the American dream, that the West holds all promise. Rather, that novel, like many of his others, suggests that a new dream must replace the old, that Americans must learn a new commitment to one another and the world they share. Steinbeck once wrote that he always had a dread of the West and a love of the East. Always, he ran counter to the crowd.

After checking into the National 9 Inn in Salinas, receiving from the manager my complimentary wine ticket for the East of Eden Restaurant, and dropping my bags in a room that smells as if it is liberally sprayed with Lysol each morning, I head off to meet Pauline Pearson, a fifty-year resident of Salinas, a former librarian, and the author of the guidebook to Steinbeck country. We're not related, but the possibility that there may be some relationship far in the past induces her, perhaps, to give one more tour. "This is my last tour," she says. "I'm retired now." I suspect that she loves this country and Steinbeck too much to retire from her search for new connections between his stories and the area, but I feel lucky to be on what may be the last for a while at least.

We meet, appropriately enough, outside the John Steinbeck Library in Salinas, in front of a 500-pound statute of the writer. The statue is about six inches under Steinbeck's actual six feet, the left hand is akimbo in an effeminate gesture, and the disproportionately large head sits tipsily on the undersized body. The only thing the sculptor seems to have gotten right was the cigarette in the writer's right hand. According to a friend of Steinbeck's who still lives in the area, the statue offers "Mickey Rooney's body and Steinbeck's head on a bad day." But Pauline Pearson tells me that the statue, done by a Long Beach State graduate student, has served its purpose. Open season was declared on it shortly after it was placed in front of the library. It has been decorated with everything from toilet paper to bras and sunglasses. This, more than anything, might have pleased Steinbeck.

When Steinbeck grew up in Salinas shortly after the turn of the century, the population was 2,500. On his last trip there in the 1960s, the population had risen to 80,000. Now it is 104,000. Steinbeck's fear that the population would leap "pell mell on in a mathematical progression" to 200,000 in ten years was a prophecy that did not come true, but it is growing, and so is the Steinbeck lore and legend.

Pauline Pearson meets me with her husband, Merle. He is the driver; she is the guide. They make a handsome team and a perfectly compatible one. She has absolute confidence in his sense of direction, and he lets her do the talking. They are both in their early sixties, and neither seems ready for retirement. Merle's white hair and Swedish rectitude make him the perfect choice for a chauffeur. Pauline's attire has a religious aura to it; she is all in purple, her jumpsuit and shoes, earrings and even her glasses and handbag. She's like the color-coordinated pilgrim in *The Canterbury Tales*. And pilgrim seems to be the right image for her; she has given seventeen years to gathering research on Steinbeck and the places he wrote about. Like many of his readers, Pauline always felt that he had something special to say to her, that he was speaking directly about her experience.

In the 1930s, around the time *The Grapes of Wrath* was written, Pauline came from Oklahoma to Salinas. She was eight years old, too young to be affected by his writing. That happened later, gradually and powerfully. She was an Okie, although maybe not a typical one. Her grandfather, who worked as a laborer, lived in Salinas and had built a little house in town. Pauline's family left Oklahoma because her father had drunk some "jake," what many during the time considered a medicine. He got what depression-era people called "jake-itis" or "jake-leg," a debilitating paralysis, and was never able to work outside the home again. Pauline thinks of her family as different from the typical Okies for two reasons: they had relatives to come live with in California, and it was her father's crippling illness, not the Dust Bowl, that sent them west. But her family was treated like all the other Okies—with condescension, anger, or suspicion. They were pariahs in the town. Steinbeck described it in *The Grapes of Wrath:* "In the West there was panic when the migrants multiplied on the highways. Men of property were terrified for their property. Men who had never been hungry saw the eyes of the hungry. Men who had never wanted anything very much saw the flare of want in the eyes of the migrants. And the men of the town and of the soft suburban country gathered to defend themselves; and they reassured themselves that they were good and the invaders bad.... They said, These goddamned Okies are dirty and ignorant. They're degenerate, sexual maniacs. These goddamned Okies are thieves. They'll steal anything."

But, like the Joads, Pauline's family had a great sense of pride. They were on the charity list with the other immigrants. "We were listed with the poor," Pauline says. "With those who needed help.

When I was in school and they sent home a box of food, my father sent it back. My parents did everything they could to keep us together. It was us against the world, just like Steinbeck's Okies. My mother worked as a substitute teacher, then she worked in the hospitals, and finally, because it paid more, she worked packing lettuce in big lettuce sheds. My father did everything he was able to do—worked at home keeping boarders, did the cooking, planted a garden. We were fiercely independent. There are still parts of *The Grapes of Wrath* that I can't read aloud and get through them. They mean too much to me."

As we drive along a road that skirts the foothills of the Gabilans, a high grey-flannel fog, like the one Steinbeck described in "The Chrysanthemums," closes off the Salinas valley from the rest of the world. In the fields heads of lettuce lie like disembodied skulls, and the water spraying from irrigation pipes rises in a ghostly mist in the distance, white under the darkening clouds. The elevation, a sign tells me, is fifty-five feet, but we are winding our way up to Corral de Tierra, a "suburb" of Salinas, about eight miles outside of town, that Steinbeck wrote about in his second book, *The Pastures of Heaven*, a series of ten interconnected stories about the destruction of the peaceful farming community. Although it was the second book he published, it was actually the third one he wrote, but it was the first book to focus exclusively on his homeland, on the land and people he knew so well.

We drive past the country club and onto what was once the Walter Markham Ranch and is now a subdivision for millionaires. I'm curious about who can afford these sprawling mansions nestled in the sides of the mountains in Corral de Tierra. When I ask, Pauline just smiles, but Merle raises his eyes into the rearview mirror and says, "Only the growers can afford this kind of opulence. The doctors live in the foothills below." Near one house is an incongruous cluster of palm trees, which I'm told is a badge of affluence around here. Merle raises his eyes again: "At $10,000 apiece for those trees I'd call that affluence." It seems that Steinbeck's prophecy at the end of *The Pastures of Heaven* has come true. The epilogue of that book describes a sightseeing bus and its passengers. Steinbeck shows the tourists gazing into the valley, and one businessman in a "tone of prophecy" says, "If I have any vision, I tell you this: Some day there'll be big houses in that valley, stone houses and gardens, golf links and big gates and iron work. Rich men will live there—men that are tired of working away in town, men that have made their pile and want a quiet place to settle down to rest and enjoy themselves. If I had money, I'd buy the whole thing. I'd hold onto it, and sometime I'd subdivide it." Some speculator has read Steinbeck very carefully because that's exactly what someone has done. It has been turned into what the locals call "monument valley."

Although Pauline doesn't like what has happened to the Markham Ranch, there are two things about the area that make her eyes sparkle. The first is the old McNerney place, a ramshackle frame house that looks more like an ancient barn, standing in the front driveway of a multi-million-dollar house owned by a grower. It was part of the development deal that the old weather-beaten house, the model for the home in Steinbeck's story "The Murder," would retain untouched. And there it stands, like a good joke or a monumental irony near the palm trees and swimming pools and Mercedes Benz. "That hovel has a face," Pauline says. "It's haunted. Steinbeck was a mystic. He always had a ghost or two wherever he lived. I'm glad he left one behind to haunt the rich."

As we drive back to town, Pauline points out Red Pony country. This is where Gitano came to die. Or this is Castle Rock, Steinbeck's Camelot when he was a boy. I have to admit it looks like Camelot. She loves the mountains as much as Steinbeck did. "I feel as he did," she says. "These mountains are like a mother's lap you want to climb up into." We pass Spreckles Sugar Company, where Steinbeck worked as a young man, and a motel where they filmed parts of *East of Eden*. Each site she mentions she seems to discover again, as if she's seeing it for the first time. After fifty years in Salinas, she's still a "newcomer," an outsider, an Okie. Her roots in the valley are in Steinbeck's words as much as they are in the soil.

Back in town Merle drives through the Alisal area, once called "Little Oklahoma" and now known as "Fly Hill." "Mostly Mexican-Americans live here now," Pauline says. Merle drives even more rapidly through the old Chinatown section and along California Street, the former red-light district. I'm warned to stay away from this area. "There are at least two stabbings a week." I make a note to come back later.

We pass the spot where they burned *The Grapes of Wrath* on two separate occasions. During one of the strikes in Salinas they built a bonfire and threw multiple copies of the book in. "This is a company town and *The Grapes of Wrath* was the final blow," Pauline says, squinting out the car window as if she can still see the fire. "They thought by throwing the book into the blaze they could take care of it. They were saying 'We own this town.' And, of course, in a sense they did. Sadly, his own home town was one of the few places that never sent him a congratulatory note when he won the Nobel Prize."

Our last stop is the Garden of Memories Cemetery on Abbott Street. On March 4, 1969, his ashes were buried here near his mother's family, the Hamiltons. There, with his mother, father, sister, and Uncle Will, John Steinbeck is buried, no inscription, just the dates, 1902-1968. Like Bill Appleton of Oxford, Mississippi, Pauline Pearson walks through the cemetery as if she's visiting old friends and is reminded of old stories. She points out the grave of Steinbeck's adored grandfather, Samuel Hamilton, near a eucalyptus tree and looking toward the drought-choked Gabilan Mountains.

Pauline stops me in front of Mary Jane Reynold's grave; she was a famous local prostitute, probably the prototype for Jenny in *East of Eden* and Flora and Fauna in *Cannery Row* and *Sweet Thursday*. "There were different kinds of prostitutes in his stories. Most of them had hearts of gold. Cathy in *East of Eden* was the exception. She was crippled on the inside. And I believe she was modeled after Steinbeck's second wife. But then there were also four families in Salinas whose sons married prostitutes. Each one read the book and said, 'This is our son.' You can see why it wasn't a big hit around here."

I head off for the Steinbeck House on Central Avenue, the writer's boyhood home, now a nonprofit restaurant and gift shop. I wave goodbye to Merle and Pauline as they linger in the cemetery, no longer attending to Steinbeck but to the grave of their own son who died when he was eighteen years old. Even then, Pauline had told me earlier in the day, Steinbeck's books had helped her through that time.

The Steinbeck House, across the street from the Steinbeck Plaza, an office building bulging with attorneys and mortgage companies, and near Steinbeck Flats Condominiums, is a spotless Victorian with spires and gables and widow's walks. It looks as if it were painted yesterday. The lawn looks as if it's manicured by a hairstylist. Even the red bougainvillea bush on the side of the house seems more sculpted artifact than plant. Down the street the houses get a bit smaller, the paint fades, and the bushes regain a wild independence. Outside the Steinbeck House is a California tour bus. The driver tells me that there are over 2,000 tour companies in the state and most of them come to or drive past the Steinbeck House in Salinas. The Best Cellar, the gift shop below the restaurant, is crowded with browsers, searching among the doilies, cups, and postcards for something unique. A few look over the books. "Yeah, I remember that one," a middle-aged man says, holding up a copy of *The Red Pony*. "It was required reading in high school. But I loved it." He takes it toward the cashier, intending either to read it again or to bring back some memory of what it was like to be sixteen.

Inside the restaurant, each waitress could pass for Steinbeck's mother. They are all grey-haired Salinas matrons. The workers, except for the cook and dishwasher, are all volunteers. The menu changes every day, but today, for six dollars, it is goulash. Mrs. Steinbeck would have been proud, although I'm not sure she would have been pleased by the conversation at the table next to mine. Three local women sit there discussing their husbands' business ventures, the price of new cars, and a recent school board meeting. Then the talk turns to Steinbeck:

"Have you seen the movie *The Grapes of Wrath?*"

"I saw part of it once, but it was so depressing."

"I know what you mean." (A meaningful look at the plate of goulash.)

"I really ought to read the book; so many people make reference to it."

Their conversation soon turns to other less depressing movies.

Near the restaurant is the Steinbeck Library, which houses the Steinbeck Archives. Mary Gamble, who has been the archivist for eight years, is an attractive woman in her late thirties. Most of her day she spends like a female version of Dostoyevski's underground man in the cement-and-brick-wall basement of the library. Her office is a little cubicle next to the fenced-in archives area, which contains tapes, videos, letters, and manuscripts. I spend the next three hours, under Mary's watchful librarian's eye, viewing rare tapes of Steinbeck speaking for the cameras. His voice is rough, like an old Nantucket sea captain, and he fidgets and squirms in front of the cameras like a boy forced to act in the class play. On my way out of Mary's office I take one more glance around at her vault. There are two pictures on the wall—one a drawing of Steinbeck and the other a famous photograph of Hemingway in his later years in Idaho, walking alone, his right foot raised balletically, just after he has kicked a can. Mary doesn't see any irony in having Papa's image guarding the gates to the Steinbeck archives. "Somebody sent it to me," she says, "so I thought I should put it up." Steinbeck probably would have been amused. Mary, who has a nice smile which sneaks out occasionally, takes things literally and doesn't seem to be one to laugh unless it's truly called for. Unlike Pauline Pearson, whose interest in Steinbeck's work and life and legend appears to spark from her eyes and to be built into every gesture, Mary Gamble tells me, "I haven't viewed all these tapes. They don't pay me to watch them. Just to take care of them." Steinbeck might be amused by that as well.

Arthur Miller once said that Steinbeck had a "blessed naivete," and Jackson Benson, Steinbeck's biographer, argued that he carried a certain amount of innocence about his work and the critics' reaction to it with him throughout his life. Certainly, he had enough ego and arrogance about his abilities to survive in a highly competitive field. But, given his stature as a writer, he had an atypical humility. At the peak of his career he was frequently confused with Hemingway, but they had little in common. Steinbeck was a shy and private man. He was never one to seek or relish stardom. All he ever wanted to be was a writer.

If, as Steven Millhauser says in *Edwin Mullhouse*, genius is the ability to be obsessed, then Steinbeck had genius. He never lost a childlike innocence, a capacity for wonder. He was always curious, searching for new subjects and unusual ways of expressing himself. As his biographer points out, "Each of his novels was different, an attempt to broach a new subject, a new approach, a new form." His interest in literature started perhaps when as a young child he read Malory's *Morte d'Arthur* with his sister Mary. An individualist with a strong social conscience and a clear sense of morality, Steinbeck drew part of his code of ethics from that book and another favorite, *Don Quixote*. Courage, loyalty, kindness, and responsibility were the cornerstones of his code of behavior.

He never lost his sense of chivalry. His first love, *Morte d'Arthur*, was also one of the last books he worked on before he died. During his last years he worked on his version of Malory in his little study in Sag Harbor, Long Island, in a room he named "Joyous Garde," after the castle to which Lancelot took Guinevere. The director's chair he sat on to do his writing had "Siege Perilous" written on the back. In *Morte d'Arthur* Steinbeck found all he held important: "All the vices that ever were—and courage and sadness and frustration, but particularly gallantry—perhaps the only single quality of man that the West has invented. I think my sense of right and wrong, my feeling of *noblesse oblige*, and any thought I may have against the oppressor and for the oppressed, came from this secret book." Like Mark Twain, Steinbeck constantly reimagined his past, and as Jackson Benson says, Steinbeck's love of Malory was "all tied together with the love he had for his sister, his family and parents, and the nostalgia for a world created in childhood." He was a man who cared deeply for the unrepresented, the voiceless, the beleaguered in our society. *The Grapes of Wrath* and *Of Mice and Men* attest to that. But he was also a man with a playful sense of humor. *Tortilla Flat*, *Sweet Thursday*, and sections of *Cannery Row* and *Travels with Charley* dramatize this part of his nature. He never lost the child in himself— the sense of outrage or the sense of play.

Steinbeck was born on February 27, 1902, in Salinas, California, at that time a small town of 2,500 people set in the coastal mountains in the northern part of the state. It was middle America, more rural than Hemingway's Oak Park but with most of the same values. Salinas was at the center of a farming and ranching community but near one of the most beautiful sections of the United States—Carmel, Carmel Valley, and Big Sur National Forest. Unlike many of his contemporaries who became writers, Steinbeck had a family life that was loving and stable, and like Faulkner and Hemingway his family history was a romantic one.

About the middle of the nineteenth century his paternal great-grandfather emigrated with his wife, two sons, and three daughters in a mini-crusade from Germany to Jerusalem, with a plan to convert the Jews to Christianity. What the family encountered were hardship, illness, rape, and murder. The story of his great-grandfather's journey to the Holy Land—the death of one of his sons from tuberculosis, the rape of his wife by marauding Bedouin tribesmen, the murder of another of his sons, the destruction of his home, a shipwreck on the way back to America, and the death of his daughter—is a narrative that combines the misery of Job with the romantic adventures of Steinbeck's own first novel, *A Cup of God*.

His paternal grandfather, John, and his grandmother survived these hardships, simplified their names from Grossteinbeck to Steinbeck, and settled in New England, then Florida, and finally on a farm near Salinas, California. Steinbeck's father's life was far less adventurous. He was an accountant, a plant manager, and the treasurer of Monterey County. But he had a lasting effect on his son and his values. Steinbeck said his father was "strong rather than profound." His father was most likely a model for many of the powerful, silent westerners like Billy Buck who, as one critic pointed out, "are made stern by the effort to carve out a life under difficult circumstances."

Steinbeck's mother was also a strong, competent person, a woman like Mrs. Joad in *The Grapes of Wrath*. Like Frost's mother, Steinbeck's mother, Olive Hamilton, was a schoolteacher who persevered with less-than-eager students. In describing his mother's years as a teacher, he said, "What light and beauty could be forced down the throats of her reluctant pupils, she forced." According to most accounts, she was a formidable, practical, and strong-willed woman. The Hamiltons left Northern Ireland in the 1850s and settled on a ranch near King City, about sixty miles south of Salinas. In *East of Eden* Steinbeck immortalized his maternal grandfather, Samuel Hamilton, depicting him as a man of great faith and compassion, a common man who is also a hero. Warren French called him "a kind of fisher-king" and Louis Owens said he is a man who "has been forced to accept the harsh reality of his land, and he respects and loves the land."

Steinbeck inherited important traits from both sides of his family. His idealism, imagination, unyielding social conscience, and loving compassion were characteristics found in both the Hamilton and Steinbeck clans. From his father, Steinbeck inherited self-discipline and resolution. From his mother, he gained a love of reading. As a young man he read *Crime and Punishment*, *The Return of the Native*, and *Madame Bovary*, remembering them not as books "but as things that happened to me." With books like *Tortilla Flat* and *The Grapes of Wrath*, he would produce the same response in many of his readers.

His school years were not ones of noticeable achievement for him. He did not do exceptionally well in his classes, was not particularly popular, and although he would have wished otherwise he was not a good athlete. According to his biographer, during these years he was big and awkward and lazy. He was shy and outside all the popular cliques. From the outset he was a bit different from his peers in Salinas. In his freshman year in high school he decided to become a writer, and he never deviated from his course over the next fifty years. As a youngster he fell in love with words, with the private and secret worlds they could create; it was a youthful infatuation that turned into a passion that he kept right up until his death at age sixty-six.

Once he made his decision to be a writer, school held little attraction for him. As Jackson Benson wrote of these years, "He couldn't see how another four years of schooling could help him become the Jack London he dreamed of becoming." After high school he attended Stanford University on and off from 1919 to 1925. He never graduated, but diplomas and degrees never held much fascination for him. He took the courses that he thought would help him accomplish his one and only goal: to become a writer. Like Faulkner at Ole Miss, Steinbeck took only those courses that interested him. His preferences were also reflected in his grades—an *A* in feature writing and a *D* in news writing. During those six years he generally worked half the year and went to school the other half. He learned as much outside the classroom as he did in it. He was a ranch hand, bench chemist, and laborer. He worked at the Spreckles Sugar Plant in Salinas and on ranches in the valley. There he was educated as much as he was at Stanford. Instead of professors, there were bindle stiffs, hobos, and cannery workers who taught him enough about human nature to help him create George and Lennie in *Of Mice and Men* and Mack and his companions in *Cannery Row*. Working among these people he learned a great deal about the hungry and desperate dreamers in the golden land.

Unlike Melville, Steinbeck had his whaling ship and his Harvard too, but eventually there was no more for him to learn at Stanford. After his years of on-again, off-again course work, about halfway through his junior year he left a note for his roommate: "Gone to China. See you again sometime." He never got a berth to China, but he did spend time in San Francisco and Oakland and the ranches below Salinas, and he began to see even more clearly the sad face of America that he would write about in *The Grapes of Wrath* and other novels. It may have been his experiences during this time that helped sharpen his social conscience, acquainting him with the plight of the poor and hopeless in the land of opportunity.

For Steinbeck, rebellion was man's highest state. For all the naturalistic elements in his fiction, he was a romantic. He valued honor, charity, strength of character, and kindness. He was also a realist, casting a cold eye on the world of poverty and degradation he saw around him. These two distinct impulses, toward an angry realism and a chivalric idealism, may help account for what many see as a strange discrepancy between novels such as *Tortilla Flat* and *A Cup of Gold* and *The Grapes of Wrath* and *The Long Valley*. The two impulses ran together in his belief in the spirit of humankind, his belief in men's capacity for courage and decency. This view of man never changed from his first novel in 1929 to his last work in 1962. As he said in his Nobel Prize acceptance speech: "The ancient commission of the writer has not changed. He is charged with exposing our many grievous faults and failures, with dredging up to light our dark and dangerous dreams for the purpose of improvement. . . . I hold that a writer who does not passionately believe in the perfectibility of man has no dedication nor any membership in literature."

For a few years after college Steinbeck did a variety of odd jobs, but he was always working toward making himself a writer. He moved to New York City and took a job as a laborer on the construction of Madison Square Garden, pushing a hundred-pound wheelbarrow filled with concrete along the scaffolding. With the help of a wealthy uncle he got a job as a reporter on the *New York American*, but his *D* in news writing came back to haunt him. He spent most of his time getting lost in Queens or Brooklyn, sent on story assignments that he found himself getting involved in emotionally. He was not made to be a reporter. After his inevitable firing, he returned to California and worked as a caretaker on an estate near Lake Tahoe. Like Faulkner and Hemingway, Steinbeck was inclined to exaggerate his past. Describing his time in Tahoe, he wrote: "I went into the mountains and stayed two years. I was snowed in eight months of the year and saw no one but my two Airedales." It was his Thoreauvian excursion into the wilderness, but—like Thoreau—he actually had a number of visitors and a few vacations. But the job did give him leave to write his first novel, *A Cup of Gold*, a historical romance with an existential twist. It's not a very good novel and Steinbeck knew that even before it was published. He started it with enthusiasm but ended it with a sense of duty. A story of the pirate Henry Morgan, *A Cup of Gold* seems an odd beginning to a career that produced *The Grapes of Wrath* and *Of Mice and Men*. Like Bernard Malamud's *The Natural* or Eudora Welty's *The Robber Bridegroom*, *A Cup of Gold* is a beginning that does not foreshadow what is to come.

During his time in Tahoe he began to impose a rigid discipline upon himself, writing every day, recording the number of words he wrote at the end of each effort. He had come to believe then what he later said: "Work is the only good thing." He was persistent, as all great writers must be, but unlike most American writers, who seem to feel a great pressure to make a grand financial success of their careers, Steinbeck was proud of his ability to get along with very little money. He was actually afraid that money and success would ruin his writing and destroy his artistic independence. He was very uneasy from the start of his career about writing anything that sold well.

While Hemingway was in Paris writing about the lost generation, Steinbeck was in San Francisco. Steinbeck's strongest work, like Faulkner's, came when he found his home ground as a subject. Steinbeck's Yoknapatawpha was the Salinas Valley—the farm communities, the canneries, the ranch hands, drifters, migrant workers, and bindle stiffs. His themes were man's loneliness and his search for love, the desperate fight against oppression, and the capacity for endurance. He spoke for the dispossessed—the Okies of *The Grapes of Wrath*, the *paisanos* of *Tortilla Flat*, the bums of *Cannery Row*, and the hobos of *Of Mice and Men*.

In the early years he struggled financially. Married in 1930 to Carol Henning, he lived in his parents' cottage in Pacific Grove, a seaside community near Salinas. His father gave him a small allowance each month so that he could continue writing. In 1931 he published *The Pastures of Heaven*, his second novel, a series of interrelated stories about the Corral de Tierra area west of Salinas. This was his true beginning. The little valley became, for him, a microcosm of American life. He had discovered his subject in his backyard. Around the same time he made one of the most important friendships of his life—Ed Ricketts, a marine biologist who became the model for Doc in *Cannery Row* and *Sweet Thursday*. Ricketts's Pacific Biological Laboratory was transformed by Steinbeck into Western Biological Lab, and Ricketts's openness and innocence made him, for some, after the publication of *Cannery Row*, a cult figure. As a number of critics have suggested, perhaps Ricketts was the embodiment of Steinbeck's notion that the best people in our society are often condemned for being different. The outcast may appear to be corrupt to middle-class society, but there may be a generosity and goodness of spirit that goes unrecognized. One of Steinbeck's key ideas is that the best among us and the best in us are often misunderstood and defeated by a callous society.

The Ricketts-Steinbeck friendship was an attraction of opposites. As Jackson Benson points out, "One basis for the friendship might have been that Ed's personality acted as a tranquilizer for Steinbeck's rage. He was very loving and accepting, almost completely without malice, yet he had a kind of sure, inner toughness that contrasted him with John's sentimentality." Steinbeck gathered much material from friends. He once admitted, "I'm a shameless magpie anyway, picking up anything shiny that comes my way— incidents, situation or personality." From Beth Ingels he gathered many of the stories that appeared in *The Pastures of Heaven*, from Ed Ricketts he developed some of his natural philosophy, from Joseph Campbell (another member of the Monterey group during the 1930s) he gained an understanding of world myths. He was a great collector of stories and his comrades during the time—Henry Miller, Bruce Ariss, and Charlie Chaplin—provided him with a lot of stimulation. One of Steinbeck's most famous images—Rose of Sharon's breastfeeding the starving migrant worker at the end of *The Grapes of Wrath*—came from a story that he bought from a hobo.

In 1935 his success began with his third novel, *Tortilla Flat*, and it reached its peak four years later with the Pulitzer Prize-winning *The Grapes of Wrath*. Never again would he achieve the same combination of critical and popular success. But, as his biographer makes clear, it was during those succeeding years that he achieved "the fame and fortune he didn't expect, didn't want, and learned to regret." Because Steinbeck was always afraid of losing his freedom to fame, he adamantly refused to become a public personality. Unlike Hemingway he was not very egotistical. For him, fame was always "a pain in the ass." But after he published *The Grapes of Wrath* his life was never the same.

After he wrote *Of Mice and Men* Steinbeck was asked to write a series of articles on migrant farm labor for the *San Francisco News*. This research led to his novel about the Okies, the emigrants from Oklahoma, Texas, Arkansas, and other states that constituted the Dust Bowl during the Depression, farmers and small businesspeople who tried to escape the poverty and hardships of their areas by moving to the land of milk and honey, California. Their reception on the West Coast was hostile. They were mistreated shamefully, and *The Grapes of Wrath*, the story of the Joads' painful journey from the dying Dust Bowl to the tainted Promised Land, eloquently dramatized the plight of 300,000 farm workers and their families. The big farms controlled wages. Working and living conditions were miserable. The laborers were treated little better than slaves.

Many Californians were afraid of the strange new group of settlers, of what they were like and of what their presence would do to the economy.

Steinbeck did intensive research into the lives and conditions of the Dust Bowl emigrants. He talked to them, lived in the camps, and worked alongside them. *The Grapes of Wrath* sprang from journalism. Steinbeck said in a letter to his agent, "I'm trying to write history while it is happening...." And he did, as William Howarth has recently said, producing a "fiction that melded idea and fact, invention and reporting." His idealism burst into anger over the migrant workers' situation. In his notebook he wrote: "Present-day kings aren't very inspiring, the gods are on vacation and about the only heroes left are the scientists and the poor.... But the poor are still in the open. When they make a struggle it is an heroic struggle with starvation, death or imprisonment the penalty if they lose. And since our race admires gallantry, the writer will deal with it where he finds it. He finds it in the struggling poor now." That the dramatic version of *The Grapes of Wrath* won the 1990 Tony Award suggests that the story has much to say to us over a half century later.

It was a difficult story for Steinbeck to deal with. He tried a number of times to write it, but he was not able to contain his anger and gain some distance from the material. For two years he tried to do something important with the material he had gathered from the farm workers. He wrote a seven-part series titled "The Harvest Gypsies" for a San Francisco paper, began a novel called *The Oklahomans*, and started a satire about the wealthy landown- ers that he called *L'Affaire Lettuceburg*, but they were all prelimi- naries, warm-ups for the five-month explosion of creative energy in which he wrote the 200,000-word manuscript of *The Grapes of Wrath*. He never fully escaped sentimentality even in his best books, but for those who love his fiction, that is never more than a minor flaw, never outweighing his great compassion and honesty. When he finished his masterpiece, he was thirty-seven years old and had written one of the great American novels of the twentieth century, but he would write for another twenty-seven years and the critics would never let him forget that each of his works should live up to his story of the Joads.

Steinbeck said he wrote the novel to protest what he had seen at the Visalia Migrant Workers Camp, the suffering of thousands of families: "I saw people starve to death. That's not just a resounding phrase. They starved to death. They dropped dead." Some readers of Steinbeck's work feel that his experiences in Visalia, California, were the equivalent of Hemingway's experiences in Fossalta, Italy, a wounding that cut to the creative source. Literary critic Robert DeMott said of the book: "Like other momentous American novels that embody the bitter, often tragic, transition from one way of life to another, *The Grapes of Wrath* possessed, among its other attributes, perfect timing. Its appearance permanently changed the literary landscape of the United States."

In *Working Days: The Journals of The Grapes of Wrath*, Steinbeck's struggle is recorded. The journal is like a battle record, showing a man in conflict with himself and a story, always fighting and maneuvering to gain control. At one point, on June 22, 1938, he wrote his next day's plan: "Start with Tom and his mother...to the return of the men and...the conference of the men. And the reports and circulars and ads for labor. (Got her done. And I'm afraid she's a little dull). Think. Think tonight and tomorrow work harder but get sleep tonight. Need sleep." *The Grapes of Wrath* became his *Moby Dick*, his *Huckleberry Finn*, his *Walden*, and his *Scarlet Letter*. It became his obsession. Toward the end of the writing of the novel, he said in his journal: "I wish I would write only one page a day but I can't. Got to go on at this rate or suffer for it. It must go on. I can't stop. . . . This book is my sole responsibility and I must stick to it and nothing more. This book is my life now or must be. When it is done, then will be time for another life. But, not until it is done. And all the other lives have begun to get in. There is no doubt of that. That is why I am taking so much time in this diary this morning—to calm myself. My stomach and my nerves are screaming merry hell in protest against the inroads." This is the voice of a man pushing himself on, developing strategies along the way to get one step farther along.

The writer, like the Joads themselves, had undertaken an arduous journey. For Steinbeck, always the chivalric knight, the work itself became the grail. He hoped only that he was worthy of the work. He continually reminds himself in his journal entries: "Make the people live. Make them live. But my people must be more than people. They must be an over-essence of people." Nathaniel Benchley, a good friend of Steinbeck's during this time, remembers his once saying that in order to write well about something you either had to love it or hate it very much. Steinbeck had both in *The Grapes of Wrath*—a hatred of the system that destroyed people and an admiration for the courage and dignity of the migrant workers. Steinbeck sensed the significance of what he was attempting. About halfway through the novel, he wrote in his diary: "Once this book is done I won't care how soon I die, because my major work will be over."

These words may have been prophetic. In its first year of publication, the novel sold about 430,000 copies in hardcover at $2.75 apiece. In 1941 the Sun Dial press issued a one dollar hardcover that sold over 500,000 copies. Steinbeck became rich beyond his dreams. But the dream soon turned into a nightmare. Like Mark Twain, Steinbeck was always caught between two worlds, courting success and withdrawing from the consequences of it. He once told a friend that the two things he wanted most were freedom from respectability and freedom from the necessity of being consistent. But now he was an honored member of the club. On January 18, 1939, he was received into the prestigious National Institute of Arts and Letters, along with William Faulkner.

The success of *The Grapes of Wrath*, unmatched by an American novel besides *Gone With the Wind*, brought with it the curse of fame he so feared: abusive telephone calls, hate mail, and hero worship. Tap-dancing children and aspiring writers appeared at his door. At one point things got so bad that he wrote to his agent: "Something has to be worked out or I am finished writing." Steinbeck, like Doc in *Cannery Row*, had to learn how to deal with adoring hordes. Neither ever truly did. From the time he wrote *The Grapes of Wrath* on, he was a rich, respectable writer, and the critics expected him to write more books just like it. When he didn't, his career was written off as remarkable but erratic.

There was a tremendous uproar over the publication of *The Grapes of Wrath*. One congressman declared: "I say to you, and to every honest, square-minded reader in America, that the painting Steinbeck made in his book is a lie, a black, infernal creation of a twisted, distorted mind." To many, like the congressman, the book was obscene, communistic propaganda, or merely cheap sensationalism to make money. To others, it was one of the most poignant, honest, and powerful novels ever written by an American.

At the same time he was trying to deal with the success of *The Grapes of Wrath*, he was also trying to hold his marriage to his first wife, Carol, together. The marriage eventually fell apart, but his renewed friendship with Ed Ricketts and his writing helped him keep his sanity. After his divorce from Carol in 1942 he left for New York City and married his second wife, Gwyn Conger. Some have speculated that the breakup of his first marriage and his move from his spiritual homeplace destroyed his career, that he never again wrote anything to compare with his Pulitzer Prize winner. But the truth is that, although *The Grapes of Wrath* is his certain masterpiece, he wrote many fine books after 1939—*Cannery Row*, *The Pearl*, and *Travels with Charley* among them.

He refused to repeat himself, no matter what the critics wanted, and although his pet name for them was "lice," he generally held his sense of humor and perspective under the barrage of critical fire he had to endure for most of his novels after 1939. He was criticized for his naturalism, denigrated for his emphasis on man's animal nature, and lampooned for his sentimentality. He was mocked for his anti-intellectuality and accused of being a Marxist or not being enough of one. Usually he reserved his anger for the wealthy and the uncaring, the complacent and the bigoted, and he was merely amused by what the reviewers had to say. But the criticism may have taken its toll because it took twelve years for him to brace himself to write his next big book, *East of Eden*. But if after *The Grapes of Wrath* the critics and professors had a field day denouncing his work, always looking for *Grapes Redux*, he didn't show too much resentment. Writing, for him, was always a personal challenge, and he didn't worry too much about what others had to say. In a letter to the novelist John O'Hara, Steinbeck wrote: "You know I was born without any sense of competition. Consequently I have never even wondered about the comparative standing of writers. I don't understand that. Writing to me is a deeply personal, even a secret function and when the product is turned loose it is cut off from me and I have no sense of its being mine. It is like a woman trying to remember what childbirth is like. She never can."

During World War II he spent time in Europe as a war correspondent and wrote a book for the Air Force. He was in the midst of quite a bit of fighting, but there are no accounts of him, a la Hemingway, creating a vigilante brigade and setting up his own headquarters. He remained a writer, always. Besides, about war Steinbeck always seemed more the pacifist than Hemingway and less the romantic than Faulkner.

When he returned home from the war, he returned imaginatively to the security of home and wrote *Cannery Row*, about the outcasts who lived along the Monterey docks. In *Cannery Row* he was doing more than return to his geographical origins; he was going back to his literary beginnings, to his interest in Arthurian legend. *Cannery Row* is Camelot with a sardine smell, and Mack, the boys, and Doc are well-tarnished contemporary knights. During these years his two sons—Thom and John IV—were born. But after five years his marriage to Gwyn began to fall apart. Despite the fact that he was inducted into the American Academy of Arts and Letters with Faulkner in 1948, it was a tragic year for him. He was divorced from Gwyn, and his best friend, Ed Ricketts, died in a car accident. Steinbeck tried to return to California to start over again, but as he wrote to his long-time friend and editor Pascal Covici, "Living is people, not places.... You see this isn't my country anymore. And it won't be until I am dead." He was right: except for his brief return during the research for *Travels with Charley*, he never lived on the West Coast again.

In 1950 Steinbeck married Elaine Scott, the former wife of film star Zachary Scott. The marriage lasted for the rest of his life and brought him some of his happiest years. If he had played Arthur to Gwyn's Guinevere, with Elaine he was Lancelot. A few years before his marriage to Elaine, he had begun writing *East of Eden*, what he thought would be his "largest and most important work." He was half right: it was his longest novel by far. But it was not his best or most important fiction. As Warren French has said, "*East of Eden* is a novel that is more satisfactorily explained than experienced." But if the novel has major inconsistencies and flaws, it is an interesting attempt to fuse family history (the Hamiltons), local history (the Salinas Valley), and allegory (the story of Cain and Abel).

East of Eden, originally titled *The Salinas Valley*, was Steinbeck's attempt to write his big book about home and history. It was a profound attempt but also a profound failure. It was a novel that he wanted to be both highly personal, something to leave his sons, and universal, something that spoke to all readers. To a friend he wrote: "I have put into it all the things I have wanted to write all my life. This is 'the book.'" Arthur Miller saw Steinbeck, like himself, as a writer in a country in which there is no continuity and little community. According to Miller, Steinbeck was "trying to find a community in the United States that would feed him, toward which he could react in a feeling way, rather than merely as an observer or a commentator. And I don't know if there is such a place left in the world. Faulkner tried to keep it alive, in Mississippi, but him apart, I don't know if it is possible." In *East of Eden* the blend of allegory and family history never fully comes to life.

In 1955 Steinbeck bought a summer home in Sag Harbor, Long Island, where he spent many of his happiest days. During the last decade of his life he spent his time in New York City, Sag Harbor, and traveling. Steinbeck had always had a voracious appetite for travel, but in his last years he gorged himself, spending as much time abroad as he did at home, in either New York City or Sag Harbor. In the next few years he wrote a number of books that confounded or dismayed the critics. Always the individualist, he wrote what he wanted, the critics be damned. But, even for Steinbeck, the novel *Sweet Thursday* was an unusual production. The book, a sequel to *Cannery Row*, was written with the idea of its adaptation to the musical-comedy stage. When the reviewers attacked the book, Steinbeck's response was typical. "I am constantly impressed," he wrote, "with the fact that reviewers do not read carefully. They always seem to read with a preconception of what it might be or might have been. And I wonder why they are so obsessed with my immorality. They feel that I am letting them down by not giving a good god dam about it. And also they do not want me to have any fun. They say I enjoyed writing *STH* [Sweet Thursday] as though it were some kind of crime."

Steinbeck was not concerned with any obligation to respond to the critics, but he was concerned about his responsibility to readers. His literary values were similar to those of Norman Cousins, the editor of *Saturday Review*, ". . . namely, that the main purpose of the novel was to tell a story and not just bare one's soul; that the obligation to the reader was primary; that writing was a craft imposing stern requirements on the writer."

In 1962 he published *Travels with Charley*, his last full-length book. In the same year he was awarded the Nobel Prize for literature. Before writing *Travels with Charley* he had suffered two strokes, and knowing that his next could be his last, there was a sense of urgency in his pilgrimage, a search for his country and for himself. It had been a long time since Steinbeck had achieved such critical and popular success as he did with *Travels with Charley*. Its publication proved that he was that rare writer who could capture the American imagination over a period of three decades.

His response to winning the Nobel Prize was a typical expression of his humility: "In my heart there may be doubt that I deserve the Nobel award over other men of letters for whom I hold respect and reverence—but there is no question of my pleasure and pride in having it for myself." He went on to explain why literature was important to him: "Literature is as old as speech. It grew out of human need for it, and it has not changed except to become more needed."

There was a vituperative critical reaction in the American press to Steinbeck's winning the Nobel Prize, and because of the criticism or perhaps simply as a result of the honor itself, he underwent an imaginative paralysis after receiving the award. He spent his last years as a cultural emissary, an adviser to presidents, and an internationally honored novelist. He died on December 20, 1968, after a severe heart attack. His ashes were buried in Salinas. He had returned home, and his words to Johnny Garcia in *Travels with Charley* now seemed right: "The place of my origin had changed. . . . I was the ghost."

In the Salinas Valley, in Monterey, and along the peninsula, Steinbeck's images and words are hauntingly present. It's not possible to stroll past the shops along Cannery Row without imagining Doc, Mack, and Flora's girls. Samuel Hamilton still seems to walk the hills outside King City. The Mexican-American scions of the Joads are bent in the fields around Salinas. This is literally Steinbeck country; his words are rooted in the very soil, in the buildings, and in the people's faces. The United Farm Workers' Union Hall on Wood Street in Salinas is a drab building with a large anteroom and six or seven offices off a narrow corridor. I ask for Beto, and a man who looks something like Desi Arnaz with a blacksmith's forearms and a third-rate fighter's nose squints his eyes and asks defensively, "Who wants to know?" When he's convinced that I mean no harm and have no connection to the growers, he extends his hand: "I'm Albert Gonzalez. I'm Beto."

I feel something like Jim Nolan in *In Dubious Battle*, walking into the union organizer's office: "The wallboarded walls were bare. Only one chair was in the room, and that stood in front of the typewriter. . . . Mac's lips were dry and cracked. He looked at Jim as closely as he was being inspected." This is the same room, this is Mac, and he eyes me carefully as we speak.

Before we even sit down (once he's brought another chair into the room), he grabs my elbow and looks me in the eye: "*The Grapes of Wrath* hasn't changed; it's only changed its face a little. I have proof. I've lived it. Conditions are the same fifty years later." He fixes his eyes on a painting of strawberry pickers, the only decoration on the walls, and tells me about the typical pay (five dollars an hour), the typical benefits (none), and the usual conditions in the fields (no toilets and no fresh drinking water). Only 8 percent of the workers are under union contract, and some don't make minimum wage. They do piecework. "A majority of the workers don't know the law and nobody tells them their rights," he says. "That makes them slaves of the growers."

As Beto sees it, the source of the problem is clear. The growers are greedy. He wouldn't disagree with Steinbeck's synopsis of California history in *The Grapes of Wrath*: "Farming became an industry, and the owners followed Rome, although they did not know it. They imported slaves, although they did not call them slaves: Chinese, Japanese, Mexican, Filipinos. . . . And it came about

Migrant workers in Salinas

that the owners no longer worked on their farms. They farmed on paper; and they forget the land, the smell, the feel of it, and remembered only that they owned it, remembered only what they gained and lost by it." However, Beto would violently disagree with Steinbeck's portrayal of the strike in *In Dubious Battle*, a novel that was bitterly rejected by Communists and anti-Communists, by strikers and bosses. As Warren French has said, *In Dubious Battle* is a book that "refused either to follow a strict Party line or to denounce the striking workers as un-American." The book indicts both sides, one for cruelty and the other for zealotry, each of which leads to exploitation and inhumanity. As French says, the battle in the novel's title is "dubious," not because there is doubt about who will win, but because there is a serious question about the merits of both sides.

Beto most assuredly gives me his "party line." I understand that that's his job. He tells me about the growers living in multi-million-dollar houses. He tells me about their use of pesticides. He offers an example, one of many: last year, one of the growers had a lettuce field sprayed with Malathion. The pickers were moved to another field for their protection, but the next day when the price of lettuce rose from seven dollars to fifteen dollars, the grower moved all the pickers back immediately, disregarding any health hazard to the workers or the public. "Somebody apparently ate a lot of Malathion," Beto says and smiles up at the picture of the strawberry pickers.

"They put dark glasses on people's eyes so they can't see," he continues. "A grower up the road just dropped his wages from seven dollars an hour to five. But *he* lives in a $3-million-dollar house. The people who work for him are forced to live like animals. Then he uses that as an argument that they are not human anyway. Most workers don't make more than $8,000 a year, less than he probably spends on his electric bill and pool maintenance. These families are forced to live together. Even though it's illegal in this town to have more than five people in a two-bedroom house, the migrant workers are forced to have fourteen or fifteen people living together. It's the only way they can pay the rent. This is the richest section of California— Carmel and Carmel Valley. Forget 1939. This is the Middle Ages right now. Farm workers are the lowest class, whether they're blacks or whites, Indians or Mexicans. They are serfs. The growers are the lords of the manor."

This is certainly Steinbeck country, the land of plenty, a twenty-minute drive to the $200-a-night hotel rooms and $50-a-meal restaurants in Monterey and the half-million-dollar handyman specials in Carmel; in this Eden of curvaceous hills and gentle breezes, large numbers of people still go hungry and without hope. The anger Steinbeck felt and wrote about still hangs in the air like smoke.

Beto has worked for the migrant workers for over thirty years. He became involved in his first strike in 1959 in the Imperial Valley. He had just returned from an eight-year tour of service in the Marines. Before he had gone into the Marines, the pickers had been making $1.25 an hour. In 1959 the workers were getting sixty-five cents an hour. He helped organize the wildcat strike that brought them back to $1.25.

He spent sixty days in jail for his part in that strike, and then he headed back to Mexicali to stay with family for a while. One morning at about four o'clock he was awakened by two men, one of whom was Cesar Chavez's cousin Manuel. From that moment on he's worked for the UFW, except for the brief periods he takes off every five years or so to regain his strength. "I don't know how Cesar did it this long," he says. "It's so emotionally draining. We're bucking a system that's been in place so long. I have to get away now and again to rest." His jaw sets hard and he stares beyond me for a moment. Then the telephone rings, but the one in his office doesn't work, so like Mac at the end of *In Dubious Battle* he shivers, seems to break the frozen jaw loose, and goes to speak on the phone in the hall. "No, no, no, David, that's not good enough..." he begins tiredly.

That evening I drive down to Chualar Labor Camp with Tom Joad's famous statement to his mother singing in my ears, telling her not to worry about him, that no one has a soul of his own, only a piece of a common soul: "Then I'll be aroun' in the dark. I'll be ever'where—wherever you look. Whenever they's a fight so hungry people can eat, I'll be there. Wherever they's a cop beatin' up a

Children of migrant workers in Chualar Labor Camp

guy, I'll be there. . . . I'll be in the way kids laugh when they're hungry an' they know supper's ready. An' when our folks eat the stuff they raise an' live in the houses they build—why, I'll be there. See?" Joad is surely a more romanticized figure than the doomed Jim Nolan or the pragmatic Mac of *In Dubious Battle*, but in Beto this other truth also comes to life, this tenacious idealism that must make the growers shiver even on the warmest summer evenings.

The Chualar Labor Camp has a typewritten list of rules nailed to the office door. Some of them seem reasonable enough, but most could be readily used to stifle any union activity. As I'm reading rule #24 ("Solicitation of money or sale of merchandise or distribution of any literature in working area without company permission is forbidden"), a young girl peeks her head shyly out one of the doors. This place is aptly named "labor camp"; it looks like the sort of location criminals are sent to do hard labor. The building is a big frame dormitory separated into a number of smaller units. Two older Mexican men sit with their door open and play cards. The door with the young girl behind it opens again. This time Mario Robles, eighteen, comes out and smiles hesitantly at me. He's followed by Romaldo, his seventeen-year-old brother, then Thomas, who is fifteen, then Isela, seven, and Alejandra, Romaldo's twin sister. The family has spent three years in Chualar in this three-bedroom unit of the labor camp. The phrase "three-bedroom" is deceptive, though, for the whole place is the size of an efficiency in New York City. Mr. Robles acts as the camp maintenance man; therefore, the family has been able to stay on, living next door to a succession of Mexican men who drift in for one picking season or another. This is not the suburbs.

A nineteen-year-old cousin, Jesus Torres, recently from Mexico, comes out next, then the father, and finally the mother. She stands in the back of the crowd and looks over the shoulders. I have the feeling that there are more cousins and aunts and uncles in the shadows, but they remain where they are. The migrant workers pay ninety dollars a week for the room and board. After they pay for a few beers and some gas in their trucks, that doesn't leave much extra, so it's typical to see cousins, friends, even strangers sharing space.

Mario Robles, the oldest brother, will be the first to graduate from high school and speaks the best English. This makes him the natural spokesperson. Through him, they smile, tell me they like it here, that it's better than Mexico. Everybody but the youngest works in the fields when school is not in session, but they don't suggest that it's drudgery. This doesn't seem to be Beto's picture of this world. Mario will leave for Phoenix, Arizona, in the fall to study computer-aided drafting, taking an eighteen-month course at High Tech Institute. Two years in a row he has won first place in the technical illustration competition in his school district. He goes inside and comes out to show me some of his drawings—of an astronaut, of Jerry Rice of the San Francisco 49ers, of a housing complex. His family looks on proudly. Then each talks about his or her specialty—the guitar, football, spelling. The others smile.

Mario walks me to the car, and we talk for an hour or so. It is then that he tells me his dreams—to buy his family a house, to get away from this labor camp, to give up picking in the fields. I ask him about Mexican-Americans he knows who have done just that. He doesn't know any. He's angry that the boss cheated his cousin on a paycheck. He's angry that his mother has to work in the fields. He's angry that he has saved only $300 of his tuition thus far.

I look back across the dusty road (four years of drought make dust seem to be a permanent part of the landscape) and glance at the crumbling frame building. It appears to be only a bit more permanent than the Hoovervilles of the 1930s. But the Robleses seem to me as permanent as the Joads.

The next morning I spend in the fields just outside Salinas. The foreman, Jose Molina, tells me I have to get the supervisor's permission to stay. But as he tells me this, the supervisor's white pickup leaves the front gate. "No problem," Jose says, "He's on his way to Watsonville. You can stay as long as you want."

Luckily, today it is cloudy and cool. This makes it easier for the workers who bend in the fields over strawberries or lettuce for ten or eleven hours a day. This is a strawberry field, like the one in the picture on Beto's wall. And the colors are just as vibrant. The workers wear layered clothing, jackets and sweatshirts tied around their waists. They're ready for any change in the weather. The women wear straw hats and scarfs around their faces, one to protect them from the sun and the other to ward off the pesticides. The men wear baseball caps and perhaps are more fatalistic about the spray. But both men and women eat some strawberries when they are hungry enough. One man with a black baseball cap with "Avoid the Noid" written on it gives me a strawberry-toothed smile and goes off down one of the rows bending to his work and listening to the World Cup soccer match.

"We have seventy-five workers here," Jose tells me, "but today a few men came too drunk to work. They drink because they get tired." He laughs. "Some drink too much. Eee aaah. These Mexicans— watch out." Jose was born in Juarez, but after twenty years in California he's started to think of himself as a United States citizen. Next year he plans to become one. But when he retires in fifteen years, he plans to go back to Mexico and open up a little shop. "I'm an electronics engineer in Mexico, but they don't pay, so I'm here. American companies steal the money from the Mexicans. That's why I'm here."

According to Jose the rest of the workers are happy here. In Mexico they make five dollars a day in a factory. In Salinas they make $4.58 per hour, plus a seventy-cent bonus for each big basket they fill. Jose picks up a strawberry, turns it over in his hand, and tosses it into the batch to be used for juice. It's too red. He picks up another and says, "The bosses say if they bring the unions in here, they'll be no picking. They'll close down. Nobody wants that."

This grower does not provide housing; therefore, the migrants have to find their own places, and the typical place in Watsonville costs about seven hundred a month. Again, this forces a few families or a group of men to live together. Most men leave their families in Mexico and come to work for the six months that U.S. Immigration allows. "That man over there," Jose says, "left six sons and his wife in Mexico. That one over there is from Oaxaca. That's where the short people live. He has twelve sons." He laughs. "I don't know how he did it."

It is 10:30 in the morning, time for the lunch break. A truck pulls up and the people take out the money to buy tacos and enchiladas. One woman, whose stature suggests that she too is from Oaxaca, entertains the crowd with jokes and funny faces. The faces I understand but the jokes elude my high school Spanish. Again Jose tells me that he is an electronics expert. I can't help thinking of Connie in *The Grapes of Wrath* and his dream of repairing radios and televisions. "I went to Edison Institute," Jose says. "I was a picker for ten years." He grimaces, then groans, then reaches back with both hands and arches his back, "I like it better in Mexico. I'll open a shop with a little money. I can live on five dollars a day there."

Without either Jose or me realizing it, the supervisor's truck has returned. Jose's face loses all its color. He edges away from me and I stand alone in the road cut between the rows of strawberries. In order to avoid any problems for Jose, I say I just arrived and would like to observe the work. He tells me firmly that I must leave now. I am reminded that paranoia is one of the principal emotions here and has been for many years. In a letter shortly after *The Grapes of Wrath* was published, Steinbeck wrote to a friend: "Let me tell you a story. When *The Grapes of Wrath* got loose, a lot of people were pretty mad at me. The undersheriff of Santa Clara County was a friend of mine and he told me as follows: 'Don't go into any hotel room alone. Keep records of every minute and when you are off the ranch travel with one or two friends, but particularly, don't stay in a hotel alone.' 'Why?' I asked. He said, 'Maybe I'm sticking my neck out but the boys got a rape case set up for you. You get alone in a hotel and a dame will come in, tear off her clothes, scratch her face and scream. They won't touch your book but there's easier ways.'"

Steinbeck probably had good reason to worry. He had painted a picture that the moneyed interests in California would rather have kept veiled. In *The Harvest Gypsies*, the book version of the series of articles he wrote back in the 1930s for the *San Francisco News*, he described "a disgraceful picture of greed and cruelty." And the growers, for less pure reasons, have to worry too. They need to keep the truth hidden from the public, from the workers, and through a series of slippery rationalizations, from themselves as well. Steinbeck ended *The Harvest Gypsies* by saying: "The new migrants to California from the dust bowl are here to stay. They are of the best American stock, intelligent, resourceful; and, if given a chance, socially responsible. To attempt to force them into a peonage of starvation and intimidated despair will be unsuccessful." Albert Gonzalez, the Robles family, and the men and women I saw bent in the fields suggest that this is still true.

My last morning in Salinas I spend on Soledad and Market streets, roaming the territory Pauline Pearson warned me about. The warning was just too much of a temptation. At night the area is raucous and lit by beer signs and police cars. Last night, when I drove past, I saw two hookers dressed like twins, each unromantically clad in short black shirts and halter tops with silver chains dangling in the breeze. Both showed a dispiriting amount of cellulite. They stood leaning unenthusiastically against a car as two other equally bored young women strolled by. Suzy of *Sweet Thursday* was not among them. Flora's girls were not in sight. Men who looked like Mexican bandits in 1940s Hollywood films stood in front of the bars.

In the daylight the next morning there seem to be fewer dangers but far more undaunted ugliness. As I step out of the car and head down the street where what's left of Saturday night stretches and yawns, I think of the words of the protagonist of Preston Sturgess's *Sullivan's Travels:* "I don't know where I'm going but I'm not coming back till I know what trouble is."

I meet two men who have spent the night in a vacant lot near Lake Alley. There's no lake in sight, just bars, a bodega, and the railroad tracks. The lot has been developed by transients, who have constructed cardboard shelters and built fires in trash cans. I meet two men who bear an uncanny resemblance to the bindle stiffs Lennie and George in *Of Mice and Men*, except the tall one has his wits about him and the short one rattles on incoherently. And unlike Lennie Small and George Milton, there's no friendship here, just a passing acquaintance.

Stephen Roy Aiken is about six feet three and as thin as a whipsaw. He's spent the last two nights sleeping in the doorway of "The Swinging Door," a community center for hobos. That's where I find him this morning, using his duffel bag with the 101st

Airborne insignia as a pillow. He's bearded, his matted hair has down feathers clinging to it, and his hands and clothes are dirty, but there's something foppish about him. The origins of the word "hobo" are unclear, but some have suggested that it is a sarcastic, rhyming reference combining the greeting "ho" with the tongue-in-cheek "beau." As Stephen carefully combs back his thick brown hair with his greasy hand, a vagrant Beau Brummel, the etymology comes to life.

After two tours of duty in Vietnam, 1968–71, and after a few unsuccessful battles with alcohol and drugs, the forty-two-year-old Aiken gave up on his career in air conditioner service and installation. For over a decade he's ridden the rails. He shows me his duffel bag, tells me to heft it (it's heavier than my rental car) and then tells me to feel his bicep (which explains where the cliche "hard as a rock" comes from). He lifts his bag up with an ease that I find embarrassing and recounts some of his journeys: "I was in L.A. this spring and I saw Sylvester Stallone. He's a little shit, you know. All that Rambo stuff is such bullshit. I still have flashbacks to Vietnam, twenty years later." He was a staff sergeant in the war and tells me about a little Vietnamese girl who made herself into a human bomb, walked into his camp, and exploded, killing two of his men. He can't stop that picture from coming into his mind.

We walk along the railroad tracks together. He punctuates his sentences by patting the duffel bag on his back. He calls it his "home." He uses the word without any irony. Last Sunday he was arrested in Santa Cruz, but it wasn't the arrest that upset him as much as the police opening his duffel bag without a search warrant. "This is my home," he says. "They had no right to open it without a warrant. But they did and poured out my vodka and knocked me down." He lifts his pants leg to show me the purple bruises.

As we walk along the tracks, kicking at the weeds, he tells me about the defoliant the railroad company uses, the same stuff the army used in Vietnam, and I ask him where he's heading next. But he says he's just wandering: "I don't know where I'll be at noon, let alone next week." He's been on the road as long as Ulysses, but

Stephen Roy Aiken in Salinas

there's no home to return to—there's no family left in Greenville, South Carolina.

We stop in front of a chemical car, and he shows me the territory, like a man showing a visitor around his neighborhood. There is a space in the back of the car, about the size and shape of a porthole, that is just large enough for a man to squeeze in. He calls it a "pooch belly," and caresses the syllables as if he's saying "womb." He shows me the darkened interior. There are a cardboard mattress and a few empty cans. "Somebody rode in on this one," he says.

Sitting in front of the pooch belly he shows me some of the contents of his "home." He unravels his sleeping bag and shows it off like a suburban housewife with a new sofa. He rubs his Red Wing boots as if they were a shining BMW. But this is not the middle-class exurbs. Like George in *Of Mice and Men*, the countryside he travels in is filled with solitude and loneliness. The hole he travels in is smaller than a linen closet. His cloudy blue eyes are streaked with red, and a jagged scar is chiseled into the bridge of his nose. There are no savings accounts or specific plans for the future. He knows one thing, though: "I'm not going back to the VA hospital. All they got there is slant-eyed doctors that want to take your blood and de-program you."

Very carefully he takes out a big bag of tobacco. His hands shake a bit as he rolls a perfect cigarette. "This is cheaper than buying them," he says and laughs. Beneath his burnt skin and wrinkles, I can see the boy who was once there, before Vietnam and before the rails.

"The trains are the backbone of America," Stephen says, intoning like a spokesperson for Amtrak. Then he smiles again, shows me his MARTA pass from Atlanta, and climbs into the pooch belly, as I look across the tracks at the darkening slopes of the Gabilans.

Monterey is Steinbeck country, but it's a different world from Salinas. In *Cannery Row*, Steinbeck described it as "a poem, a stink, a grating noise, a quality of light, a tone, a habit, a nostalgia, a dream. Cannery Row is the gathered and scattered, tin and iron and rust and splintered wood, chipped pavement and weedy lots and junk heaps, sardine canneries of corrugated iron, honky tonks, restaurants and whore houses, and little crowded groceries, and laboratories and flophouses." He said that the inhabitants were whores, pimps, gamblers, sons of bitches, saints, angels, martyrs, and holy men. The crowds are still there but whether they're angels or sons of bitches, they all go by the name "tourist" now.

Early morning is still a time of magic in Cannery Row. The tourists haven't emerged yet from the ever-growing hotels and bed-and-breakfasts. The fog hovers and, as Steinbeck said, it is a "gray time after the light has come and before the sun has risen, the Row seems to hang suspended out of time in a silvery light." In a matter of minutes, it seems, the sun burns away the clouds and, as if the doors to a bargain basement have swung open, the crowds appear on the streets. Most people are headed towards the end of the row, in the direction of the old Hovden Cannery, which was remodeled in 1984 as the Monterey Bay Aquarium. It's a good choice with its unusual exhibits and interesting re-creations of what a diver would see beneath Monterey's tides. The drawback is the gauntlet of fudge shops and wax museums that one encounters on the way down the avenue. The old canneries have all gone. "They disappeared," a long-time resident told me, "along with the sardines and the prostitutes." Actually, when the bay was fished out in the 1940s, the canneries died out. The workers left and naturally the prostitutes did too. The Hovden Cannery was put to good use, but the rest of the places became restaurants, singles bars, wine-tasting rooms, or boutiques. La Ida's Cafe and Brothel is now Halisha's Restaurant. The name is more exotic, but the merchandise is less so. The Old General Store, once Lee Chong's Market, no longer sells frogs from the Carmel River.

There's only one of the original locations left that Steinbeck alluded to in his fiction, Ed Ricketts's old laboratory at 800 Cannery Row. It looks pretty much the same as it did fifty years ago. A group of doctors, lawyers, businessmen, and artists from the area bought the building in the early 1970s for twelve thousand dollars. Recently they were offered over a half a million, but they have kept it a private men's club for nearly twenty years, and they don't intend to sell at any price. Some members of the group were part of Steinbeck's and Ricketts's informal club a half-century ago and joined in the legendary parties with Joseph Campbell, Charlie Chaplin, or others. According to recent accounts, there have been some legendary parties among the members in the last few years as well.

The paint on the building is fading, and the numbers on the door frame are missing, the "800" just a ghostly shadow. As I sit on the rickety steps, waiting to meet with the artist Bruce Ariss, a resident of Monterey and a friend of Steinbeck's in the 1930s, a woman comes up and takes a photograph. Of me? The building? I never get to ask because Bruce Ariss appears in front of his mural of Cannery Row, one of the street-long line of murals painted on the wooden construction fence. Tall and broad-shouldered, Ariss has a wide smile and white hair that looks as if it has a will of its own. His hands are huge, looking more like they belong to Michael Jordan than to one of the most renowned muralists in California. He walks across the street, leaning on a cane, one of the few telltale signs that he'll be eighty next month.

Ariss, who is a member of the club, lets me in, gives me a tour of Ricketts's old lab downstairs (only two specimens are left—a dried snake and, as Ariss says, "someone's kidney"), and then we relax in the main room upstairs. The room is decorated with posters, collages, and a few paintings depicting Ricketts and friends and is furnished with the best from flea markets in the area. It seems worlds away from the tourists and the present-day Cannery Row outside.

Bruce has a portfolio of his work to show me and enough stories to entertain me for days. Like Samuel Hamilton in *East of Eden*, he "eats stories like grapes." And, also like Hamilton, he has a courage and sense of perspective that are gratifying to be near. The house that he built on Huckleberry Hill, which some theorize was the location of Tortilla Flat, and is the home he's lived in for over forty years burned down last month. He had dropped the insurance because the rates had gotten too high. So all he's left with is ashes—sixty years worth of paintings went up in flames. When I ask him about it, his laconic, smiling reply is, "I guess I was getting complacent. It's time to start over."

I notice that his thick hands are calloused and his fingernails are dirty. With help from friends and neighbors, he's started to

Bruce Ariss in front of his mural on Cannery Row

rebuild his house, all five thousand square feet of it. He had built his old house with discarded timbers from local buildings and shipwrecks. Now, he'll have to rebuild with new lumber. The local newspaper calls him a legend and says, "As Ariss watched his home burn, he got out paper and pencil and started sketching." At this Bruce laughs, his neatly trimmed white moustache curling slightly at the ends, and says, "That's not exactly true, but it makes a good story, eh? This town is a lot like Steinbeck described it in *Sweet Thursday*—'The communications system on Cannery Row is mysterious to the point of magic and rapid to the speed of light.'" He smiles again. "But they don't always get the story right."

Ariss and his wife Jean, who is a novelist (*The Quick Years* and *The Shattered Glass*), spent many a night with Steinbeck and his first wife Carol in Ed Ricketts's lab. Like many of the area residents who were indignant about Steinbeck's description of people and places in *Tortilla Flat* and *Cannery Row*, Ariss is not an unqualified fan of the man or his work. He looks innocently over the rim of his glasses, which have slipped slightly on the bridge of his nose, and says, "He was meaner than cat shit at times. All you had to do was catch him on the wrong day." As Ariss remembers him, Steinbeck had a lot of fey, Irish humor and some darker, more sour German traits. Doc Ricketts, on the other hand, was a saint. It was Ricketts's reputation, among other things, that first drew him to Monterey.

Ariss was born in 1911 on an Indian reservation in Washington, on the Columbia River. His father, who was in the logging business, soon went into a construction partnership with Henry J. Kaiser in the San Francisco Bay area. According to Ariss, his father had fairly gained the reputation for being "the hottest-tempered guy in California," and in order to protect themselves Bruce and his brother became boxers. But even with a six-foot four-inch frame and the hands of a blacksmith, boxing was only a hobby. He wanted to be an artist. "I didn't want to become a goddamned construction worker but a painter. But my father looked at me—a big, strapping kid—and said, 'What do you want to become an artist for? You're not a cripple.'"

At eighteen Bruce left for the University of California at Berkeley, where he got interested in writing and other things. "One morning I woke up in the sack with a great beautiful Amazon," he recalls, "the most beautiful girl I had ever seen. She said 'Today's my birthday,' and I asked, 'Wonderful, darling, how old are you?' I fell out of bed when she said, 'Fifteen.'" They got married when she was eighteen and didn't need her parents' permission. He tells his five children, the six nieces and nephews he helped raise, and their dozens of grandchildren, "If this beautiful young gal hadn't smiled at me on a spring morning in 1930, none of you would be here." Telling me that Jean has always been a striking beauty, he says, "But fortunately she didn't know it. She always wondered why men were so clumsy, always walking into walls and tripping over their feet. I never told her it was because they were looking at her."

After making two hundred dollars mining for gold in the California mountains, Ariss left with Jean for Monterey, which had a reputation as an artists' community. There they met Ricketts and Steinbeck. The Arisses lived in a ten-by-twenty-foot garage near the beach. They owned a copy of *Walden*, two rice bowls, and a pair of chopsticks. They lived well on eight dollars a month, and for two years his gold-digging financed their honeymoon. They roamed the beach, ate lettuce and sardines and carefully dried seaweed, and spent evenings with Ricketts's crowd. "At that time," Ariss says, "I had a big beard and looked like a cross between Jesus and Man Mountain Dean. The Monterey Peninsula back then was a wonderful place to be poor in—you had seafood, odds and ends, vegetables, and great company. You could even buy two damaged cans of sardines at a cannery for a nickel." The former center for the University of California's basketball team was living the life he had dreamed about.

When the WPA came into the area, he got jobs painting murals, some as big as ten feet high and 150 feet long, in Pacific Grove and Monterey. During the war he went back to the Oakland area and worked in the building trades, and after the war he returned with three children. He started mural painting again, began a local magazine, became editor of another, and eventually spent a number of years as an art director for the studios in Hollywood, commuting back to home and family on weekends.

"I've got a million stories," Ariss says. "They're all around me." He's right, of course. Right now, he's sitting under an oil painting that depicts a beach party with Doc Ricketts, his girlfriend Susy, Steinbeck, Tal Lovejoy (standing naked on the beach), and Bruce and Jean Ariss in the background kissing. "I remember that party well," he says but instead tells me about a science fiction novel he's working on (the manuscript, along with his wife's current draft, was recovered from the fire). He already published one fantasy novel, *Full Circle*, in 1964, about a post-nuclear world in which native Americans briefly regain their birthright. This book, titled *The Voyeur*, explains exactly where UFOs come from. He asks me not to divulge the secret. But the subtitle is "Sex and the UFO."

We step out the back door to stand where Doc Ricketts must have spent much of his time pondering the great bay. The day has cleared perfectly, and it looks like a description from a Steinbeck novel: "It was one of those days in Monterey when the air is washed and polished like a lens, so that you can see the houses in Santa Cruz twenty miles across the bay and you can see the redwood trees on a mountain above Watsonville. The stone point of Fremont's Peak, clear on the other side of Salinas, stands up nobly against the east." There are buildings to block some of this view, but this day is as clear as Steinbeck's, and there's a quality of light that makes you believe you can see as far as your heart will allow.

Out front, Bruce and I stand hesitating on the top of the steps. On the sidewalks the tourists squirm along in groups that would rival the schools of sardines once in the bay. "During its heyday in the thirties," Ariss explains, looking down on the crowds, "the sardine industry brought in about $10 million dollars a year. A quarter of a million tons of sardines were processed annually by thousands of workers." The workers have been replaced by tourists, the smell of fish by Polo cologne. The harbor is thick with pleasure boats. But Bruce Ariss doesn't seem easily discouraged by fires or tourists. He's heading back to his land to begin again, as if the westering spirit that Jody's grandfather in *The Red Pony* spoke so eloquently about is a hunger that never died in this man.

† † †

This morning I check out of my motel room in Salinas and narrowly avoid a fistfight with the Iranian manager. He wants to charge me more than the price we agreed upon, and when I object he pulls the charge slip out of my hand. We exchange some heated words, and I suggest we let the police arbitrate. He tears up the slip, throws it at me, and screams, "Get out of my motel!"

After picking up the torn piece of paper, I oblige. The photographer who is traveling with me is certain that the manager has taken down my license number and is calling the state police, saying I refused to pay. For the next two days in the area, I'll have a keener appreciation of Steinbeck's paranoia after the publication of *The Grapes of Wrath*. Before I'm even out of Salinas on my way back into Monterey, I'm picturing myself as Robert Donat in *The 39 Steps*, unjustly accused and hounded by the police.

Steinbeck's powerful story "Flight" was set in the mountains around Big Sur, and my own flight from tourists and wax museums in Monterey, Iranian motel keepers in Salinas, and even expensive boutiques in Carmel takes me south on Route 1. A travel writer recently suggested that there seems to be some unwritten federal decree that wherever spectacular scenery exists, there must be gift shops. The number of gift shops rises exponentially according to the beauty of the scenery. But this coastline has a primal beauty and has somehow avoided gift shops.

Big Sur is one of those locales, like Yosemite or the Grand Canyon, that is literally breathtaking. The high cliffs, jutting rocks, and wind-swept seas all contrive to stun any traveler into silent contemplation. It's one of those places where human beings feel simultaneously humbled and elevated by nature.

About fifteen miles south of Carmel I find a spot that seems made for escape. In my mind is Pepé from "Flight" as I climb down a narrow cliffside path, framed by wild rosemary and unyielding chaparral, toward the rocky beach. It's about a mile to the bottom. I know the trip back up will be twice as hard, so I squeeze myself between two boulders and rest, watching the surfers and sea otters play. Sea kelp rises like a monster's dark hair in a watery green world, and white spray leaps against the rocks into the salt-soaked air.

The sun begins to go down and the cool evening is coming on.

Before it gets dark, I climb back up the spiraling path. After reaching the top, sweating and panting, I head back through Salinas, disguised in a "Columbus, Mississippi pig roast" baseball cap and a pair of dark sunglasses.

The disguise apparently works because I'm not arrested or gunned down. The next morning I drive to San Juan Batista and then the eleven miles up the mountain to Fremont's Peak. Originally called Gavilan Peak, named after the hawks that made their home there, it is the highest point in the Gabilan chain at 3,169 feet. The peak was later named for Captain John Charles Fremont, who planted the United States flag there in 1846. Fremont was on an exploring expedition in the area, and when the local Mexican authorities ordered him to leave, he built a log fort on the mountaintop and on March 6, 1846, raised the U.S. flag. But before the Mexicans attacked, the flag blew down. Fremont, who may have been a bit superstitious, took this as a bad omen and left the area for the San Joaquin Valley. He might not have been sure at that point if the territory was worth fighting for.

The early history of California suggests a similar ambivalence. The Spanish were the first Europeans to come in the mid-sixteenth century. They weren't too impressed. They hoped to find spices and gold. Instead they found a rocky coast. Searching for Eden, these sixteenth-century Spaniards named the land "California" after the imaginary treasure island in Garcia Ordonez de Montalbo's story "Las Sergas de Esplandia." At first glance, the land didn't appear to match their expectations. Nearly 300 years later Spanish California was a failed experiment. Not counting native Americans, California had a population of 8,000. Aside from a few otter traders and some trappers like the famous Jedediah Smith, Americans were not swarming into California either.

But within a few years things changed quickly. Fremont came and then the war with Mexico, but when gold was discovered in the American River, near Sutter's Fort, all hell broke loose. The golden dream of California had become a reality. In a short time over 80,000 Americans were crawling over the territory looking for gold. As Steinbeck phrased it in *The Grapes of Wrath*, "A horde of tattered feverish Americans poured in. And such was their hunger for land that they took the land—stole Sutter's land, Guerrero's land, took the grants and broke them up and growled and quarreled over them, those frantic hungry men."

California from that day forward became the land of golden opportunity—and it continued to be for Steinbeck's Okies in the 1930s and for the young people flocking to Haight-Ashbury in the 1960s. But the dream of prosperity or escape had some strings attached—overcrowded and polluted communities, cities inundated with drugs, oil spills in the harbor. But Steinbeck's world is still strongly present—in the migrant workers, in the ranch hands, in the homeless, and in the free spirits that seem as much a permanent part of the landscape as the smog in Los Angeles.

In *Travels with Charley* he said, "I knew that strip angled against the Pacific better than any place in the world." And from Fremont's Peak the whole strip is visible, the long line of valley, the mountains, Monterey Bay. I stand in the same spot Steinbeck did as he took his last view of his homeplace. Monterey Bay still shines like a blue platter and the wind blowing up from the valley smells of wild oats. A man sitting on the precipice a few feet from me carving a stick into a good imitation of a Bowie knife for his young nephew tells me that a half an hour ago he watched two ranchers in the foothills below shoot a coyote. The man comes up to the peak whenever he gets a chance, for it gives him a perfect view of the life around him and the solitude and distance to see it. Steinbeck would have understood him very well.

My drive back to San Francisco airport is uneventful, no roadblocks at least. I stop in a redwood preserve on the way back and perform the task Charley was so reluctant to perform on his journey. But I have had three sodas and besides am an outlaw already.

I spend the night in San Francisco with George Moley, an old friend from New York City who has lived in California for the past twenty years, spending the last twelve as a brakeman on the cable cars. We visit many of the Irish bars in his neighborhood near Golden Gate Park, but spend most of our time in O'Shea's, where the motto is "We cheat tourists and drunks." Like Steinbeck in his reunion with Johnny Garcia in *Travels with Charley*, I feel as if I've encountered a "bucket of ghosts." By four in the morning I have played enough pool, heard enough Irish accents, consumed enough beer, and listened to enough Irish jokes ("My brother-in-law was sentenced to sixty days in the electric chair") to refresh my memory and to make me realize, as Steinbeck did, that these neighborhood bars were the same—I was the ghost.

Homer once said that there's nothing worse for mortals than a wandering life, but as I look forward to my next trip, the journey to Hannibal, Missouri, and think of the excited faces of my young sons who are eager to join me on the last leg of the journey, I wonder if the old poet was speaking the truth. Maybe he was just trying to keep the roads open for wayfarers like himself.

7 Boyhood and Forgotten Dreams: Twain's Missouri

All over the world, wherever men can read,
everyone knows Hannibal. Everyone has lived
here for a precious moment and there are few
men who do not revisit it still in search of
forgotten tranquility and lost dreams.

Russell Baker, "The Observer,"
in the *New York Times*, August 26, 1963

All American literature comes from one book by
Mark Twain called *Huckleberry Finn*.

Ernest Hemingway,
The Green Hills of Africa

The reports of my death are greatly exaggerated.

Mark Twain in a cable from London
to the Associated Press in 1897

MOST PEOPLE have never been to Hannibal, Missouri. It's out of the way, no matter which way they're heading. It's a little river town of peeling paint and long-forgotten high hopes. Even the most sanguine Hannibalians must realize that the population has moderately but steadily decreased for over a half-century and that Mark Twain's success story, no matter how much they wish for it, will not be theirs.

But, as Russell Baker remarked, everyone knows Hannibal. For in our dreams Hannibal is that town of our youth, where time was like an island, motionless against the currents of days or weeks or even years. Summer was an eternity. It was lazy and dull and exhilarating and mysterious all at once. And it would not change. Nor would we. That is the town that Mark Twain gives us in *Tom Sawyer* and *Huckleberry Finn*, that is the place he remembers in *Life on the Mississippi* as a "white town drowsing in the sunshine of a summer's morning." It is the town we wish to remember, whether we grew up in the Bronx or St. Charles, Utah. It is a town situated more in time than in place, and it offers most of us the excitement and security of childhood and home. Twain remembers

> the streets empty, or pretty nearly so; one or two clerks sitting in front of the Water Street stores, with their splint-bottomed chairs tilted back against the walls, chins on breasts, hats slouched over their faces, asleep—with shingle-shavings enough around to show what broke them down; a sow and a litter of pigs loafing along the sidewalk, doing a good business in watermelon rinds and seeds; two or three lonely little freight piles scattered about the "levee"; a pile of "skids" on the slope of the

stone-paved wharf, and the fragrant town drunkard asleep in the shadow of them.

And, of course, he remembers the "majestic and magnificent" Mississippi.

In America, Twain was enormously popular as a funny man, but his great success surely goes much deeper. He is our Homer of boyhood, remembering for us the places and people, the splint-bottomed chairs and sleeping men, the wide waters and darkened graveyards. As one of his biographers, Justin Kaplan, has explained, the very word "drowsing," which Twain uses over and over again to describe Hannibal, conjures up an "image of childhood purified by the years, a state of idyllic innocence which could be recaptured only in the imagination." Our river may not be the Mississippi but Long Lake in Maine. Our town drunkard's name may not be Finn. Our frightening adventure may have been in a subway and not a cave. But the memories are the same. Twain's are universal, mythic, and most certainly American—filled with adventure and guilt and dreams of glory.

So the road to Hannibal may not be an interstate, but it is an important road, nevertheless, a road each of us has traveled at least in memory.

The drive from Virginia Beach to Hannibal is about one thousand miles. My traveling companions are my two younger sons—Ian, who just turned thirteen, and Owen, who is eight. Each of us has his own reasons for wanting to go. I want to see what Hannibal has made of Twain after all these years and perhaps discover whether his books have anything to do with it anymore. Ian wants to find basketball courts along the way. As I carry *Tom Sawyer*, he takes the *Back in Your Face Basketball Book*, which traces the best places to play the game throughout the country. We're surprised to find one listed in Hannibal. Owen comes for the thrill of travel and to see what the Holiday Inn will offer. He's seen color brochures, picturing a game room with a whiffle ball golf course, pool tables, and shuffleboard. I can read his mind—"Who knows what other adventures lurk in the corridors of that 250-room motel?" We all come wondering about Cardiff Hill and the cave and the Mississippi River.

And we all come with games and adventures in our minds. I remember *being* Tom Sawyer and Huck Finn and experiencing the separations of childhood, both real and romanticized. Most of us, at some time in our lives, play intensely, with all our energy. For me the time was the late 1950s and early 1960s, and the place was New York City. My games were not Tom Sawyer's and my escapes were not Huck Finn's, but they were not all that different either. We played Johnny-on-the-pony and ring-a-leavio, hunter and hide-and-seek, and every conceivable game that could be played with spaldings. Those pink rubber balls covered the gray city skies, as I remember it. They ricocheted off the brick walls and exploded into the alleys, off stoops and garbage cans and fire hydrants.

My sons are suburbanites. As I did, they play basketball and touch football, but they look to net guppies in the nearby pond, store pinecones for mock wars, and ride bikes around the cul-de-sacs. For them, as for me and Tom Sawyer and Huck Finn before them, time is a river as thick and slow-moving and sweet as honey. They even still chant "One Mississippi, two Mississippi" for any game that demands a count, as if in honor of Twain's memory.

I felt lucky to have my own Tom and Huck along for the ride. We'd advanced since the 1830s: our raft was a 1986 Plymouth Voyager, our river the highway. But just as Huck said that it was lovely to live on a raft, it's pleasant to pass the days floating along the highway, to be in the world and separate from it at the same time, listening to two boys spend the afternoon making up their universe, devising games and characters to fit the flow of time. They imagined themselves to be sports figures and politicians and detectives, going through more disguises than Huck Finn in the course of his adventures. They didn't let a moment go by unaccounted for. Annie Dillard's admonition in *Pilgrim at Tinker's Creek* was not one they needed to hear: "This is how you spend this afternoon, and tomorrow morning, and tomorrow afternoon. *Spend* the afternoon. You can't take it with you." Like Tom and Huck they knew how to spend their time.

Shortly before we left, I read *Tom Sawyer* to them. Twain said he intended it mainly for "the entertainment of boys and girls," but I'm convinced that it's really a book for adults who are remembering their childhoods. My thirteen-year-old listened attentively but asked often when they would get to the cave (he's seen the movie), but the eight-year-old said he didn't get most of it. He stared politely into space. Phrases like "caitiff carcase" and words like "incantation" and "odious" came too frequently for his taste. I think he felt a bit like Twain's narrator in *The Innocents Abroad*, persecuted with abstruse prepositions framed in a language no modern boy could appreciate. There was just too much of a "luxuriance of syllables" for him.

We leave Virginia on Saturday morning and drive through a blinding rain all the way through West Virginia and into Kentucky. As we leave Virginia Beach the streets have already begun to flood and like Noah and his family we seem to have two of everything— bonkers and *Sports Illustrated* and basketballs and biographies of Twain. My route is clear and simple: Route 64 west to St. Louis and then 61 north to Hannibal. My son Ian has a more complicated plan—stops at the outdoor basketball courts known as The Dell at the University of Virginia in Charlottesville; the Donnally Interstate Courts in Charleston, West Virginia; Douglass Park in Lexington, Kentucky; Igleheart Park in Evansville; and Don Mattingly's Restaurant in the same town. The bumper-to-bumper traffic along Route 64 away from the beach dampens some of our enthusiasm. Because of the rain, everyone from Ohio, Michigan, and Pennsylvania leaves with us. There are even a few Missouri plates speeding away from ruined vacations.

The Blue Ridge Mountains are shrouded in fog, and the lush valleys of western Virginia seem as thick as rain forests. By the time we reach West Virginia, it's late afternoon and the rain and the factory smokestacks spewing mushrooms of yellowish clouds into the air, blanketing the valley, the river, and the people in a malevolent-looking smoke, leave us silently questioning our choosing to travel. In *Life on the Mississippi* Twain wrote, "I was a *traveler*. A word had never tasted so good in my mouth before." But things are turning sour for us. It helps a little that the sky clears and the smokestacks of West Virginia vanish, replaced by the sculpted horse farms and rolling hills of Kentucky. But when we reach Evansville, Ingleheart Park is empty, the rims are rusted, and Don Mattingly's Restaurant is closed. This is beginning to resemble Twain's description of his trip on the *Quaker City*: "Perhaps it was a pleasure excursion, but certainly it did not look like one."

At night we stop in a motel outside St. Louis, brush the radioactive West Virginia dust from our clothes, and settle in to dream about Twain's "peaceful village." But the morning begins where the night left off. I turn on the faucet to get a drink, but whereas we may like color in our sports shirts, we usually demand a less exotic hue in our drinking water. Things have not changed much in one hundred years; Twain's description of the water in a St. Louis hotel still seems to apply: "A score of years had not affected this water's mulatto complexion in the least."

The Jefferson Arch in St. Louis, the gateway to the West, greets us first thing in the morning, its rainbow shape suggesting better things ahead. The first sign we see for Hannibal says ninety-four miles. The road narrows and gets bumpier, and the abandoned gas stations along the roadside become more frequent. The ones that remain open have an indolent, lonely appearance. A few homemade "for sale" signs are staked in the road, apparently unacknowledged. The highway seems to twist and turn for more than ninety miles, and as Route 61 unrolls, Ron Powers's remark that no one finds himself in Hannibal without seriously intending to get there seems a remarkable understatement. Hannibal is one of those little river towns that had high expectations but technology and circumstances left it sitting in the middle of nowhere. But there are more Hannibals than Chicagos or Atlantas in the United States. Route 61 is a vein leading to the heart of America, hidden away from the big cities. Such towns are anonymous, sometimes dreamily peaceful, and often filled with despair. Many of the roads branching off from 61 are not even given names. They are simply called *DD* or *FF*, as if the engineers or town fathers had given up on possibilities and accepted the most banal realities of life in the area.

But not everyone has accepted defeat gracefully. Mark Twain was a tireless and successful self-promoter, and the business community in Hannibal has tried desperately (and often pathetically) to follow in his footsteps. The first billboard we see, miles from Hannibal, announces that the Mark Twain Cave is "Open All Year

Round." The closer we get the more Twain's name and characters come out of hiding. Mark Twain Lake. Injun Joe Campground. Sawyer's Creek General Store and Putter's Golf. Mark Twain Outdoor Theater. Huck Finn Shopping Center. Pudd'nhead's Mini-Mall. Hotel Clemens. Tom 'n Huck Motel. The list could go drearily on for pages, but some credit should be given to these nomenclators, if not for ingenuity at least for tenacity. Everything in town, it seems, is named for Twain, from a horse-drawn wagon ride to the Mark Twain fried chicken at the, of course, Mark Twain Family Restaurant. As Tully Mars, a character in Jimmy Buffett's story "Take Another Road," says, "I do believe that if Mark Twain had never drawn a breath, the Hannibal Missouri Chamber of Commerce would surely have invented him to support the tourist economy."

But as we enter the town, it's clear that the promotion is not fully successful. The economy is not thriving. Staring out the window at the worn little town which seems more lifeless than tranquil, Owen says, "There's something funny about this place." I have to agree with him and with Ian who says, "They don't seem to be doing very well even *with* Mark Twain."

The town has its charm, though. The Garth Woodside Mansion, built by Colonel John Garth in the 1870s as a summer home, is a stately Victorian structure not unlike the homes Twain was to own in Connecticut later in his life. The Rockliffe Mansion, now a museum, and the Missouri Territory Restaurant, once the state's second-oldest federal building, rise magnificently above everything around them. The town is situated on a number of hills overlooking the Mississippi River. The 400-acre Riverview Park has an idyllic quality.

Then there's the rest of Hannibal, a few nice homes on the cliffs but mostly modest dwellings and stark circumstances. In his reminiscence *White Town Drowsing* Ron Powers called it a "cartoon of its former self, a parody of its past. Hanniballand. Twaintown. Haunted. Step right up." Very little of what it was remains to make Twain's description of it under the name Dawson's Landing seem accurate today:

In 1830 it was a snug little collection of modest one- and two-story frame dwellings, whose whitewashed exteriors were almost concealed from sight by climbing tangles of rose vines, honeysuckles, and morning glories. Each of these pretty homes had a garden in front fenced with white palings and opulently stocked with hollyhocks, marigolds, touch-me-nots, prince's feathers, and other old-fashioned flowers; while on the windowsills of the houses stood window boxes containing moss rose plants and terra-cotta pots in which grew a breed of geranium whose spread of intensely red blossoms accented the prevailing pink tint of the rose-clad housefront like an explosion of flame.

Twain's pseudonymous Dawson's Landing has lazy cats stretching out in the sun along the brick sidewalks, white fences, and quaint stores. The clear Mississippi washed up to the hamlet's front. Of course, the blemish of greed, murder, and slavery are the corrosion beneath the whitewash in his story.

However, Hannibal today doesn't seem to have even the white-wash. The great Mississippi, the "father of waters," stretching over 2,000 miles from the frozen North to the steamy Delta, may have enough chemicals and sewage in it to allow even the most ungodly to walk across the waters. Recently an article in *Newsweek* said, "Somewhere along its shores, virtually every environmental prob-lem known to civilization can be seen, except for the destruction of whales, and if the Mississippi had whales, they'd be in trouble there, too."

Hannibal, like the river, has its troubles. It had its peak popula-tion in 1930 when it could brag that it had 22,761. For the last sixty years it has steadily declined. The population, last count, was 18,881, more than a 16 percent drop since 1930. Industry is not thriving, and the young people are leaving as soon as they are able. The closest city, a little less than 120 miles away, is St. Louis. Many young people head there. The more daring strike out for Chicago, 300 miles away, or Detroit, which is about 600 miles east. More than 20 percent of the citizens are over sixty-five, compared to a national average of under 12 percent. The most recent record indicates that the vast majority of Hannibal's citizens make under $25,000 a year, and its households making under $10,000 are double the national average. Hannibal is not so much the white-picketed town Twain describes in *Pudd'nhead Wilson* or the pleasant hamlet drowsing in the sun in *Life on the Mississippi* but rather the "poor little shabby village of St. Petersburg" he mentions in *Tom Sawyer*.

But the shabby village has always aspired to greater things. "Hannibal has forever been dreamily in love with its unrequiting past," Ron Powers said. And Mark Twain has been the town's blessing and its curse. The town has attempted to capitalize in every way imaginable on the Twain legend. It's as if the town fathers looked to Twain, whose image Ron Powers says is easy to confuse with God's in Hannibal, trying to imitate his promotional magic. Twain was a master. As Justin Kaplan points out in *Mr. Clemens and Mark Twain*, after publishing *The Innocents Abroad* Clemens began

> to enact the legend of Mark Twain: the rocket rise, by way of the best seller and its nettling web of values, to celebrity, money, the grandest house in town, the gaudiest style of living. It was in his deliberateness, his promotional sagacity and sheer doggedness, that he departed from the dazzling pattern he set for American writers after him. Unlike the archetypal writer who leaves his creative solitude to find himself famous, Clemens was in part the father as well as the child of the circumstances that made him.

The town of Hannibal has tried everything to find the right incantation magically to restore the city's sagging hopes. It is a town which literally has a primitive and childlike belief in the power of naming. Twain. Twain. Twain. But no cave doors open to reveal a hidden treasure. However, it seems that without tourism the town would disappear. Most of the tourists come from St. Louis and the majority from Missouri and surrounding states, and they come not because of magazine or television ads but because Twain's writings have drawn them. They come to see the source for his peaceful St. Petersburg.

Hannibal's beginnings were not all that peaceful, however, as Hurley and Roberta Hagood point out to me. The town started with an earthquake and a smooth-talking salesman. I'm sitting in the Hagoods' modest home on Wyaconda Street in one of the

The old police station, Hannibal

subdivisions on the outskirts of town, listening to them recount the history of the place they clearly love. Both are in their eighties, born shortly before Mark Twain died, and both grew up in Hannibal in a time when its star was on the rise.

For forty years, until they retired in their sixties, the Hagoods lived in California, where Roberta was the director of placement for Chapman College and Hurley was a professional Boy Scout leader. When they retired, they returned to Hannibal, and it became their "usable past." They have spent the last decade writing two histories of the town and county, and Hurley hopes to start soon a history of Hannibal-LaGrange College, the small Baptist institution up the road from their house.

The Hagoods are the sort of good, decent people that unfortunately seem strangely out of place in the modern world. They are soft-spoken and hold hands as they talk. They smile at one another and have the ability that some couples develop after years together to make their individual statements and ideas blend together. They don't interrupt each other, but instead by some hidden radar make their words flow into one another, creating one voice. Neither had ever written a book, but when they heard from Roberta's sister that the chamber of commerce was looking for someone to write a bicentennial history, the Hagoods interviewed for the job and received the commission to do it. As Hurley says, "We didn't have many qualifications other than enthusiasm. But we did it for the right price—free."

Between the two of them, the Hagoods weave a miniature tapestry of Hannibal's history. In 1680 the first white man set foot on the cliffs overlooking the clear waters of the Mississippi, near the section that would become Riverview Park, but for the next century and a half Hannibal entertained only a few Indians and an occasional fur trader. A cataclysmic change began in 1811 but it had little to do directly with the settlement of Hannibal. During the winter of 1811–12 southeastern Missouri was rocked by massive earthquakes, at least one which was the largest ever felt in the United States. Probably the equivalent of 8.7 on the modern-day Richter scale, it was more severe than the San Francisco quake a century later, though few people were hurt because the area was so sparsely populated. The most devastating shocks reportedly came on February 7, 1812, hurling the Mississippi River to great heights and changing the land faster than a greedy developer and an overzealous construction crew. Lakes sprung up where forests once grew, chasms rent huge fields, rivers vanished. The Mississippi River braked to a stop, as we believe rivers can do only in cartoons, and ran backwards for a time. Towering trees split as neatly as kindling. The shock waves, attended by broken windows, smashed dishes, and frightened animals, shattered the calm as far away as St. Louis and Cincinnati. The tremors shook Detroit, Boston, and New Orleans.

Hannibal was settled by people with "earthquake certificates." "It was nothing but raw land then," Hurley explains to me, "and St. Louis was nothing but a small town. This was the government's first welfare program, granting people who lost their land in the earthquakes up to 650 acres in certain locations." There weren't many takers in the Hannibal area until Moses Bates came along in 1818. According to the official town history, handed out by the tourist bureau, Bates was a "successful contractor from St. Louis." Ron Powers describes him as the town's "first impresario, the frontier fixer who first spotted the area's dollar potential." Whatever the case, the slick-haired, goateed Bates convinced Thompson Bird to file a claim in the area with his father's earthquake certificates, which he did on the land near the confluence of Bear Creek and the big river. A few years before, the team of surveyors had named the stream Hannibal Creek. The town took its name from there, but the creek went back to the bears.

Over a decade passed and Hannibal's population barely reached thirty. By 1840, however, there were one thousand people, but promotional wizardry didn't account for the change. It was simply an accident of fate. In this case William Muldrow, described by Hurley Hagood as a "super salesman," was the agent of destiny. Muldrow had helped raise thousands of dollars for Marion College and had sold, sight unseen, $180,000 worth of lots in Marion City, Missouri. He persuaded buyers that the city would be a Chicago west of the Mississippi. The site for the town was about eight miles north of Hannibal. Muldrow was a masterful salesman, but he wasn't much of a planner. The town he envisioned was unfortunately built on mud and sand, and when hundreds of settlers came out to their new Eden it was flooded. They quickly moved to higher ground, the hills around Hannibal. The high hills brought high hopes, and in 1839 it brought the Clemens family.

For a time, it seemed some of those dreams would come true. The lumber industry helped the early economy. By 1850 Hannibal was a big town, mainly because of the Hannibal-St. Joe Railroad. By 1870, thanks to entrepreneur John Cruikshank from New Orleans, there were twelve lumber companies in Hannibal. Railroads, sawmills, pork packing and shoe manufacturing followed the $3 million lumber industry, and according to Ron Powers, "For a few thunderous decades, Hannibal boomed and boomed." Six railroad lines came through the town in the last decades of the nineteenth century. International Shoe Company was one of the biggest shoe manufacturers in the world, employing 3,000 people. In its heyday 1,200 riverboats a year steamed into Hannibal.

Appropriately enough, perhaps, the tourist bureau's summary of Hannibal's history ends with a paragraph on Twain's arrival in the town in 1839, as if nothing happened for the next 150 years. Not much did, except for the town's rise to its modest peak in the early twentieth century, when the population stretched over 22,000, the lumber industry was still alive, and shoes and cement were the area's pride and source of wealth. Hannibal's golden age was slow in coming but fast in departing. By the time the Mark Twain Memorial Bridge was opened in 1936, linking the town to the Illinois side of the river, Hannibal had been on the decline for a number of years.

Now the shoe factories are gone. The largest employer, besides the tourist industry, is American Cyanamid, which employs 370 people. There are only two railroad lines left running through the town. The bridge that spans the river into Illinois leads to cornfields and brings little community wealth. Besides, most of the residents cross it only warily, placing bets on when it will most likely fall into the muddy waters below.

Despite its dismal history, Roberta and Hurley have a great affection for Hannibal, and ironically, given all they have told me, are optimistic about its future. They take me to the graveyard Twain wrote about in *Tom Sawyer* and point out Injun Joe's tomb and the Clemens family plot. We drive past Twain's boyhood home and through Riverview Park, stopping to gaze at the Mississippi twisting far below, what Eliot called "the River God" slithering like a dark green snake in the sunlight. Behind us stands a majestic statue of Twain, near a row of cottonwood trees. The inscription reads: "His religion was humanity and a whole world mourned for him when he died." They drive over to the foot of Cardiff Hill and point up at the memorial lighthouse that was placed on a crest of the hill at the ceremonial beginning of the Mark Twain Centennial in 1935. President Roosevelt himself touched a gold key in the White House, lighting the beacon in the edifice, which seems oddly out of place on this cliff far from the possibility of any practical use. The Hagoods' last stop is near the riverboat dock. There we sit watching the water flow by as they tell me about the college expansion (although I noticed a few burnt-out buildings on campus), a new hospital, and the flood wall (which seems as necessary as a lighthouse in this town of many hills). But one thing is certain, they say: "The Mark Twain industry is expanding." They're right.

After leaving the Hagoods I stroll into the center of "Twaintown," as Powers called it, to visit the house where Sam Clemens grew up. Mark Twain's Boyhood Home and Museum, on Hill Street in Hannibal, is the hub of a dizzying wheel of Twain attractions, and like most of them it's disappointing. Twain liked P. T. Barnum, the master showman, and exchanged curiosities with him; Twain believed, according to Justin Kaplan, that "a man without publicity was a tinkling cymbal." Well, this is beyond Barnum, a whole brass band of salesmanship—the Tom Sawyer Dioramas Museum, the Molly Brown Dinner Theater (starring Mark Twain), the Haunted House on Hill Street (featuring life-sized figures of Twain, his family, his fictional creations, and a few corpses and skulls for good measure), and the Becky Thatcher Bookshop. There's even a sign for Huck Finn's House in front of a North Street duplex. It's a white frame house, typical of the homes in the area. On the side of 213 North Street a young woman hangs baby clothes on a line. On the front porch of 215, the other half of the duplex, a man whose sad eyes are shaded by a Coors baseball cap stares past a woman sitting next to him who reaches one weathered hand to prop up her

Statue of Twain on the outskirts of Hannibal

face against the railing. The sign reads: "This is the hovel described in the book." I can't help but wonder if the sign lowers the price the rental agent might ask for the place.

There's Mark Twain Avenue and the Mrs. Clemens' Shoppe, but the Twain House is the center of this universe. It's the place everyone comes to see, where we can be reminded that the American success story sometimes really happens. The "Lincoln of our literature," as William Dean Howells called Twain, left behind him poverty and a clapboard house to occupy a place of architectural splendor and to achieve fame and wealth that defied all categories.

Henry Sweets, the curator of the Twain House and Museum, has a tongue, as Twain once said of someone else, "that worked easily in the socket." In his Converse sneakers, jeans, and short-sleeved plaid shirt, he looks more like a member of the construction crew that is renovating the house than its curator. Sheets of plastic cover the building making it look more like a haunted house than the one up the street. The laths and beams are all exposed, the back end has been disassembled, and plaster powder seems to be a permanently fixed mist in the air. Before I talk with Sweets, Ian, Owen, and I pay our entry fee and "tour" the house. Tacked to the lathing are "photographs" of what it *should* look like. In certain rooms there are little machines that resemble parking meters, and for ten cents you can hear Hal Holbrook imitate Twain or listen to the author's favorite songs. Outside the house is "the fence Tom Sawyer painted." Even that seems smaller than the boys imagined, but we're just grateful we didn't have to pay another dime to see it.

Henry Sweets looks like Gomer Pyle with glasses, but he doesn't have the twang and is fond of using words like "dendrochronologist." He talks about the house as if he were rebuilding a skeleton. He thinks of himself as an archaeologist in his own back yard.

Sweets grew up in Hannibal and after finishing an M.A. in history at the University of Delaware he took the job as curator of the Twain House twelve years ago. He talks about many things in our short conversation, but one stands out: he wants to see the return of the rivertown appearance that Hannibal had during the

1840s; he envisions a mini-Williamsburg. He expects that Hannibal may end up being a crossroads of two major highways. Of course, this expectation has lurked in the shadows of the town for fifty years. Besides, ironically, Sweets's goal may have already been realized. Hannibal appears to be just like "the poor little shabby village of St. Petersburg."

Standing outside Twain's home as I leave are a young black couple, and in Hannibal with its steadily decreasing black population, this is an unusual sight. But I'm reminded of Twain's return to his Hannibal when he was writing *Life on the Mississippi*. "On my way through town to the hotel," he said, "I saw the house which was my home when I was a boy. At present rates, the people who now occupy it are of no more value than I am; but in my time they would have been worth not less than five hundred dollars apiece. They are colored folks." Some have suggested that Twain is implying some racist irony here, but although some see a tangle of intentions because he was raised on the southern code and later nurtured in an abolitionist environment, he was clearly no racist. To William Dean Howells he was "the most desouthernized Southerner I ever knew," and as Shelley Fishkin has explained, "During the years when he was struggling to complete this troublesome manuscript [*Huckleberry Finn*], he was also attempting to combat the destructive legacy of slavery by supporting the undergraduate and professional education of several promising black students."

For a time at least my sons and I need a respite from Twaintown, so we decide to find the gymnasium mentioned in Ian's book. But there's no escaping Twain around here. The Admiral Coontz Recreation Center is next to Clemens Field. Around the field is a ten-foot-high wall with sections of barbed wire. The field and the armory, turned recreation center, were once a camp for German POWs. The barbed wire that lingers over the main gate of the wall may suggest a fond memory of the military past, a skepticism about German goodwill, or simply a serious attitude about baseball. Nobody knows why it's there.

Inside, the recreation center is equally anomalous. Four basketball courts stand vacant (even here Hannibal didn't live up to expectations), retired people walk around the perimeter of the gym, and a nineteenth-century hearse wagon that is ready to be auctioned off sits incongruously at the far end of the building. Jim Burtnett, a nineteen-year-old Hannibal High graduate, is washing the floors. Unshaven and dressed in a sweat-stained old button-down T-shirt and ratty sneakers, Jim could pass for a modern-day Huck Finn. He's as pragmatic as Huck and holds no romantic views about the town he grew up in. "There's no middle class in this town," he tells me. "If you make $12,000 around here, you're doing well." A freight train, running from the east, crawls by the open garage doors at the back end of the gymnasium with a melancholy clicking. "Hannibal is going downhill slowly. If you want industrial drudgery, Hannibal has a job for you, but my dream is to move out of here." I almost expect him to say, "light out for the Territory," but Jim doesn't seem to be that familiar with Twain's work.

"I'm not an ardent fan of Twain's just because he lived here a few years," he says. "In a way it seems as if this town invented him just to exploit him, but this isn't an amusement park. It's a real place. There's drinking and drugs. I got caught up in some of that and am just getting myself straightened out now. The dream here is *escape*." As he talks, Jim slides his mop from side to side until he's standing next to the hearse. One of the elderly walkers who is ambling around the perimeter of the courts, stops and smiles, then says, "Whyn't you lie down in there, Jim, and take a rest. Ha, ha, ha." Jim shakes his head, and as I leave, I see them setting up a stage for a "senior-citizen hootenanny." Maybe the joke was just a warm-up for the afternoon's festivities.

The Mississippi River flows through much of Twain's work. After his training as a riverboat pilot, the river became for him "a wonderful book—a book that was a dead language to the uneducated passenger, but which told its mind to me." For Twain, and for generations of readers after him, it was the "great, majestic, magnificent Mississippi," mythical and coursing through American folklore, culture, and history. The pilot was also a mythic figure, "calm, imposing, the envy of all," a man who nobly combined memory, judgment, and courage to perform his job. And what a wonderful job Twain made it seem to be:

And it [the river] was not a book to be read once and thrown aside, for it had a new story to tell every day. Throughout the long twelve hundred miles there was never a page that was void of interest, never one that you could leave unread without loss, never one that you would want to skip, thinking you could find higher enjoyment in some other thing. There never was so wonderful a book written by man; never one whose interest was so absorbing, so unflagging, so sparingly renewed with every reperusal.

Like Melville before and Hemingway after him, Twain sounds the trumpet for experience. It is a patently American chord but typical of Twain; his "twain-ness," as Justin Kaplan has called it, comes out later in the same passage when he longs for the romance and beauty of the river. He wonders which should take precedence, the practical or the poetical, utility or beauty, and questions "whether he has gained most or lost most by learning his trade."

It is a trade still followed by some on the river. Twenty-five-year-old Greg Brown has the pink-skinned, scrubbed good looks of a blond-haired, blue-eyed surfer-turned-management-trainee, but he's actually a modern-day riverboat pilot. He has an east Tennessee drawl as casual as the meandering river and a playful sense of humor as deceptive as Twain's. As he stands behind the wheel of the boat, attentive to scores of details, he talks to me and the passengers in the same easy, ironic tone, which has the twang and cadence of the airline pilots described by Tom Wolfe in *The Right Stuff*, a poker-hollow tone that has a particular down-home calmness that is so exaggerated it begins to parody itself. I can imagine his calm voice if the boat sprung a leak and began to sink in the middle of the river: "I'm sorry folks but we're experiencing a minor inconvenience. Notice, by the way, on your left, the cliff called Lovers' Leap, described by Mark Twain. . . ."

The glass-enclosed wheelhouse aboard the *Mark Twain* riverboat is much the same as it was when Clemens was a pilot, the big wheel and the Olympian view. In this sanctuary the pilot still stands royally alone. But the depth finder, the speakers, cassette deck, and surface radar shake the nostalgic illusion. There's no leadsman riding the bow throwing in a line marked with a piece of cloth tied at twelve feet— "mark twain"—calling the depth of the channel in bass tones. There is no longer a steady traffic of steamboats, a few each day coming into Hannibal, curious children waiting for their arrival. But for Greg Brown there's still the romance of the river and the profession. "Originally these guys were the astronauts," he says, looking toward Jackson's Island just south of us, which has become a fleeting area, a parking lot for barges. "There used to be an old saying, 'What's the use of being a river pilot if you can't tell everyone to go to hell?'" But before he can follow his subversive line of thought, he realizes that it's time to change roles from pilot to tour guide, and he performs this transformation as easily as Sam Clemens turned into Mark Twain. He picks up the microphone and, tongue firmly planted against cheek, tells the legend of Lovers' Leap, the lovesick young Indian, the chief's beautiful daughter, Romeo and Juliet on the Illinois-Missouri shores. His speech slows, the drawl thickens, the microphone clicks off. Turning to me, he smiles and says, "Pretty fucking sad, huh?"

Four times a day he makes his hour-long cruise, four times a day he tells his stories and watches actors from the Mark Twain Theater shoot blanks at the boat, but neither tourists nor the routine seem to have diminished the character of the job for him. "Technology or not, we're still flying by the seat of our pants on the river as much as Twain was in his day," he says. "It's still the fickle Mississippi, and in order to get licensed you have to know the river in the dark, every curve and stump. Radar is optional, but you're not supposed to use electronic devices as your sole means of making decisions."

Brown was a cub pilot on the *Robert E. Lee* and other sternwheelers on the Tombigbee River and got his master's license in 1986. There's no school for piloting on the river, just what he calls the "knowledge box." His Horace Bixby was Steve Gadiz and his bible was Twain's *Life on the Mississippi*. He remembers reading Twain's chapter on a pilot's needs:

> One cannot easily realize what a tremendous thing it is to know every trivial detail of twelve hundred miles of river and know it with absolute exactness. If you will take the longest street in New York, and travel up and down it, conning its features patiently until you know every house

and window and lamppost and big and little sign by heart, and know them so accurately that you can instantly name the one you are abreast of when you are set down at random in the street in the middle of an inky black night, you will then have a tolerable notion of the amount and the exactness of a pilot's knowledge who carries the Mississippi River in his head. . . . Next, if you will take half of the signs in that long street, and *change their places* over a month, and still manage to know their positions accurately on dark nights, and keep up with these repeated changes without making any mistakes, you will understand what is required of a pilot's peerless memory by the fickle Mississippi.

He's read the passage over many times since he's been on the river and agrees with it more each day.

He grew up as a military brat in Knoxville, Tennessee, and other places, and maybe some of the military influence is still reflected in his short blond hair, starched white shirt, and spit-shined black shoes. He ended up on the river, though, by accident. After high school he got a job as a deck hand. "I was just killing the summer as a kid, but once it gets inside you, you can't believe it," he says. By the time he took his master's test, he knew he never would leave. In order even to take the ten-day written exam, a cub pilot must have 365 days of service and be endorsed by three other pilots. "You have to be able to draw the river in twenty-five-mile sections," he explains. "The pilot's test is all written. The only thing you don't have to prove to them is that you can steer a boat." As he talks to me he steers the boat downriver, past a barge on the Illinois side, answers a call from the engine room, puts a cassette in the tape deck, and spies a boy leaning against the side chain. He puts his head out the cabin door, saying, "Hey, get off of that chain." Inside, he says, "Bonehead. He's going to fall off and bust his head like a pumpkin."

But he seems to do everything in slow motion, even release his anger. He doesn't fight the river but rather finds its flow, engages its drifts, discovers the friendly winds. "You're not a pilot until you've run aground," he tells me. "The trick is to aim so you can readily get off. The river teaches you a lot about accepting the larger currents in life, finding a way to become a part of them. This boat weighs two hundred tons. You have to be patient. Whatever a boat this size does, it's going to do slow. If you're a pilot, you learn not to be in a rush. Twain was right when he said a riverboat is as slow as an island and as comfortable as a farm."

He's learning the river slowly and apparently in a different manner from the way Twain did. As a boy Sam Clemens knew the river as a poem, as a bewitching dream, noting all the "glories and the charms which the moon and the sun and the twilight wrought upon the river's face." But Brown read the river initially as a book of science, learning its snags and wrecks and sandbars. Now, he's become more interested in its mystery and reads everything he can about the Mississippi—fiction, folklore, oral histories. On the old leather sofa behind the wheel is a copy of Harlan Hubbard's *Payne Hollow: Life on the Fringe of Society*, which begins, "Maybe it isn't the river itself that made the folks along the Mississippi a little bit different. Maybe it was just God's way of kinda' keeping a lot of the world's eccentrics all in one place where he could watch 'em."

Just as there are two ways of reading the river, there seem to be two sides to Greg Brown, who looks like a young banker but who has the instinct to move slowly yet inexorably against the mainstream. There's also a part of him, as there was with Twain, that relishes stardom, and in this little waterfront world, Brown is a star—the handsome riverboat pilot. As we're leaving what Twain called "the sumptuous glass temple," two young women ask Greg to be photographed with them. I take the picture, as he smiles and hugs them both.

"We'd send you photos," one says shyly, "but you probably wouldn't want them."

Greg smiles and shakes his head, as if to say it doesn't matter. Then he says, "Well, as long as they don't appear on 'America's Most Wanted.'"

When I step across the gangplank and look up at the pilot house before I leave, I notice Greg still standing there in the doorway to his "office," as if he's caught between his two roles, pilot and entertainer. Everything in Hannibal and everything connected to Twain seems to suggest a conflict of interests. Ron Powers once said that Mark Twain was Hannibal's *blessing* and its *curse*. Those two words open the door to Twain's story as well.

† † †

Samuel Langhorne Clemens was born on November 30, 1835, in the dusty hamlet of Florida, Missouri. He was the sixth of seven children born to John Marshall and Jane Lampton Clemens. Mirroring the history of Hannibal, Missouri, where the Clemenses moved in 1839, Sam's family had high hopes and fading prospects. The moderately successful John Clemens was part of the gentry in east Tennessee. He was trained as a lawyer, served as a county commissioner and clerk of the circuit court, and owned a store. He had a profession and a few slaves, and in the hill country of Tennessee this made him part of the local aristocracy. But when hard times struck the area, he left, daydreaming about riches. Besides, he had purchased for about $400 a little over 75,000 acres of Tennessee land reputedly rich in copper, coal and timber. Whatever happened, he believed he would leave his family secure. But as Mark Twain says in his *Autobiography*, "Thus with the very kindest intentions in the world toward us, he laid the heavy curse of prospective wealth upon our shoulders. He went to his grave in the full belief that he had done us a kindness. It was a woeful mistake, but, fortunately he never knew it."

John Clemens became a county judge in Florida, Missouri, and for the remaining decade of his life he retained the title like a southern gentleman while his circumstances steadily declined. According to Justin Kaplan, the pattern he followed was poverty, dispossession, bankruptcy, exhaustion, and finally hopelessness. He failed in everything he put his hand to, from land speculation and the legal profession to slave trading and storekeeping. He was a silent, austere, and proud man, described by Twain as "stern and unsmiling." From him Twain may have inherited his easily outraged sense of rectitude and his agnosticism, which later turned to a dark naturalism. John Clemens died in 1846, when Sam was twelve, leaving his son forever haunted by the specter of debt. Years later in an obsessive attempt to acquire enough wealth to banish forever even the remote possibility of poverty, Twain would ironically follow in his father's stumbling footsteps. Like his father, Twain would have a history of business failures that replayed his father's story of misplaced faith and dreamy expectations.

John Lauber, in *The Making of Mark Twain*, a biographical account of Twain's first thirty years, writes, "Life in poverty, or under its perpetual threat, left Sam with a lifelong horror of debt. But it did more than that: it made him constantly aware of the need for money, of the humiliating discrepancy between family pretensions and family realities; forced him to yearn to be really rich, even when he was already a wealthy man, and to indulge in obsessive, ruinous speculating."

According to Twain, his mother had a "sunshiny disposition" and "the heart of a young girl." He saw her as a woman full of playfulness and laughter, spontaneous and impulsive. Twain would recall that her most memorable trait was a "strong interest in the whole world and everybody in it." The sense of playfulness and laughter he fell heir to he used in most of what he wrote. He also inherited her red hair, although he might have described its color differently, for as his Connecticut Yankee said, "When red-headed people are above a certain social grade, their hair is auburn." But Jane Clemens was also a zealous Presbyterian who never fully convinced her son of God's place in the universe but certainly left him with a generous capacity for guilt and an often overworked conscience.

Sam Clemens's boyhood days in Hannibal, from the time he was four until he turned seventeen, became the geography of his soul and the heart of his work. He once said that when he was younger he could remember everything, "whether it happened or not." Albert Bigelow Paine, Twain's friend and first biographer, has suggested that Jane Clemens was the original of Tom Sawyer's Aunt Polly, that Huck Finn was based upon a local boy named Tom Blankenship, and that a whole score of characters from his novels are based upon his boyhood associates. John Lauber agrees that "there can be no doubt that much of *Tom Sawyer* is taken from life: probably young Sam gave painkiller to the family cat, swindled his friends into whitewashing the fence, clobbered his younger brother for tattling, escaped a whipping by calling out to his mother to look behind her." As Lauber points out, Tom Sawyer was clearly modeled on the young Clemens, but surely Huck at least equally reflects the adult Mark Twain. Ron Powers once remarked that Hannibal was Tom Sawyer's town. In some ways Mark Twain *was* Tom Sawyer, nostalgically remembering Hannibal and anxious to return, after having lived the life of a pirate, with his pockets full of gold. The other part of him was Huck Finn, a realist and a loner, with few ambitions to secure an honored place in the community.

Hannibal was the imaginative source for the remembered serenity, the fragile security, the forbidding churches and schools, the excitement of gilt and glass steamboats, the occasional but nightmarish violence, and the realities of caste and class that were an integral part of all southern towns, for Hannibal was southern by inclination if not by geography. And if Hannibal was the imaginative source, the Mississippi River was the lifeblood coursing through all Twain felt and imagined about the town.

The river offered escape to the larger world, away from the often dreary existence in the town, away from the poverty, away from some of the local nightmares. The young Clemens saw things he would never forget. He saw the corpse of a murdered man lying in his father's empty law office. He witnessed a man after he had been shot down in the street, "the grotesque final scenes—the great family Bible spread open on the profane old man's chest" and in his dreams he reimagined the man as he "gasped and struggled for breath under the crush of that vast book." But most horrible of all, he apparently witnessed his own father's post-mortem. In one of his notebooks he recorded that in 1847 he peered through a keyhole to watch his uncle's autopsy, but as John Lauber makes plain, he had no uncle who died then. It was *his father* who died in 1847. "It seems, then, that the eleven-year-old Sam looked through that keyhole," Lauber says, "and saw the naked corpse of his father under dissection—a shameful, unforgettable violation of John Clemens' austere dignity."

Clearly, as Twain said, everyone is a moon and has his dark side. Perhaps Van Wyck Brooks sounded the truth when he wrote of Twain's dual personality, one side allied to the Victorian notion of success and respectability and the other to a romantic idea of rebellion and creativity. Samuel Clemens, the master of personas, eventually transformed himself into his best creation, his other half, Mark Twain.

Behind all the facets of his personality, however, was the Puritan work ethic. Despite the jokes he made about his own laziness, Twain always worked hard at whatever he did. His schooling apparently ended when he was about fourteen, shortly after his father's death, although this was probably a typical age for most boys to begin work in such frontier communities as Hannibal in the mid-nineteenth century. He was apprenticed to the publisher of the *Hannibal Courier-Post*, a weekly newspaper, to learn the printer's trade. Benjamin Franklin had made the printing trade an acceptable avenue into literary pursuits, but at this point Clemens showed few signs of such an interest. According to John Lauber, the printing office was "the poor boy's college," where a young man could learn spelling and grammar and something about writing and current events. Sam learned his trade and even published a few articles under the byline "SLC."

But Hannibal was too small to hold Clemens for long. Before he turned eighteen he left for New York City with less than twenty dollars in his pockets. Only rarely after that did he return to Hannibal except in his imagination, where the town became the Edenic St. Petersburg, representing a universally understood age of innocence. After getting a taste of itinerant work, he wound up in Keokuk, Iowa, in his brother Orion's printing shop, and he spent the next year and a half there, doing his job and dreaming of escape. Finally he did escape, heading for the Amazon, Brazil, and a fortune in cocoa plants. He never made it to Brazil. Instead he ended up in Cincinnati in the printing trade once again. Then in 1857 he escaped once more, heading probably for the gold fields, but he ended up as a pilot on the steamboat *Paul Jones*, under the tutelage of Horace Bixby, a pilot he would make famous in *Life on the Mississippi*. For $100 down, with the remaining $400 to be paid from Clemens's first earnings, he was able to convince Bixby to take him on as a cub pilot.

As Twain said in *Life on the Mississippi*, "Pilot was the grandest position of all. The pilot, even in those days of trivial wages, had a princely salary—from a hundred and fifty to two hundred and fifty dollars a month, and no board to pay. Two months of his wages would pay a preacher's salary for a year." The pilot had a princely salary and a king's status, but the job was no sinecure as Twain soon learned. After a few months he thought he was ready to take a boat down to New Orleans, but Bixby taught him otherwise. In *Life on the Mississippi* Twain tells the story:

One day he turned on me suddenly with this settler:

'What is the shape of Walnut Bend?'

He might as well have asked me my grandmother's opinion of protoplasm. I reflected respectfully, and then said I didn't know it had any particular shape. My gun-powdery chief want off with a bang, of course, and then went on loading and firing until he was out of adjectives.

On April 9, 1859, after two years of apprenticeship Clemens received his pilot's license. This was the golden age of steamboating and Twain would remember his two years as a pilot as the best of his life. Later he was to say that if he had to live his life all over again, he would start out as a cub pilot, by and by become a pilot on the Mississippi, "and remain one."

Twain learned the river and he "learned" the people on it as well. Those were happy years for him, a time when expectation and actuality seemed to flow together, but there was also tragedy. His younger and beloved brother Henry was killed in an explosion on the steamboat *Pennsylvania*, a boat that Clemens had recently left after a fight with its pilot. Perhaps because fate had decreed that he would survive and the "blameless" and "poor sinless" Henry was to be scalded to death, Clemens felt that his younger brother's death was to be a recurring pattern in his life. He felt guilt for his son's death, his daughter's, for the death of a prisoner in the Hannibal jail when he was a boy—he may have had a trained Presbyterian conscience but he usually carried enough guilt around to be a good Catholic.

The steamboat was Twain's Harvard, but his education came to an abrupt end with the Civil War. By 1861 everyone was taking sides, but Clemens, true to his past and his future, was divided. The loyalties within his state were confused, his family had held slaves, and his brother Orion had campaigned for Lincoln. Clemens, however, joined the Confederacy, a military stint that lasted for about two weeks of quarrels, rain, mud, false alarms, and unnecessary retreats. His troop seems never to have fired a shot, and when Missouri finally declared for the Union, he went home without having to face charges of desertion. After his "campaign that failed," Clemens went out west to the Nevada Territory with his brother Orion, who had been appointed secretary of the newly formed state. Clemens was heading in the right direction: although his future was in the East, his identity and fame were in the West. It was in Nevada and California that Mark Twain would be born. He started out as a miner but found more gold in the long run in journalism. He began contributing letters, signed "Josh," to the *Territorial Enterprise* of Virginia City, Nevada. Soon he was a reporter for the paper, making twenty-five dollars a week. Virginia City was a frontier and gold-mining town, which meant it was rich and unfinished and violent. In the matter of a few years it had transformed itself from tents and shanties into a town of frame houses and a population of 15,000, mostly grizzled prospectors. There was always news for a young reporter, it seemed—claim jumps, fights, murders.

It wasn't long, however, before Clemens's special brand of humor, which could be uproariously funny and vicious at the same time, began to be appreciated. Here is his description of a woman to whom he had taken a dislike: "I conceived an aversion for her the first time I ever saw her. A strange and vanity-devoured detestable woman! I do not believe I could ever learn to like her except on a raft at sea with no other provisions in sight." He began writing under the pseudonym "Mark Twain," a riverboat term for two fathoms, or safe water. As many historians have pointed out, the pen name was a custom of the time and could be discarded or reserved for print as the writer's following grew. In any case it pointed out a clear distinction between literature and life, between the writer and the persona he created. However, in Twain's case the pseudonym, as Justin Kaplan and others have suggested, seems to have had a deep hold on the writer's personality. Eventually Clemens was to use his pseudonym even in letters to his wife and close friends. He took on a new identity in a new world. "In the same way the fop journalist Walter Whitman put aside his frock coat and became Walt Whitman, 'one of the roughs,'" Justin Kaplan writes, "Sam Clemens put aside his river outfits in favor of 'a damaged slouch hat, blue woolen shirt, and pants crammed into boot-tops,' and he was on his way toward becoming something other than what he had been." The first comic piece in the *Enterprise* to be signed with his new name read, "Yours, dreamily,

Mark Twain." With those four words, the man who was to become America's most famous writer rose from the shadows of his own subconscious.

He began contributing letters to the San Francisco *Morning Call* and after the fiasco of an aborted duel with a writer from a rival newspaper, he moved to San Francisco and took a job for the paper at an increased salary of forty dollars per week. According to Nigey Lennon, the San Francisco of the 1860's was "a boomtown with a thyroid problem, a punk kid rapidly growing too big for its britches." In other words, it may have been the perfect place for Mark Twain to create himself. He was a good reporter and as the months went on a better humorist. On November 18, 1865, "The Celebrated Jumping Frog of Calaveras County" was published in the New York *Saturday Press*. Mark Twain was on his way to literary stardom. "Jumping Frog" was in the tradition of southwestern humor, but it was a superb example. In it Twain mastered the American vernacular and created a wonderfully effective frame with the stilted language and pretensions of the gentlemanly narrator crashing comically into the simple, plain, if garrulous, speech of the uneducated frontiersman Simon Wheeler.

By 1866 he was a correspondent for the Sacramento *Union*, traveling in the Hawaiian Islands. After the freedom of his Hawaiian adventure, daily journalism would never suit him again. When he returned he delivered a few lectures in what was to become his patented deadpan delivery. As he once said, "The first virtue of a comedian ... is to do humorous things with grave decorum and without seeming to know that they are funny." He would spend a large part of his time over the next quarter of a century on the speaker's circuit, and, along with Charles Dickens, would become one of the most popular lecturers of his time.

Toward the close of 1866, the San Francisco paper the *Alta California* told its readers that Mark Twain would be its correspondent, sending back letters from his journey around the world on the *Quaker City*, a luxury cruise ship embarking from New York City. Two important things were to come from his excursion. First, *The Innocents Abroad*, the book comprising his collection of letters written while he was on the *Quaker City* tour, was destined to be his first great success. Second, while he was on board ship he met

Charles Langdon, a seventeen-year-old boy who had been sent on the grand tour by his father, a wealthy coal dealer in Elmira, New York. Charles showed him a cameo portrait of his sister Olivia, and Twain fell in love, it seems, like a character in a Walker Percy novel, at first sight and from thousands of miles away.

But before he actively began his courtship, he struggled to transform himself once again, from writer to author. He accepted an offer from Elisha Bliss of the American Publishing Company of Hartford, Connecticut, to print *The Innocents Abroad* as a subscription book. Like encyclopedia sales today, subscription books were sold not through advertising or reviews but through the canvassing of salesmen, mostly disabled war veterans, schoolteachers, and clergymen. As John Lauber explains, they went out armed with enticing illustrations, prospectuses, tables of contents, sample pages, and their order forms. Profit was the motive and hard sell was the technique. Lauber also says that subscription publishing had a lifelong effect on Twain, teaching him "to consider his books as merchandise; to satisfy the need for sheer bulk, he might extend them far beyond their proper length, stuffing them with irrelevant or inferior material, as he did with *Roughing It* or *Life on the Mississippi*." His first great success, *The Innocents Abroad*, is a prime example of a book too long by at least a half. Even Twain recognized this flaw when he said that he felt about the book much the same as God probably did about the world: "The fact is, there is a trifle too much water in both."

Early on, Twain was pigeonholed as a humorist, but, as his biographers have made clear, perhaps the way his books were sold did as much as anything else in allowing his genius to go unrecognized by the literary establishment. But if *The Innocents Abroad* didn't find the critics, it certainly found an audience. Sixteen months after its publication it had sold 85,000 copies. As Clemens proudly announced to his future wife, Livy, "Nothing like it since *Uncle Tom's Cabin*, I guess."

On February 2, 1870, Twain married Livy, moved to Buffalo as part owner of the Buffalo Express, and was astonished by Jervis Langdon's gift of a Victorian mansion, furniture, and carriage. Twain had come a long way from the frame house in Florida, Missouri, and within a few years he had another mansion in

Hartford, Connecticut, a house of "spectacular opulence unknown to American writers before," as Justin Kaplan phrased it. It was in the Nook Farm community, near the homes of Harriet Beecher Stowe and Charles Dudley Warner, an enclave of wealth and idealism. The house could be called a Victorian mansion but it seemed to defy architectural definitions. Kaplan describes it:

> It presented to the dazzled eye three turrets, the tallest of which was octagonal and about fifty feet high, five balconies, innumerable embrasures, a huge shaded veranda that turned a corner, an elaborate porte-cochére, a forest of chimneys. Its dark brick walls were trimmed with brownstone and decorated with inlaid designs in scarlet-painted brick and black; the roof was patterned in colored tile. The house was permanent polychrome and gingerbread Gothic; it was part steamboat, part medieval stronghold, and part cuckoo clock.

Mark Twain had arrived in all his splendor. The house had nineteen rooms, five baths (with indoor plumbing, which was uncommon for the time), inlaid woodwork, opulent furnishings, a glass conservatory, and even a third-floor billiard room, where Twain could indulge in two of his passions, smoking cigars and playing pool.

In the years that followed, Twain transformed himself once again. He had been a typesetter, riverboat pilot, gold miner, newspaper reporter, and travel writer. Now he would become family man, entrepreneur, and "author." In 1872 he published *Roughing It*, which, although not as commercially successful as *The Innocents Abroad*, was a better book, as he acknowledged himself, "much better written." He continued to be a star lecturer and in 1876 published *The Adventures of Tom Sawyer*, what one critic called his "paean to boyhood." With this book he began to change his status as literary comedian and to move from fictionalized autobiography to autobiographical fiction. As he says in his preface to *Tom Sawyer*, "Most of the adventures recorded in this book really occurred." He began to mine the gold in his "usable past." In *Huckleberry Finn*, his masterpiece, a book he described as a story in which "a sound heart and a deformed conscience come into collision and conscience suffers defeat," and in *Life on the*

Mississippi, which is like a non-fiction twin of the novel, he continued this process.

During those years he was also becoming a family man. Livy gave birth to a son, Langdon, who died at two years old, and to three daughters, Clara, Jean, and Susy. Livy, who had been an invalid throughout her late teenage years, the victim of some unnamed Victorian ailment, was basically healthy and strong during those years, although later she had sporadic spells that incapacitated her. A loving husband and father—although his children later seemed to remember his quick anger and sharp tongue—Twain was living out his fantasies. As his close friend William Dean Howells said of him, a large part of Twain's dream was absolute financial security, and to accomplish this he needed more and more money "to fill out the spaces of this dream." He was like a Horatio Alger character whose talent, hard work, and genius for self-advertisement made his dreams materialize in the hard light of day.

But not even the hard light of day saved Clemens from falling under the spell of James W. Paige, an inventor who had supposedly created a typesetting marvel that could do the work of ten men. Like his brother Orion, whom he consistently upbraided for being flighty and whimsical, Twain inclined toward poor investments and questionable inventions—everything from a history game and a perpetual calendar to a bed clamp and a fire extinguisher that worked like a hand grenade. Like Orion's schemes, Twain's ventures usually failed and cost him thousands of dollars. Unlike Orion, however, Twain had his talents as a writer and a speaker to fall back on. Through his talent Twain was more than "twice-born," as one critic called him. He was born again and again, falling into debt, recovering himself with a best-seller, going into bankruptcy and paying off his creditors by earning vast sums of money on the lecture circuit. He had, it seems, the Midas touch; at one point, everything he touched turned to gold. He was actually frightened, he said, at the "proportions of my prosperity."

But there was never *enough* money. As Justin Kaplan points out, "By 1881 Mark Twain's scale of living was so high that just running the house and providing champagne, canvasbacks, fillets of beef, and ice-cream cherubs for his procession of visitors cost about as much as he earned from royalties and investments." His own publishing company was never truly successful, his inventions sputtered and clanked to a halt, even his Hartford palace forced him, as Justin Kaplan said, into a "style of living and earning more like that of a robber baron than that of a writer." But the biggest financial drain of all was the Paige typesetting machine, costing him hundreds of thousands of dollars for nearly two decades, beginning in 1880 with his initial $5,000 investment.

He continued to write during this time—*The Prince and the Pauper* in 1882, *Life on the Mississippi* in 1883, *Huckleberry Finn* in 1884, *A Connecticut Yankee in King Arthur's Court* in 1889, and *Pudd'nhead Wilson* in 1894—but financial difficulties eventually took their toll. He went bankrupt, and even though he was not legally liable to pay back all his creditors, he paid back every penny, saying, "Honor is a harder master than the law." It took him years of grueling lecture tours, but although he had cleared his debts and started on his next fortune, the demons had been loosed and a darker Twain was emerging. As he said of *A Connecticut Yankee in King Arthur's Court* in a letter to Howells, "If it were only to write over again there wouldn't be so many things left out. They burn in me; and they keep multiplying; but now they can't ever be said. And besides, they would require a library—and a pen warmed up in hell."

He had other reasons during these years to become cynical and despairing. In 1895 his youngest daughter, Susy, died suddenly of meningitis. It seemed to take the life out of Livy and him, and he said, "It is one of the mysteries of our nature that a man, all unprepared, can receive a thunder-stroke like that and live." Livy never fully recovered from the blow and declined steadily until her death in 1902. In another sense, Twain never recovered either. His writing became darker, angrier, more naturalistic. His good friend Howells worried that he ate too many meals on the lecture circuit and did too little writing. His humor, which had always been sharp, became caustic and left little hope for human beings or the world.

By this time, early in the twentieth century, Twain, the roots of his identity reaching deep into folklore, had become a worldwide celebrity, a part of his own mythmaking. He had defied the literary establishment, had proven that there are some second acts in American literature, had made and lost and remade a fortune, and had demonstrated that American humor could have sources and intentions as deep as any literature. For the last ten years of his life he was, in Kaplan's words, "a semi-retired man of letters who no longer kept notebooks but instead pocket diaries in which he recorded a few literary ideas and a lot of social and business engagements." He had realized one of his ambitions, to be "the most conspicuous person on the planet."

A few months before his own death, fate dealt him one final blow. His middle daughter, Jean, died after an epileptic seizure in her bath. Twain did not last much longer. He had once said that a man without publicity was a tinkling cymbal, and as if he had waited for the return of Halley's Comet, which had appeared in the year of his birth, he departed with the streak of light across the universe to announce his passing.

His fame never faded, and this genius of publicity became, after his death, the object of a sales pitch in his boyhood hometown that could have been the subject of one of his satires. In a sense, though, he is the man who corrupted Hannibal. The streak of fame he left in the sky was too much for the town to resist. I remember a conversation I once had with Justin Kaplan in which he said to me, "The two worst things that happened to Hannibal were the Mississippi River, which regularly overflows its banks into the business district, and Mark Twain." The more I see of Hannibal, the less exaggerated his remark seems to me.

One of the advertised highlights in Hannibal, the Mark Twain Cave, touted on billboards fifty miles away, is our destination. The Mark Twain Cave, called McDougal's cave in *Tom Sawyer*, is still a vast labyrinth of crooked aisles that run into each other and lead nowhere. Twain said that a person could wander days and nights through the tangle of rifts and chasms and never find the end of the cave. During Twain's time, no man "knew" the cave, but most young boys and girls knew parts of it.

Now, like the rest of Hannibal, it's been made into an artifact, sterile and safe. Rows of lights dot the passageways and tour guides lead the way, using the same overdescriptive names Twain mentions in Tom Sawyer—"The Cathedral" or "Aladdin's Lamp." The tour guide batters us with awful puns about rocky marriages begun in the cave and other assorted stone jokes. In the spirit of revenge, Ian and Owen seem to pattern their behavior on the tourists in *The Innocents Abroad* who play the game that, as Twain says, "has vanquished so many guides for us—imbecility and idiotic questions." But the best revenge would be to escape, and they whisper to me, "Let's slip down this darkened passageway and explore on our own." Luckily, before I have to decide between the spirit of escape and the inclination to conform, the tour guide says, "This is what the cave looks like without lights." He shuts off the lights and the darkness is unlike any we're used to—it is total, absolute. I'm unable to see my hand when I hold it inches from my face. None of us wishes to get lost in this blackness. We continue with the tour guides, following the lights and bad puns.

The cave, a marvel of lithographic limestone, is about fifty degrees all year round, too cool for snakes and rodents. It's easy to imagine how exciting it must have been for young girls and boys to drift in here, unchaperoned, to explore, candles in hand in the potential blackness. Perhaps the cave has become a mirror of the times. Discovered in 1819, in Twain's day it was part of the natural landscape. Twain most likely explored the cave as Tom Sawyer did. At some point during Twain's boyhood, the cave took on a macabre connotation. He explains in *Life on the Mississippi:*

> There is an interesting cave a mile or two below Hannibal, among the bluffs. I would have liked to revisit it, but had not time. In my time the person who then owned it turned it into a mausoleum for his daughter, aged fourteen. The body of this poor child was put into a copper cylinder filled with alcohol, and this was suspended in one of the dismal avenues of the cave. The top of the cylinder was removable; and it was said to be a common thing for the baser order of tourists to drag the dead face into view and examine it and comment upon it.

There are no copper cylinders or dead bodies (perhaps the private owners of the cave haven't yet realized the marketing possibilities in this direction), and I could only guess how my fellow tourists might respond. In the 1950s the cave was a civil defense fallout

Owen and Ian Pearson, looking out onto Bear Creek, Hannibal

shelter, stocked with water and food, a haven against the Communist curse. Today it is just another tourist trap, another item sold in the carnival. It's the age, as Daniel Boorstin said, of the pseudo-event and maybe of the pseudo-place, as well, the place that once had some authenticity and vitality and has now been made into a mild parody of itself.

On our way across town to Cardiff Hill, we stop in the Becky Thatcher Bookstore, hoping maybe to pick up a few of Twain's books and shed the present. They had most of his works, but they were sandwiched between cram cassettes for *Huckleberry Finn* ("In one hour you will know: complete plot, characters, and themes") and a row of Harlequin romances—*Silk and Satin*, *Passionate Warriors*, *Hot Flashes*, and *Lady of Conquest*. Our appetite for reading quickly fades.

At the foot of Cardiff Hill, also called Holiday's Hill, is a statue of Huck and Tom. With all the statues of Twain and his fictional creations, with all the images that plastered billboards and posters and brochures, it was becoming painfully obvious that Jim would never become one of the town's icons. It was clear once again that Ron Powers was right: this was Tom Sawyer's town.

There's a man leaning against the statue. In the falling dusk he at first seems to be a bronzed third figure. When we ask him about the lighthouse on top of the hill, he warns us about the "riffraff" that "lounge around" up there at night. Before he can go very far in his sermon about change, young people, and the loss of morality, we excuse ourselves to climb the hill. A few steps up I turn back and he is still there, like one of Twain's characters in *The Innocents Abroad*, "a sanctimonious old iceberg who looked like he was waiting for a vacancy in the Trinity."

I'm a bit wary as we climb the steps because I recall Twain's anecdotes about the boyhood pranks performed on Holiday's Hill. He describes one in which he dropped a watermelon shell on his brother's head and another in which, with some friends, he pried loose a boulder. When it broke free, it nearly crushed one boy, then smashed a good-sized tree, leaped straight over a terrified man with his mule and cart, and wrecked an empty shed before burying itself in the dirt at the bottom. I keep a watchful eye for even loose rocks heading in our direction.

There's a crowd of sorts on top of the hill, five young men, a teenage girl, a baby, and enough mosquitoes to compete with a square mile of Costa Rican jungle. In *Life on the Mississippi* Twain remarks that two Louisiana mosquitoes could whip a dog and four could hold a man down. What little these Hannibal bugs might lack in strength, they make up for in numbers. But the teenagers seem undisturbed and swat only occasionally with the lazy indifference of a dog's tail flicking against the inevitable onslaught.

As we arrive, one young man, eighteen-year-old Brandon Lamont, his young wife, Amy, and their year-old baby girl, Brean Nicole Lamont, head down the hill. Of the four teenagers who remain, two are black and two are white, an unusual balance in this town. Mark Lamont, Brandon's seventeen-year-old brother, is the most talkative of the group. It seems he's used to attention from the media: a little over a year ago his brother was the object of a feature for a Detroit newspaper on modern-day Tom Sawyers. "He made a good picture," says Mark, "with his blue punk haircut and leather jacket. We've got the picture hanging at home." Since the story, Brandon has gotten married and had a child, but despite marriage and fame he still meets with the old crowd on Cardiff Hill on summer nights.

Mark is eager to talk, as if the publicity spirit so pervasive in Hannibal has caught fire in him too. He has the freckled good looks we might expect of Tom Sawyer, but he does not evoke the past. His baseball cap, which he bought in a local video shop, says "MGM/UA," and his brown Banana Republic T-shirt, black Reeboks, and the two earrings in his left ear suggest a Tom Sawyer on the brink of the twenty-first century.

The four boys have been friends for a long time. Their fathers work in the local factories or on county work crews. They seem to believe that the best luck they can expect is to do the same. Sitting on the bench atop Cardiff Hill, in the center of what they call "Bug Nation," is the only escape they imagine. I have to admit there's a magic to the place at night. Ian, Owen, and I even forget about the bugs as we sit in the gathering darkness, listening to the boys talk, hypnotized by the yellow lights that line Main Street below, making it appear to be a Hollywood set for *The Wizard of Oz*.

None of the boys can afford cars, so they can't cruise Main Street, which is the principal form of entertainment for the older teenagers in town. Instead, like overage Tom Sawyers and Joe Harpers, they plan "mischief" from their vantage point on Cardiff Hill. Or they talk about the other groups of teenagers in town: the jocks, the skaters, the preps, the ricks. Shawn's T-shirt, which lists all the dead skate parks across the United States, implies his affiliation. The skaters, I guess, are the closest thing to surfers you can find over 1,000 miles from the nearest ocean. Their other classifications are fairly clear and are probably ubiquitous, as common in Beverly Hills, California, as they are in Yulan, New York. It's the "ricks" that make me pause and wonder. At first I hear "wrecks" and assume they're talking about some slimy, desperate, slovenly breed known only in Hannibal. Actually, it's less unusual and funnier than that. The name "ricks" stands for all farm boys and rednecks in the area, but there's an etymology to the word. It seems there's an actual "Rick," a burly, red-headed epitome of all that the stereotype means to them, but he's too big and hot-tempered for anyone to let him know that he is the eponymous source.

When they're not talking about "ricks," they are talking about jobs, or the lack of them. "Grandma is trying to get me to work out at the old age home," one complains. Another talks about his two-week career at Hardee's, the seven days he worked, the three days he skipped, the three days he was suspended, and the day he quit. The others talk about possible jobs at Watlow Industries, Hannibal Carbide Tool, and Buckhorn Rubber Products, but their talk seems to be idle conversation and has even less enthusiasm than their fly swatting.

Even some small towns unused to economic struggle have fallen on bad times recently. Family farms seem to be a thing of the past and young people are lured to the big cities. Once-prosperous hamlets are turning into ghost towns. Of the 19,000 incorporated cities in the United States, more than 13,000 have fewer than 2,500 people. After Illinois and Iowa, Missouri ranks third with the largest number of small towns. As Mark and his friends see it,

Hannibal is just one of many. It's no different from the rest of the world.

For them, not even Mark Twain's haunting presence makes it different. "I was fifteen before I went to Mark Twain's house," sixteen-year-old Chris Barnard tells me. "It's kind of like living in New York City and never going out to the Statue of Liberty, I suppose. You know it's there, but, well, you don't care enough to actually go see it." For the rest, Twain's books are just that—books, things they associate with school, like rulers and erasers and detention. Most evenings they spend on Cardiff Hill, unaware of Twain's description of the place, unconcerned about the anomaly of the lighthouse behind them, and only vaguely concerned, it seems, about the future that lies under the yellow lights in the streets below. In *Life on the Mississippi* Twain remembered, "When I was a boy, there was but one permanent ambition among my comrades in our village on the west bank of the Mississippi River. That was to be a steamboatman. We had transient ambitions of other sorts, but they were only transient." For these young men the riverboats are just a tourist ride, like a kiddie train in an amusement park. Skateboards are just a sad surrogate for vanished expectations.

That night Owen and Ian read a basketball magazine together on the bed in the Holiday Inn. Their heads angle toward one another, making a triangle of light from the lamp behind them. Their eyes are bright with enthusiasm as they discuss David Robinson and Michael Jordan. They exchange a few basketball cards and talk about which are most valuable and which will be in the future. Behind their words their dreams are clear and sweet as the waters of the Mississippi once were.

The next morning we meet Mark and his friend Shawn Williams in the country near Bear Creek. Both hold filled-out applications for work at Revcon. Neither seems optimistic about getting a job. They expect to get together in the evening on the crest of Cardiff Hill, to watch the lights and the miniature cars and people below, to sit like Yeats's Chinamen with gay and glittering eyes, to spend the evening making jokes about "ricks," to wait for the next day. Now, standing on the country bridge above the trickle of water named

Mark Lamont and Shawn Williams on a bridge over Bear Creek

Bear Creek, Shawn makes jokes about "bare" creek and Mark talks about his sonnets and about a long short story he has written. It's about two boys who get lost in a time warp in a cave. It sounds familiar.

This afternoon on our way out of Hannibal, we stop for a pack of gum at PD Sports and Liquor Store. George Rupp, who has owned the store for twenty-one years, limps up to the cash register. His store sells everything, it seems—more even than the "This and That" shop next door. On his shelves are stacked vacuum cleaner bags, Nights and Days perfume, pocket Simons, fishing nets, Ninja throwing stars, tackle, stink worms, even a "squirrel attractor." His main case displays quarts of Jack Daniel's next to Saturday night specials. We get our gum—Juicy Fruit—but not before I notice a few Mark Twain postcards as well. But the guns and liquor seem a dangerous combination to me and we make our exit.

We drive past River City Billiards, the Uniform Shop, defunct movie houses, loan establishments ("$25 and up"), and across the Mark Twain Memorial Bridge into the flatlands of Illinois. I've discovered that all this driving, even in the relative luxury of an air-conditioned Plymouth Voyager van, can wear a young body out. Owen would rather stay, perhaps live forever if he were given the choice, in the Holiday Inn. After all, it has a miniature golf course, ping-pong, a pool, shaded corridors to run along. Ian lies in the back, disregarding the scenery and reading a book about the Continental Basketball League, a second-class dream which fits the atmosphere of the place we've just visited. I think the rigors of a raft on the Mississippi would be easier, giving us all more to do and see. We are a still life in a capsule rocketing past Shell stations and cornfields. But as Huck says, there's no home like a raft, after all. "Other places do seem so cramped and smothery, but a raft don't. You feel mighty free and easy and comfortable on a raft."

Illinois, Indiana, and Ohio are a blur of prehistoric-looking bugs splatting into the windshield against a backdrop of farmland, grain silos, and tractor trailers. These states are about as flat as a coffee table and about as interesting. Late in the day lightning splits the sky into fiery sectors. The radio tells the story of Pete Rose's fall, Ohio's Oedipus disgraced and heading for prison. Somewhere in

Illinois a brown-and-yellow butterfly attaches itself to our antenna and hitches a ride all the way to New York State. In our grisly funk after driving twelve hours, we assume it's been speared in some way by the car antenna, but we park for the night and the next morning it's gone.

The ride across these states is so long and tiresome that my sons invent all sorts of dramas and games to while away the time. Owen, the eight-year-old, develops the most unusual game, something worthy of Tom Sawyer. Ian is still reading his book about the CBA in the back of the van. Owen sits next to me grimacing as if he were about to burst. Finally he looks triumphantly at me and says, "I made it. I won!" He explains: he was tickling the bottom of his bare left foot with the eraser end of a pencil, seeing how long he could stand it. This is what Ohio can do to an ordinarily sane boy.

We stop in Vermont to visit family, but Mark Twain follows us. In Laney's Restaurant in Manchester, Vermont, the first thing I see on the menu is a "Huck Finn Mississippi Mud Drink," a combination of Southern Comfort, Kahlua, and ice cream. But I don't give in to temptation because it's a long drive yet to Hartford, Connecticut, to see Twain's house in that city. We arrive in Hartford about two in the afternoon, getting stuck in the bottleneck that seems to be a permanent part of the highway system in that area at any time of the day or night. We've all been to Twain's house on Farmington Avenue before, but it seems an appropriate stop on our way home.

We get off at the exit that says "The Mark Twain House" and stop at Subway for a sandwich and directions. The roast beef looks as if it were cooked when Twain lived in Hartford and, even though his house is only down the block, they don't know where it is. "Around here?" the counterman asks. We find it on our own. As Kaplan said, it is a veritable riverboat of a house, all cupolas, roof lines, awnings, and balconies. But all the tours are filled. A glance at the guest list tells me the recent crowd has come from New York and California and France. I suppose we didn't stand a chance. In any case, it seems a fitting last stop to a trip where the expectations never quite fit the reality, as if the pieces and the jigsaw puzzle are from separate games.

As we head south, away from Connecticut and Twain, and toward my boyhood home in New York City, Owen and I start a game to block out some of the miles. We've played states and capitals before on the trip, and he seems to know Illinois and Indiana and Ohio pretty well.

"What's the capital of Connecticut?" I ask him.

A long pause and his face twists into a comical grimace. "Subway?" he says.

I am about to correct him, but we've come a long way and still have a few hours before we get to the Bronx. We'll probably hit more traffic, and I can give him the right answer later on. Besides, as Twain said, "Few things are harder to put up with than the annoyance of a good example."

8 Home

The journey, not the arrival, matters;
the voyage, not the landing.

Paul Theroux,
The Old Patagonian Express

I thought hard for us all—my only swerving.

William Stafford,
"Traveling Through the Dark"

AS WE CROSS the Tappan Zee Bridge my whole childhood comes flooding back. It has been twenty years since my last visit, except for brief stops. I feel something like Twain did upon his return to Hannibal after twenty-nine years:

> That picture of it was still clear and vivid to me as a photograph. I stepped ashore with the feeling of one who returns out of a dead-and-gone generation. . . . I saw the new houses—saw them plainly enough—but they did not affect the older picture in my mind, for through their solid bricks and mortar I saw the vanished houses, which had formerly stood there, with perfect distinctness.

The charming and peaceful waters of the Hudson River run below. It seems wider and more wonderful than the Mississippi. Twain once said that comparing the Sea of Galilee to Lake Tahoe was like comparing a meridian of longitude to a rainbow. The Hudson, I suppose, is my Lake Tahoe and the Mississippi seems to pale in comparison. There's a favorite John Cheever story of mine, "The Angel of the Bridge," in which the main character is led across the Tappan Zee by a young woman with golden hair, a harp, and a melodious voice. It's the past that sings to me, but I feel much the same as that character did: "It all came back—blue-sky courage, the high spirits of lustiness, an ecstatic sereneness."

Over the bridge are Bronxville and Yonkers, and tennis courts and suburban commonplaces that seemed to be part of a world as foreign as Iraq or Southeast Asia when I was a boy. The Bronx River flows to the right of the highway, a trickle compared to the Mississippi, but its murky, taboo waters are as laden with memories for me as the other was for Twain. The Major Deegan Express-way winds past Van Cortlandt Park, where for a moment I see myself, like the protagonist of Irwin Shaw's "Eighty-Yard Run," being a football hero, intercepting a pass in a Pop Warner game for St. Philip Neri Elementary School and running it back for a touch-down. As I get off the highway, wondering for the first time in all the years I've driven on this road who Major Deegan was, the Bronx appears, as it does to Will Barrett in *The Last Gentleman*, "all solid and sullen from being the same today as yesterday, full of itself with lumpish Yankee fullness, the bricks coinciding with themselves and braced against all comers."

The sounds and smells and sights are New York, the present. Car horns blare above motors and music and shouts. Garbage seems to grow on the streets the way shrubs once did. Graffiti is every-where, all colors, all shapes. Potholes make the streets look like the surface of the moon, and razor-sharp barbed wire embraces every parking garage and loops around some apartment buildings, as well. Buses spray mushrooms of metallic exhaust fumes into the air, and many cars advertise "No Radio" to potential thieves. This is more like my idea of Beirut than the Bronx I remember, a place of chestnut trees and candy stores, Al's Delicatessen where the five-cent pickles soaked in mouth-watering brine in wooden bar-rels, Sarah's Candy Store where egg creams were a dime and cones with sprinkles were eleven cents, stickball games on the Grand Concourse in the afternoon, and games that took us through back alleys and subway corridors and over rooftops until ten o'clock on a summer's night. The buildings remain, but everyone is gone— Molly Grossman and Jimmy Hanley and Frankie Bartoletti and Steve Tarnok.

Owen, Ian, and I stop at Drewsen's Delicatessen but keep a careful watch on the van as we step inside the store. It's still the same. Fresh-faced, freckled Irish girls and boys stand behind the counters, and as if technology and twenty years never happened, they still add up the bill on the brown paper bags before they put our order in it. The roast beef sandwiches and the German potato salad are still the best in the world. We drive past St. Philip Neri playground and down Villa Avenue. Older Italian men and women hunch on the stoops. Children shout up to their mothers in the apartments above. We eat our sandwiches near the "cool spot" across from Harris Field. I spent many summer afternoons in the shade of the oak trees that are still here. Sam Clemens had Jackson's Island, Frost the Dismal Swamp, Hemingway Key West—I had this shaded spot near the train tracks. I try not to look over at the blades of barbed wire that now protect the nearby Lehman College.

The taste of the roast beef brings back a lifetime of memories, but I know this is probably my last trip to the Bronx. I will come back, but only in my imagination, and maybe Somerset Maugham was right when he said that those journeys were by far the best. Now those years seemed so far away, like a dream, or like a book, clean and complete, something I could return to over and over, forever, a story that never changes but that I will constantly see differently, reinterpret each time I return. So we leave the land-scape, which reminds me of *The Road Warrior*, behind—the shards of tires, rusted mufflers, overturned shopping carts, fast-food con-tainers, pints of vodka, and all the shreds and pieces that may one day add up to an archeologist's dream—and head through the nightmare landscape of industrial New Jersey and into Virginia. But as I head south I'm still dreaming about California and Mis-souri and Mississippi, about Bill Appleton and Beto and Tony Tarracino. And I hear Holden Caulfield's voice at the end of *The Catcher in the Rye:* "It's funny. Don't ever tell anybody anything. If you do, you start missing everybody."

In the darkening twilight a half-moon peeks out from behind a sky flecked with light gray clouds as we make our way over the Chesapeake Bay Bridge-Tunnel and home. Like so many other nomadic Americans, for me *home* has more to do with the two sleeping boys in the van, the wife that waits for me in Virginia Beach, and those I love scattered about the country than it has to do with any specific location. *Home* too is an imagined place, but, nevertheless, the bridge lights stretch over the dark and glistening bay like a jeweled necklace.

Selected Reading List

My journey took place in books as well as on the roads. For the same reason that I couldn't mention all the people I met or describe all the experiences I had, it wouldn't be feasible to try to produce a definitive reading list. Here is a list of some of the books I consulted and enjoyed in the course of my travels.

CHAPTERS 1 AND 2 — BEGINNINGS AND VERMONT

Frost, Robert. *The Complete Poems of Robert Frost*. New York: Holt, Rinehart and Winston, 1958.

The Letters of Robert Frost to Louis Untermeyer. New York: Holt, Rinehart and Winston, 1963.

Selected Prose of Robert Frost. New York: Colliers, 1968.

Allen, Ira. *The Natural and Political History of the State of Vermont*. Louisville: Lost Cause Press, 1965.

Burnshaw, Stanley. *Robert Frost Himself*. New York: G. Braziller, 1986.

Cook, Reginald. *Robert Frost, A Living Voice*. Amherst: University of Massachusetts Press, 1974.

Cox, James. *Robert Frost: A Collection of Criticism*. Englewood Cliffs: Prentice Hall, 1962.

Cox, Sidney. *Swinger of Birches: A Portrait of Robert Frost*. New York: New York University Press, 1957.

Fisher, Dorothy Canfield. *Vermont Tradition: The Biography of an Outlook on Life*. Boston: Little, Brown, 1953.

Frazier, Ian. *Great Plains*. New York: Fawcett Crest, 1982.

Gerber, Philip. *Robert Frost*. Boston: Twayne, 1982.

Hiss, Tony. *The Experience of Place*. New York: Alfred A. Knopf, 1990.

Kemp, John. *Robert Frost and New England: The Poet as Regionalist*. Princeton: Princeton University Press, 1979.

Kinnell, Galway. *Selected Poems*. Boston: Houghton Mifflin, 1983.

Least Heat Moon, William. *Blue Highways: A Journey Into America*. New York: Fawcett Crest, 1982.

Morrison, Kathleen. *Robert Frost: A Pictorial Chronicle*. New York: Holt, Rinehart and Winston, 1974.

Morrissey, Charles. *Vermont: A Bicentennial History*. New York: Norton, 1981.

Pack, Robert *Before It Vanishes: A Packet for Professor Pagels*. Boston: Godine, 1989.

Pritchard, William. *Frost: A Literary Life Reconsidered*. New York: Oxford University Press, 1984.

Tharpe, Jac. *Frost, Centennial Essays III*. Jackson: University Press of Mississippi, 1985.

Theroux, Paul. *The Old Patagonian Express*. New York: Pocket Books, 1979.

Thompson, Lawrance. *Robert Frost*. (3 vols.; 3rd vol. with R.H. Winnick). New York: Holt, Rinehart and Winston, 1966–76.

CHAPTER 3 — MISSISSIPPI

Faulkner, William. (all Vintage paperbacks). *The Sound and the Fury*, 1929.
As I Lay Dying, 1930.
Sanctuary, 1931.
Light in August, 1932.
Absalom, Absalom!, 1936.
The Hamlet, 1940.
Go Down, Moses, 1942.
Intruder in the Dust, 1948.
The Reivers, 1962.
Selected Letters, Joseph Blotner, ed. 1977.
Blotner, Joseph. *Faulkner: A Biography*. 2 vols. New York: Random House, 1974.

Brown, Larry. *Facing the Music*. Chapel HIll: Algonquin Books of Chapel Hill, 1988.

    Dirty Work, 1989.

Gandhi, Arun. *A Patch of White*. Bombay: Thackers, 1969.

Gwynn, Frederick, and Joseph Blotner, (eds.). *Faulkner in the University: Class Conferences at the University of Virginia, 1957–58*. Charlottesville: University of Virginia Press, 1959.

Imes, Birney. *Juke Joint: Photographs*. Jackson: University Press of Mississippi, 1990.

Karl, Frederick. *William Faulkner: American Writer*. New York: Weidenfeld and Nicolson, 1989.

Loewen, James. *Mississippi: Conflict and Change*. New York: Pantheon Books, 1974.

Morris, Willie. *North Toward Home*. Oxford: Yoknapatawpha Press, 1982.

Oates, Stephen. *William Faulkner: The Man and the Artist*. New York: Harper and Row, 1987.

Prenshaw, Peggy W., and Jesse O. McKee, eds. *Sense of Place: Mississippi*. Jackson: University Press of Mississippi, 1979.

Rubin, Louis, et al. *The History of Southern Literature*. Baton Rouge: Louisiana State University Press, 1985.

Wilson, Charles Reagan, and William Ferris, eds. *Encyclopedia of Southern Culture*. Chapel Hill: University of North Carolina Press, 1989.

CHAPTER 4 — GEORGIA

O'Connor, Flannery. *The Complete Stories*. New York: Farrar, Straus and Giroux, 1971.

    3 by Flannery O'Connor. New York: New American Library, 1962.

    Mystery and Manners. New York: Farrar, Straus and Giroux, 1969.

    Conversations with Flannery O'Connor, Rosemary Magee, ed. Jackson: University Press of Mississippi, 1987.

    The Habit of Being: Letters of Flannery O'Connor, Sally Fitzgerald, ed. New York: Vintage Books, 1980.

Bonner, James. *Milledgeville, Georgia's Antebellum Capital*. Athens: University of Georgia Press, 1978.

Coleman, Kenneth, et al. *A History of Georgia*. Athens: University of Georgia Press, 1977.

Coles, Robert. *Flannery O'Connor's South*. Baton Rouge: Louisiana State University Press, 1980.

Dexter, Pete. *Paris Trout*. New York: Penguin Books, 1988.

Harris, Joel Chandler. *Uncle Remus*. Atlanta: Cherokee Publishing, 1981.

Mitchell, Margaret. *Gone with the Wind*. New York: The Macmillan Company, 1936.

Walker, Alice. *In Search of Our Mothers' Gardens*. San Diego: Harcourt Brace Jovanovich, 1984.

CHAPTER 5 — FLORIDA

Hemingway, Ernest. *To Have and Have Not*. New York: Scribners, 1937.

The Old Man and the Sea, 1952.

Selected Letters, Carlos Baker, ed. New York: Scribners, 1981.

Baker, Carlos. *Ernest Hemingway: A Life Story*. New York: Macmillan, 1969.

Browne, Jefferson Beale. *Key West, the Old and the New*. Gainesville: University of Florida Press, 1973.

Derr, Mark. *Some Kind of Paradise*. New York: W. Morrow, 1989.

Ehrlich, Gretel. *The Solace of Open Spaces*. New York: Penguin Books, 1985.

Finkelstein, Dave, and Jack London. *Greater Nowheres: A Journey Through the Australian Bush*. New York: Harper and Row, 1988.

Jahoda, Gloria. *Florida: A Bicentennial History*. New York: Norton, 1976.

Lynn, Kenneth. *Hemingway*. New York: Simon and Schuster, 1987.

McLendon, James. *Papa: Hemingway in Key West*. Miami: Seeman Press, 1972.

McPhee, John. *Oranges*. New York: Farrar, Straus and Giroux, 1967.

Malcolm, Janet. *The Journalist and the Murderer*. New York: Alfred A. Knopf, 1990.

Meyers, Jeffrey. *Hemingway: A Biography*. New York: Harper and Row, 1985.

Lennon, Nigey. *The Sagebrush Bohemian: Mark Twain in California*. New York: Paragon House, 1990.

Lynn, Kenneth. *Mark Twain and Southwestern Humor*. Boston: Little, Brown, 1960.

Percy, Walker. *The Last Gentleman*. New York: Farrar, Straus and Giroux, 1966.

Powers, Ron. *White Town Drowsing*. New York: Penguin Books, 1986.

Wecter, Dixon. *Sam Clemens of Hannibal*. Boston: Houghton Mifflin, 1952.

Wolfe, Tom. *The Right Stuff*. New York: Farrar, Straus and Giroux, 1979.

Millhauser, Steven. *Edwin Mullhouse: The Life and Death of an American Writer 1943–1954 by Jeffrey Cartwright*. New York: Alfred A. Knopf, 1972.

Pearson, Pauline. *Guide to Steinbeck Country* (pamphlet). Published by the Salinas Public Library, 1984.

CHAPTERS 7 AND 8 — MISSOURI AND HOME

Twain, Mark. (paperback editions). *The Innocents Abroad*, 1869.
  Roughing It, 1872.
  Tom Sawyer, 1876.
  Life on the Mississippi, 1883.
  Huckleberry Finn, 1884.
  Pudd'nhead Wilson, 1894.
  The Complete Short Stories of Mark Twain, 1957.
  Selected Letters, Charles Neider, ed. New York: Harper and Row, 1982.
  Mark Twain's Letters 1858–1866, Branch, et al., eds. Berkeley: University of California Press, 1988.
  Mark Twain's Autobiography. 2 vols. New York: Gabriel Wells, 1924.

Brooks, Van Wyck. *The Ordeal of Mark Twain*. New York: E.P. Dutton, 1933.

Cox, James. *Mark Twain: The Fate of Humor*. Princeton: Princeton University Press, 1966.

Dillard, Annie. *Pilgrim at Tinker's Creek*. New York: Harper's, 1974.

Eble, Kenneth. *Old Clemens and W. D. H.: The Story of a Remarkable Friendship*. Baton Rouge: Louisiana State University Press, 1985.

Fishkin, Shelley Fisher. *From Fact to Fiction*. Oxford and New York: Oxford University Press, 1985.

Foley, William. *The Genesis of Missouri: From Wilderness Outpost to Statehood*. Columbia: University of Missouri Press, 1989.

Kaplan, Justin. *Mr. Clemens and Mark Twain*. New York: Simon and Schuster, 1966.
  Mark Twain and His World, 1974.

Lauber, John. *The Making of Mark Twain: A Biography*. New York: American Heritage Press, 1985.
  The Inventions of Mark Twain. New York: Hill and Wang, 1990.

Murphy, George, ed. *The Key West Reader*. Key West: Tortugas Ltd., 1989.

Raeburn, John. *Fame Became Him: Hemingway as Public Writer*. Bloomington: Indiana University Press, 1984.

Young, Philip. *Ernest Hemingway: A Reconsideration*. University Park: Pennsylvania State University Press, 1966.

CHAPTER 6 — CALIFORNIA

Steinbeck, John. (paperback editions). *Cup of Gold*, 1929.
  The Pasture of Heaven, 1932.
  Tortilla Flat, 1935.
  In Dubious Battle, 1936.
  Of Mice and Men, 1937.
  The Red Pony, 1937.
  The Long Valley, 1938.
  The Grapes of Wrath, 1939.
  Cannery Row, 1945.
  East of Eden, 1952.
  Sweet Thursday, 1954.
  The Winter of Our Discontent, 1961.
  Travels with Charley, 1962.
  The Acts of King Arthur and his Noble Knights, 1976.
  Working Days: The Journals of the Grapes of Wrath, Robert DeMott, ed. New York: Viking, 1989.
  Steinbeck: A Life in Letters, Elaine Steinbeck, ed. New York: Viking, 1975.

Benson, Jackson. *The True Adventures of John Steinbeck, Writer*. New York: Penguin, 1984.

French, Warren. *John Steinbeck*. Boston: Twayne Publishers, 1975.

Howarth, William. "Journalism and *The Grapes of Wrath*" in *Literary Journalism in the Twentieth Century*. Norman Sims (ed.) Oxford and New York: Oxford University Press, 1990.

Kerouac, Jack. *On the Road*. New York: Viking Press, 1979.

Lavender, David. *California: A Bicentennial History*. New York: Norton, 1976.

Owen, Louis. *John Steinbeck's Re-Vision of America*. Athens: University of Georgia Press, 1985.